Archiving Your SAP® Data

 PRESS

SAP PRESS is a joint initiative of SAP and Galileo Press. The know-how offered by SAP specialists combined with the expertise of the publishing house Galileo Press offers the reader expert books in the field. SAP PRESS features first-hand information and expert advice, and provides useful skills for professional decision-making.

SAP PRESS offers a variety of books on technical and business related topics for the SAP user. For further information, please visit our website: *www.sap-press.com*.

Armin Kösegi, Rainer Nerding
SAP Change and Transport Management
2006, 725 pp., ISBN 978-1-59229-059-8

Thomas Schneider
SAP Performance Optimization Guide
2006, 522 pp., ISBN 978-1-59229-069-7

Marc O. Schäfer, Matthias Melich
SAP Solution Manager
2007, 490 pp., 978-1-59229-091-8

Markus Helfen, Michael Lauer, Hans Martin Trauthwein
Testing SAP Solutions
2007, 367 pp., ISBN 978-1-59229-127-4

Helmut Stefani

Archiving Your SAP® Data

Galileo Press

Bonn • Boston

ISBN   978-1-59229-116-8

2nd edition 2007

Translation Lemoine International, Inc., Salt Lake City, UT
Copy Editor Nancy Etscovitz, UCG, Inc., Boston, MA
Cover Design Silke Braun
Layout Design Vera Brauner
Production Iris Warkus
Typesetting Typographie & Computer, Krefeld
Printed and bound in Germany

Contents at a Glance

Contents

3 Storing Archived Data 87

4   Accessing Archived Data 143

5   Technology and Administration 181

Appendix 365

Preface to the Second Edition

Since this book was first published in 2002, the data archiving processes in the SAP environment have been developed further with regard to both functionality and quality. A large number of new functions and improvements made available by releases SAP NetWeaver 7.0 (2004s) and SAP ERP 6.0 (formely known as SAP ERP 2005) facilitate the archiving of data and actually complete the data archiving processes in many respects.

With regard to the design and concept of data archiving as a whole, the integration of data archiving into the extended context of Information Lifecycle Management (ILM) is probably the most significant of those innovations. ILM represents a holistic method to actively manage all information objects in a system across their entire lifecycle. It comprises technologies, processes, and concepts whose primary goal is to provide users with the right information at the right time in the right place and at the lowest cost possible.

Other new features that are covered in this second edition include XML-based archiving that complements the "classical" Archive Development Kit (ADK)-based archiving process in the Java and XML environment, partitioning the Archive Information System (AS) to improve the management of large tables, and Archive Routing, which enables the automatic separation of archived data, for example, in order to meet legal requirements more efficiently. Another new feature described in this book is the Archive File Browser (AFB) that supports the archive administrator in solving problems related to archive files. In addition, this book contains a new chapter on archiving data in SAP ERP Human Capital Management (SAP ERP HCM).

New topics in this edition

The section on the reporting transaction TAANA (Chapter 7) was completely updated and enhanced (e.g., by the description of the functions for virtual field catalogs and of analysis procedures in mass operations). The process of archiving data in SAP NetWeaver BI has also changed considerably as compared to its predecessor, SAP BW, due to the newly developed nearline storage concept. This is reflected in Chapter 6, which deals with archiving data in SAP NetWeaver BI, a large part of which has been added and updated. Another focus in development at SAP was the standardization and improvement of archiving logs that can now be accessed centrally via transaction SARA (Chapter 5).

In addition, the entire contents of this book have been updated to reflect the latest SAP system releases. This includes modified terminology used in this book, as well as updates of graphics and screenshots, wherever necessary.

Because of all the new and updated information available in this new edition, I am sure that this book will not only help those readers who are just becoming familiar with the subject of data archiving, but also those users who are experienced in data archiving tasks. Gook luck to all of you!

Acknowledgements

First, I would like to express my sincere thanks to the new authors who joined our team and contributed their expertise to the creation of this current edition of the book. On behalf of the entire team of authors, I would also like to thank the following colleagues for their contributions and support: Olaf Schmidt for proofreading the chapter on the Document Relationship Browser; Tanja Kaufmann for her support with the terminology and her help in writing the chapter on information lifecycle management; Harold "Ken" Campbell, without whom many of the new examples and screenshots would not have been possible; and last but not least, Dr. Ulrich Marquard, Senior Vice President at SAP, who, as an active sponsor of this project, deserves our special thanks.

Walldorf, March 2007
Helmut Stefani, editor and co-author

Preface by DSAG

Archiving data in SAP systems is an ever-changing area whose significance is continuously increasing for companies.

When maintaining SAP systems, the growing data volume and unsatisfactory performance that occur soon after the going live of a production system raise such questions as which data should be retained in the system and for how long, as well as which data must be retained and which data can be deleted. To avoid system operation problems that cause these questions to arise, data archiving must be considered at the start of an SAP project. Regular archiving activities can slow down the overall growth of the quantity of data and therefore establish an equilibrium within the system and ensure good system performance.

When considering data archiving, you need to take into account several requirements. There are legal requirements for retaining and evaluating company data, as well as user requirements for easy access to data from previous time periods. Also, there are technical requirements regarding system performance, backup and recovery times, as well as hardware and administration costs.

To take into account all of these data archiving aspects, experts from various areas of the company have to work together: system technicians; Basis support; application support; key users from the departments concerned; data center, auditing, and security department personnel; and external auditors.

These experts have to perform a number of tasks. The database needs to be analyzed and suitable archiving objects need to be chosen. Archiving processes need to be customized—which may even involve programming—and tested, right up to the first archiving runs in the production environment and throughout routine operation. These experts also need to evaluate the effects of these processes on the size and performance of the system. Finally, they need to consider dependencies between data archiving and document storage, including questions concerning authorizations, and storing and accessing archived data. The recent enhancements of the SAP data archiving functions and tools provide sufficient support to carry out these different tasks.

With the introduction of SAP/R3 Enterprise, the area of data archiving became standardized, which made administrative work much easier and more straightforward. The ability to interrupt archiving runs, a statistics function, the complete control of background jobs by external schedulers through the new XBP-2.0 interface, and the table analysis via transaction TAANA are but a few of those new developments.

In the context of SAP ERP 6.0/SAP NetWeaver 7.0, new functions such as Archive Routing, the partitioning of tables of the archive information system, and XML-based archiving have been added.

The concept of information lifecycle management (ILM) poses new tasks and challenges to all those involved in data archiving in SAP systems.

I hope that all readers of this book, *Archiving Your SAP Data*, can tap into the new possibilities of data archiving and optimize these options both in their daily work and in new projects and strategies.

Gütersloh, March 2007
Dipl-Inf. Jutta Gimpel
Miele & Cie KG
GTZ/IT Betrieb
Spokeswoman of DSAG-Arbeitsgruppe Datenarchivierung

Acknowledgements for the First Edition

In completing an extensive project such as this book, experience shows that the final version is not just a product of the authors, but also of a number of other "helpful souls" who are too numerous to mention here. The entire team of authors would like to extend their thanks and appreciation to these people.

Special thanks goes to Dr. Peter Zencke and Dr. Ulrich Marquard, without whose support this book would not have been possible. We would also like to mention Wolfgang Röder, the "grandfather" of SAP data archiving, who initiated its development and who has helped to shape it over many years.

We also would like to thank Dr. Rolf Gersbacher, who helped with many of the documents included in this book; Erik Meyers for his graphic design, documentation contributions, and terminology work; and René Bacher for providing us with valuable linguistic feedback on many chapters.

Finally, we would like to take this opportunity to thank everyone else who supported us in creating this book.

Walldorf, May 2007
The Team of Authors
Helmut Stefani, editor and co-author

Introduction

Never before has mankind created so much information—and data—as is being created today. According to a survey carried out by the School of Information Management and Systems at the University of Berkeley, California, in 2003, we produced a total data quantity of 5 exabytes[1] in 2002, while in 1999, the total was 2 exabytes. The largest part of this data—92%—was stored on magnetic media, most often on magnetic disks. Within this same timeframe, printed paper documents barely maintained a 0.01% share [SIMS2003]. Even though the information on which this survey was based is now several years old, there's no reason to expect a significant change or slowdown of this trend.

These general observations, which take into account audio and video data, also apply in the area of business software. Only a few years ago, computer systems that could handle terabytes of data were a rare exception. Today, many companies operate systems of this size. The volume of stored data, often distributed over a number of systems, has also clearly risen. There are many reasons for this increase. For example, after successfully introducing business software to certain business processes, a company will apply it to other business processes, or will extend the existing processes to include other departments or subsidiaries. As a result, additional data is created, which must be stored and managed within the company.

The current, and more importantly, future rate of data growth is primarily the result of a revolutionary expansion in the global business world, fueled by the explosive proliferation of the Internet. The worldwide networking of millions of computers enables the high-speed exchange of data between companies and across national borders, forming the foundation for electronic trade and e-commerce.

The flood of information continues to grow

---

1   1 exabyte corresponds to 1 billion gigabytes or 10^{18} bytes. For comparison: According to [SIMS2003], 1 gigabyte corresponds to a small delivery truck full of books. 5 exabytes would be the equivalent of all words that have ever been spoken by humans.

The economy of the 21st century is characterized by collaborative business models, in which all of the partners are integrated in the business process. Software solutions for customer relationship management (CRM) and supply chain management (SCM) are also becoming increasingly common, while the volume of electronic data continues to grow.

Data storage and administration continually increases in importance

The storage and administration of these enormous volumes of data represents an enormous challenge to all companies. There is a great need to develop concepts and tools that support these volumes and that take the entire data lifecycle into account. For IT managers worldwide, the organization and use of data is one of the most important responsibilities; in Europe, it has been a "Top 5" IT-critical concern for many years.

The importance of data archiving

Data archiving is an essential component for ensuring efficient data management in the SAP Business Suite, SAP's family of integrated business applications. Application data for closed business transactions that is no longer relevant for day-to-day system operation can be relocated out of the database, thereby substantially reducing data management costs.

Since system availability and administration are usually the responsibility of in-house IT departments, they will often be the first to suggest reducing the volume of stored data. However, typically, the IT department cannot assess on its own the effect that data archiving will have on the affected departments. Access to archived data is not only subject to internal requirements; taxation and legal requirements must also be considered.

Continuous enhancement

The advent of SAP R/3 3.0A made it possible for data to be extracted as archive files from the database of an SAP system, and stored on external storage media. Over time, control over the data archiving process and access to archived data have been continuously improved. Further development has been driven to a large degree by customer experience, and especially by the large data archiving working groups within SAP's user groups in Germany (DSAG) and the U.S. (ASUG). With the help of their major contributions, a very well developed and secure solution is now available—the majority of all data recorded in SAP systems can be archived in a timely manner. This solution also guarantees that there are no substantial limitations to accessing archived data.

The type of data to archive and the timeframe within which to archive can only be determined if one is familiar with the specific data types and their role in the business process. This knowledge usually resides in each individual department. IT and other departments will always have to work together when introducing data archiving to a company. This interdepartmental cooperation includes selecting data to be archived. As an efficient tool for limiting data growth, data archiving should be a part of any concept for the long-term operation of a business application, and it should be included at an early part of the planning process.

Since data archiving was first developed for deployment with SAP R/3, the business world has experienced fundamental changes because of its increased use of the Internet. With its SAP Business Suite, SAP offers a family of integrated business applications that provides numerous solutions for a vast multitude of business challenges. The level of coverage by software of business processes has been substantially increased. Within an individual application, data is now usually created in several software components, not just in one component, such as SAP ECC. This increases the need to discuss data archiving projects and elevates the importance of data archiving itself, in terms of managing the quantities of data being created.

The primary reason for writing this book lies in the increased importance of data archiving. This subject is examined from all sides. Closely related subjects, such as document storage or tax aspects of data storage, are also covered, so that the reader will have the best possible overview. All of the authors have extensive experience in data archiving in an SAP environment. They cover both technical and business aspects of data archiving, and provide many suggestions and ideas for readers who work with data archiving.

Goal and purpose of this book

This book should not be considered to be a technical document, that is, a document that contains all the details of working with data archiving. Rather, you should think of this book as a guide for day-to-day archiving practice. This book provides those of you who are new to this topic with a thorough overview, while giving experienced users the important details and firsthand, up-to-date background information they want. The many tips and recommendations provided in each chapter let the reader benefit from the extensive experience of the authors. At the same time, the reader gains the required practical know-how for implementing data archiving.

Chapter 1 describes data archiving in the context of information lifecycle management (ILM). This chapter helps you understand the rest of the book, by giving a short description of important terms and tools, and by showing how they can be applied. The chapter is self-contained and delivers the basic knowledge that should be made available to decision makers, members of project teams, and users.

Chapter 2 offers a detailed description of the processes and concepts that are of importance for data archiving. This chapter describes the fundamental process of data archiving, from creating archive files and deleting data from the database, to storing the archive files that have been created. Linkage relationships between data are described, along with the archiving sequence and the examination of data for archivability.

Chapter 3 focuses on the storage of archived data. It gives an overview of the possible concepts and technologies, while providing concrete criteria for selecting a proper storage strategy for a company. Aspects of data security and integration are also examined in detail.

Chapter 4 examines the possibilities for recovering or analyzing archived data. This information is geared towards administrators, whose task it is to implement an archived data access strategy, and to integrate this into general system operation. Two tools, Archive Information System (AS) and Document Relationship Browser (DRB), play an important role in data recovery and analysis. Their functions and implementation are described in detail.

Chapter 5 focuses on the technical basics of data archiving. By referring to utilized technologies such as the Archive Development Kit (ADK), this chapter explains data archiving and indicates how administrators can integrate data archiving efficiently into their current system operation. You will also find a wealth of practical tips and recommendations.

Chapter 6 describes data archiving solutions in individual applications of the SAP Business Suite and SAP NetWeaver components, such as SAP Enterprise Resource Planning (SAP ERP), SAP ERP Human Capital Management (SAP ERP HCM), SAP Customer Relationship Management (SAP CRM), and SAP NetWeaver Business

Intelligence (SAP NetWeaver BI). Due to the large variety of possible solutions that are available for data archiving with SAP ERP, this chapter limits itself to presenting an example that covers the archiving of financial accounting and cost accounting documents.

Chapter 7 translates the concepts presented in the previous chapters into practical examples. It is based on a proven process model that has formed the basis for planning and executing a number of successful archiving projects. This chapter also offers a large number of valuable tips and recommendations, all of which have been tested in practice.

The **Appendix** contains a checklist that can be used for planning and carrying out an archiving project. It also provides a sample description of an archiving object within the framework of preparing a project plan. Finally, it provides an overview of extensive information sources and training, as well as a detailed glossary of terms related to data archiving.

In this book, the term *SAP System* is used as a substitute for all applications contained in the SAP Business Suite that are involved in data archiving. This is especially the case whenever the description treats generic data archiving functions or processes that are the same for all components. In contrast, if data archiving in a specified component (e.g., SAP CRM or SAP ERP) is being discussed, then this component will usually be mentioned by name.

Some remarks

The data archiving documentation that is available from SAP Knowledge Warehouse (SAP Library) is referenced in several chapters. This documentation contains a broader range of more detailed information than is offered in this book. For the sake of simplicity, these references are usually limited to the short-form indication "SAP Library." Depending on the solution or component that is being referenced, you can find the data archiving documentation in the SAP Library using the paths that are indicated in Table 1 below.

References to documentation

The easiest way to access the documentation for most of the functions and programs described in this book, such as the Archive File Browser, the Table Analysis, and the Archive Information System, is to directly select **Help • Application Help**.

In addition, you can use the **i** pushbutton in Archive Administration in most cases to go directly to the specific documentation of the respective archiving object in the SAP Library.

Application/Component	Path
General documentation on SAP data archiving	**SAP NetWeaver Library • SAP NetWeaver by Key Capability • Solution Life Cycle Management by Key Capability • Data Archiving (CA-ARC) • Introduction to Data Archiving**
General documentation on SAP data archiving (XML)	**SAP NetWeaver Library • SAP NetWeaver by Key Capability • Solution Life Cycle Management by Key Capability • Data Archiving (CA-ARC) • Introduction to Data Archiving • XML-based Archiving**
SAP NetWeaver AS	**SAP NetWeaver Library • SAP NetWeaver by Key Capability • Solution Life Cycle Management by Key Capability • Data Archiving (CA-ARC) • Data Archiving in SAP NetWeaver AS**
SAP ERP	**SAP ERP Central Component • Scenarios in Applications • Data Archiving (CA-ARC)**
SAP CRM	**SAP Customer Relationship Management • Components and Functions • Basic Functions • Data Archiving**
SAP NetWeaver BI	**SAP NetWeaver Library • SAP NetWeaver by Key Capability • Information Integration by Key Capability • Business Intelligence • Data Warehousing • Data Warehouse Management • Information Lifecycle Management • Data Archiving Process**

Table 1 Data Archiving Documentation for SAP Applications and Components

You can find a regularly updated list of path names for the archiving documentation in the various SAP applications and releases in SAP Notes 71930 (ADK-based archiving) and 826000 (XML-based archiving).

This chapter focuses on the fundamental concepts, terms, and tools of data archiving. It integrates them into the concept of information lifecycle management (ILM) and provides an overview of the topics that are closely related to data archiving. In subsequent chapters, you can learn more about the processes and tools described here.

1 Basic Principles of Data Archiving

by Georg Fischer

Data archiving is no longer regarded as a separate, isolated data management method, but instead as a fundamental pillar of information lifecycle management (ILM) — the holistic concept that integrates all data that exists within a company. For this reason, the first part of this chapter focuses on ILM before we turn our attention to the concepts and processes involved in data archiving.

1.1 Information Lifecycle Management in an SAP Environment

You can probably find an article about ILM in any IT publication available today. After reading most of those articles, you will certainly ask yourself whether you can say with absolute certainty what exactly it is that ILM stands for, or rather, how an implementation of ILM would affect your SAP system. For this reason, this chapter is intended to provide you with a more detailed view of ILM and to describe the role of data archiving in this environment.

Due to the general increase of data volumes, which is primarily caused by the more rigid legal regulations for storing and handling electronic data, ILM has become an often cited word that is used by many people in different situations to describe completely different things.

ILM everywhere

Many definitions of ILM suggest that it is a tool or standard product provided by only a few specific vendors of storage systems, software products, or services. In our opinion, however, such a definition is not sufficient as it does not cover the really important aspects, namely those that are supposed to help customers carry out their transactions more efficiently.

The right piece of information in the right place at the right time

A definition that is increasingly being accepted describes ILM as a combination of processes and technologies with the objective to provide the right piece of information in the right place at the right time; all this at the lowest possible cost and with the lowest possible risk across the entire lifecycle of the data. In this context, we'd like to point out that the term "technology" as we understand it describes a complete ecosystem of supporting tools and solutions that range from business software to individual products of storage system providers.

If we take all those aspects into account, the processes and tasks in ILM can best be described as a model that consists of four phases (see Figure 1.2). The purpose of this model is to provide you with some guidelines that enable you to better understand the role of your SAP data in the overall context of information and to manage that data in a more optimal way.

But before we describe the detailed content and attributes of ILM, we think it's important to know exactly what is meant by the "lifecycle of SAP data."

Lifecycle of SAP data

Figure 1.1 illustrates the lifecycle of SAP data, as well as the frequency at which this data is accessed, depending on the age of the data.

It is rather obvious that data such as a sales order or an invoice is most often accessed as long as it is still "young," that is, at an early stage after its creation. After a certain amount of time, when the business process that involves this data has closed, end users access this data much less frequently than at the beginning of its lifecycle. In fact, sometimes they no longer access the data at all.

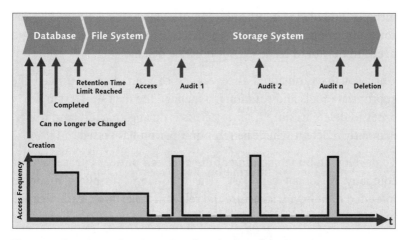

Figure 1.1 Data Access Frequency Based on the Age of the Data

From the point of view of saving space and costs, this is the time when the data should be removed from the database and stored in the file system or in an external storage system. There it can be accessed at any time whenever this is required, for example, in the context of an audit. And finally, once the retention period for this data type has expired, the data can be deleted (which is even mandatory in certain cases).

Today, efficient data and information management are not just an option for most companies, but an important prerequisite in order to keep up their business operations. The essential reasons for this change of paradigms are the constantly growing list of laws and regulations that apply to your data, as well as the risk you take when violating those regulations. At present, there are roughly more than 20,000 regulations in place worldwide that deal with the storage and management of electronic data. **Data management required to keep up operations**

However, ILM is also important because today no company can actually afford to neglect the structure of its business processes. An ILM strategy that is optimally implemented enables you to move ahead of your competitors. To achieve this, you should not only use ILM to save time, improve the performance of your system, and optimize your systems and processes, but also to identify and tap into the valuable potential that lies hidden in your enterprise data.

To put it simply, ILM represents the strategy needed to completely master the data and information that exists in a company. This **Controlling data with ILM** includes knowledge about the type of data that is generated in the company, about the location at which this data is stored, how long it needs to be stored, and when it must be deleted.

Once you have obtained an overview of your data, you need the appropriate tools and solutions to manage the data—for example, in order to delete it, store it, or to access it during an audit, and to permanently delete it when the retention period has ended.

To develop an understanding of the data and business processes in a company is not an easy task. The following four-phase model is intended to help you structure the relevant tasks into clearly defined individual steps.

Analyze Data,
Define Data Types,
Define Attributes,
Check Results
Regularly

Define Guidelines for
Attributes and Categories,
e.g., Retention Period
Legal Regulations,
Data Extracts

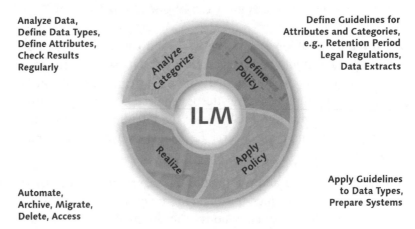

Automate,
Archive, Migrate,
Delete, Access

Apply Guidelines
to Data Types,
Prepare Systems

Figure 1.2 The Four Phases of Information Lifecycle Management

The four phases of ILM

1. In the *first phase*, you analyze and categorize your data. SAP provides various tools and functions to support you in performing this task for data in the SAP environment.

2. In the *second phase*, you must define your guidelines with regard to legal requirements, service level agreements, retention periods, etc. that apply to your company. Here as well, SAP provides useful tools, guidelines, and documentation to support this process.

3. In the *third phase*, you must apply the defined guidelines to your data and processes and prepare your SAP system, as well as interested third-party systems (such as storage systems) for the next phase.

4. In the *fourth phase*, you can finally implement the strategy you developed during the first three phases.

As shown in Figure 1.2, ILM does not represent a completely new concept from the point of view of an SAP environment; as a matter of fact, users of SAP systems have always been "doing" ILM, even though they may not have known that, or have used a different name other than ILM for it. The fact that many of the tools provided by SAP for the four phases are indeed tried-and-tested functions and applications that have already been used by SAP customers for a long time supports this theory. Other functions have been added only recently in order to support customers even better in implementing ILM, especially in terms of automation and comprehensiveness.

Data archiving and the associated tools and functions play an impor- Data archiving in
tant role for ILM in an SAP environment. In fact, data archiving rep- ILM
resents a useful example of how an essential component of the ILM strategy can be structured as it involves all four phases and requires a basic understanding of the entire lifecycle of data.

The subsequent chapters describe the relevant tools and concepts in greater detail, sometimes also from a quite technical point of view, in order to demonstrate how ILM affects your daily business. In addition, we will provide you with some guidelines, advice, and useful tips so that you can carry out your future data archiving and data management projects even more efficiently.

1.2   Data Archiving as Part of Data Management

Data archiving within the individual components of the SAP Business Suite plays a significant role in the data management of an SAP system. It enables you to relocate data pertaining to closed business transactions from the database, without having to shut down the respective system.

This data is identified by archiving objects, that is, predefined, technical mappings of actual business objects, such as sales orders or material documents. These business objects are chosen according to user-defined selection criteria, and are compressed into archive files and then written to a file system. Then the written files are read again, and the corresponding data records are deleted from the database.

Extensive checks ensure that business objects are closed and not needed by other business transactions, before they can be archived and deleted. Storage in a meta format ensures that this data can be accessed in the future, even by later software releases.

1.2.1 Benefits of Data Archiving

Given how much time, effort, and money companies invest in implementing business processes and creating business data, you might ask why data should be removed from a database? The storage area in which application data is stored—the database, which is the most valuable part of an enterprise storage system—is usually one of the most fail-safe, high-tech, and expensive storage areas within a company. Storage systems are also usually mirrored, meaning that the storage media, usually hard disks, are redundant.

High storage costs

In any case, this is not the only factor that must be considered when estimating effort. The transfer of data from a live system to another system, such as development systems, also requires consideration. It is not unusual for one data record to be replicated three or four times in this manner. The actual cost of providing storage space is, however, only a fraction of the overall storage cost. Administrative costs are five to seven times higher, even more if database administration is integrated. If we take into account these factors, it is not surprising that customers expect to pay four- and sometimes even five-figure dollar sums for each gigabyte of production disk space.

It therefore makes sense to look for alternative storage options for data that is no longer required for day-to-day business (for instance, data from past, closed fiscal years), as long as this data can be accessed, if required. SAP's data archiving system is the perfect option.

The benefits gained by using data archiving are mainly found in the following areas:

▶ System availability

▶ Resource usage

▶ Response times

▶ Legal compliance

1.2.1.1 System Availability

Operations that run without index support on the data volume of a database obviously need more time to operate, if the database or specific table area is large. This situation worsens if the operations require the application system to be shut down, or if end user access to certain areas needs to be temporarily denied. These delays could occur when switching to a newer software release, or when recovering data after a system breakdown.

1.2.1.2 Resource Usage

When dealing with fast growing or large database systems, attention often focuses solely on the storage system. However, considering the effects that this situation has on system performance, other performance parameters and resources also need to be examined—the number and clock speed of processors, and the size of the main storage area. In extreme cases, the database server will have reached its capacity and upgrade limits, so that other options need to be considered, including reinvestment.

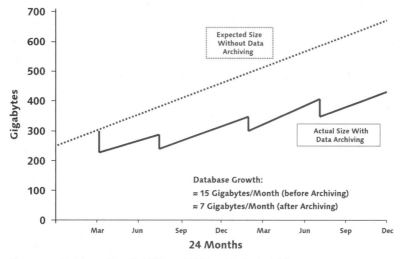

Figure 1.3 Database Growth With and Without Data Archiving

1.2.1.3 Response Times

System response times are also strongly influenced by the size of the data volume in the database. Not only does a larger data volume mean slightly longer delays in response times in user queries; but it also means that an unspecified search will lead to the selection and transfer of unnecessarily large volumes of data.

1.2.1.4 Adherence to Legal Regulations

One of the reasons for the tightened legal requirements regarding data storage discussed in Section 1.1 is that in many countries legal bodies have introduced paperless tax audits, that is, those audits are exclusively based on digital data. For example, not only does the German law covering data access and electronic data—GDPdU—which was introduced on January 1, 2002, define the object of an audit but also the type of data access, that is, the way in which an auditor must be provided access to the data to be examined. This can either be an extract of all tax-relevant data ("data preserve"), which can be interpreted outside of the SAP system, or the auditor can require direct access to the relevant data in the system. The latter includes all tax-relevant archived data as well since that data represents an essential part of each system.

Data archiving was originally not designed for the purpose of tax audits or to meet other requirements in the context of information storage, but rather to remove workload from the database. However, the role it plays with regard to legal compliance as well as in the overall context of information lifecycle management (see Section 1.1) is constantly growing (see also Section 1.6).

SAP Note 670447 provides further information on the topic of data archiving, GDPdU, and DART (see Section 1.6.2).

Data archiving represents an important component for all four areas described above, and it can help you to achieve planned improvements and goals. It is also often considered in context of data management. For more information on this, please refer to Section 1.5.2.

A brief review The functional basis for Archive Development Kit (ADK)-based data archiving in SAP R/3 3.0 and later was created in SAP R/3 2.1 and 2.2. The idea originated in the early 1990s from customers dealing with large or fast-growing databases. Without data archiving, these customers would have been forced to invest heavily in new hardware, or to accept a deterioration in system performance (see Figure 1.3).

SAP developed a data archiving solution that enabled mass data—generally transaction data—to be removed from the database during live operation, while also enabling subsequent access to this data.

1.2.2 Scope of Functions

Data that is still required from an operational standpoint must not be archived (and consequently removed from the database). To ensure this does not occur, the system checks before archiving whether this data satisfies the archivability criteria specific to archiving objects (see Section 2.1).

A two-step method is used to ensure that errors don't lead to the loss of data during archiving. In the first step, the data is copied to archive files. The data is then only deleted from the database in the second step, once the archive file has been fully written and successfully read (see Section 2.2.2). This helps to mitigate errors that may occur when transferring data through the network from the database to the archive file. Archiving can be restarted in these cases, because the data is available either in the database or in the archive file. **Two-step process**

Data is compressed automatically during archiving, in many cases by a factor of 5. However, since data saved in cluster tables is already compressed, it is not further compressed when it is archived (see Section 5.1.2). **Compressing data**

> **Note**
>
> The compression factor can deviate substantially from factor 5 described above. In addition to the statistics provided in the archiving administration section (as of SAP R/3 Enterprise), you can also apply the following rule of thumb: The higher the number of archiving objects you use from different SAP applications, the closer you get to the average factor 5.

Metadata is saved in the archive file along with the actual application data, so that the archive file can be read long after being created, and with newer releases. The metadata includes **Metadata**

▶ the names of the archived database tables

▶ the columns of each table

▶ the data type of a column

▶ the length of a column

- the codepage (ASCII, EBCDIC, Unicode)

- the number format (e.g., integer on various hardware platforms)

Using this information, the ADK is then able to automatically consider any changes in the database scheme (field types, field lengths, new fields) that may have occurred since the data was saved. Any necessary adaptation only occurs temporarily during the read access; the archive file itself remains unchanged. This is not only a useful approach in terms of performance, but also when using non-erasable storage media, for which subsequent alteration of the saved data is not possible.

This concept is one of the elementary principles of data archiving: Archive files should not need to be converted due to a hardware or software upgrade.

1.2.3   Areas of Use

Subject covering several areas

The origin and scope of functions of data archiving described in the previous section also describes its original purpose. Application data that is no longer required for day-to-day business is removed from the database, so that database resources can be used more efficiently.

Data archiving is a generic solution that should be used periodically within the framework of administrating a system, such as an SAP ERP system. What is important in data archiving is that this process must take place in close cooperation with the managers of the different user departments that are affected. This is necessary, because one requires exact knowledge of the business processes to decide (and take responsibility for) which data should be archived at a specific point in time. In the end, although data archiving is generally initiated by the IT department, it remains an interdepartmental concern. Due to the constantly increasing number of legal requirements, and primarily due to the steadily increasing retention periods, archived data plays an increasingly more important role. Even though archived data does not meet all the legal requirements per se, and additional tools such as DART (Data Retention Tool) have to be used, access to this data must be ensured over a long period of time. Other topics such as information retention management and data destruction must also be taken into account during an ILM project.

Data archiving is not a universal tool for managing financial or tax data within a company. Accordingly, adherence to documentation requirements must be clarified prior to starting an archiving project. In many cases, the presentation of data is subject to specific instructions that may require considerable effort using the tools that are available after archiving. If this is the case, the departments affected within the company must be consulted.

When data archiving is not suitable

There are also strong restrictions regarding access to archived data created in a different system. Data in the archive files have the same close link to the system from which they were archived as the data still remaining in the database. It is therefore not possible to access archive files that originate from other SAP systems.[1] If you processed archived data and data from the database of different systems simultaneously, severe conflicts caused, for example, by identical document numbers could result. Evaluations carried out on this basis would be useless and could lead to false conclusions. Database data can only be transferred to another system in the context of an internal migration project, and the same applies to archived data.

No access to external system archives

Data from a live system is often copied for use in development and test systems, for example, in order to develop or tailor processes or solutions. To build up this kind of test system, all data needs to be copied, even if only a certain time period or application area is required.[2]

Development and test system structure

Due to the high degree of integration of the SAP Business Suite applications, there is no simple, free-of-charge alternative available. Data archiving cannot really help here either. You cannot simply remove required subareas of a system, nor can data be archived and deleted "quickly" from a live copy of a test system. In the first case, the archiving objects will only rarely contain the exact data that is required for a certain project. And in both cases, it would take far too

---

1 XML-based archiving allows you to access archived data across systems, because XML DAS is able to manage archived data from multiple application systems. See Section 5.1.5 for more information on this subject.

2 For this purpose, SAP offers an appropriate service solution: SAP Test Data Migration Server (TDMS). You can find more detailed information on this solution in SAP Service Marketplace, quick link *CUSTOMDEV-TDMS*, as well as in the book, *Testing SAP Solutions*, published by SAP PRESS [HEL06].

long to circumvent the comprehensive archivability checks. Therefore, operations of this kind are generally not worth the effort.

The aforementioned reasons also explain why data archiving is not suitable for deleting organizational units from a system. This operation could be requested if a plant or a company division was sold, and the corresponding data was no longer required for continued system operation.

1.2.4 The Archive Development Kit

The *Archive Development Kit* (ADK) is the central component for controlling an archiving session. It contains functions for analyzing individual archiving objects and for administrating archiving sessions. The ADK also provides the application programs with program interfaces, and deals with handling the archive files. In other words, the ADK creates, opens, writes, reads, and closes archive files. The ADK is supplied with the SAP NetWeaver Application Server, and enables the development of archiving solutions for customer-specific business objects.

ADK functions   The ADK contains the following functions:

▶ Control and parameterization of the archiving session

▶ Creation and status administration of archive files

▶ Ensuring the long-term readability of archived data

To ensure the last function, the ADK writes metadata to the archive file, which the archiving programs can ignore. Long-term readability includes the legibility of the bit sequences and the conversion of the codepage, in case there are any deviations. The ADK also carries out automatic structure conversions, if any changes were made to the database objects. See also Sections 1.2.2 and 5.1.2 for more information.

Archivability criteria   User entries specify in detail the business objects that should be archived. The archiving program tests whether this data can be archived. This testing takes into account corresponding archivability criteria, such as residence times, deletion indicators, or integration in the business environment. The application programs implement their own complete check logic. For more information, see Section 2.1.

The ADK centrally controls access to the archive files. To do this, the ADK writes administration information into the database, which is then used to read the archived data from the SAP system.

Please refer to Section 5.1 for more information on the ADK.

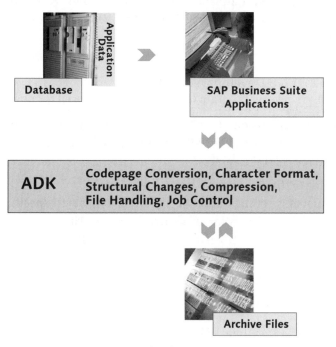

Figure 1.4 ADK Integration and Tasks

1.2.5   The Archiving Object

The archiving object is a central element of data archiving. It defines the unit that can be archived and deleted as a whole in the database. An archiving object represents a business object that has been enhanced to include the components required for data archiving (see Figure 1.5). These components are

▶ **Data Declaration Section**   Components
  All relevant data structures and database tables that characterize an application object are described here.

▶ **Archiving Programs**
  These include:

  ▶ the write program, which writes the business objects sequentially in the archive files

▸ the delete program, which deletes the business objects that were previously copied successfully to the archive file, from the database

▸ the preprocessing program (optional), which prepares the business objects for the archiving session. This could include labeling the objects that are to be archived (setting a deletion indicator).

▸ the read program, with which the archived business objects can be displayed

▸ the post-processing program (optional), which is used for post-processing after archiving, e.g., to update statistical data

▸ the reload program (optional), which loads the database objects back into the database

▸ **Customizing Settings**

The Customizing settings describe the archiving object-specific parameters that can be set for an archiving session. These settings vary, because they are aligned to suit the individual archiving objects.

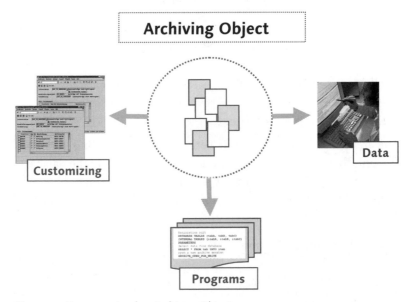

Figure 1.5 Components of an Archiving Object

Industry solutions have a special feature. In addition to industry-specific archiving objects, industry solutions often employ numerous archiving objects from SAP ERP as well. These archiving objects may be enhanced due to specific industry requirements, so that they take these requirements into account. In some cases, these archiving objects belong directly to the industry-specific components, while in other cases, they are still part of the cross-industry application component, SAP ERP.

Specifics of industry solutions

In addition to the archiving object, there are also archiving classes. These characterize data objects that have no independent business significance (e.g., SAPscript texts, change documents, or classification data), and that must be archived together with application objects.

1.3   The Data Archiving Process

Since the data archiving process is the subject of another chapter, we'll only provide you with a brief introduction here. For more information on this subject, see Chapter 2.

As previously mentioned, the task of data archiving is to remove data that is no longer required in the system, and to store it in accessible archive files outside of the database. During archiving, the write program chooses the data to be archived according to certain selection criteria. In addition to the business criteria defined by the user, such as a number range interval or a company code, these criteria include the residence time, which defines the first possible date on which an archiving object can be archived (see Section 2.1). The selection criteria differ, and depend on the circumstances of the individual archiving object. For example, accounting objects tend to contain period-based fields, whereas logistics objects will more frequently use organizational units or number range intervals.

Selection criteria

Due to the huge data volumes processed during archiving in parallel to live system operations, system and program performance clearly need to be taken into consideration. There are several ways of controlling the write and delete phases that ensure your system resources are used as efficiently as possible.

Performance

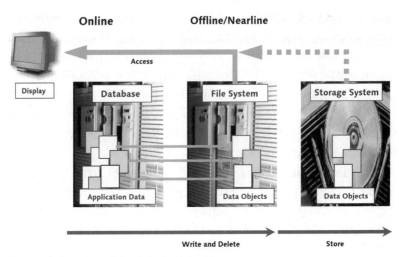

Figure 1.6 Overview of the Data Archiving Process

You can start the deletion process at the following times:

▶ at the same time as the write phase

▶ after the write phase

▶ at a later time (triggered manually or by an event)

Even if you spread the load across the aforementioned times, you should always plan to archive data when the system load is low. For more information on the performance and control of the archiving phases, see Chapter 5.

Complete archiving sessions

The archiving process—or archiving session—is not complete until the write and delete phases have been completed without error. Accordingly, an incomplete archiving session is indicated by a yellow traffic light in the archive management status field. This status does not change until the delete phase is completed, at which point the color changes to green. This status must be monitored, because if the session is incomplete, the data selected for archiving remains in the archive file and in the database once the write phase is finished. If you started an evaluation program that accesses data from both the archive files and the database, the results, such as totals, could be falsified. Therefore, despite the aforementioned suggestion regarding later file deletion, the time between writing the archive file and deleting the data from the database should be kept as short as possible.

1.3.1 Accessing Archived Data

Data that is no longer used for day-to-day business (because it originates from previous fiscal years) is usually accessed far less frequently than data from the current fiscal year. Nevertheless, you must also be able to appropriately display and evaluate this "legacy data." This is especially important with regard to the acceptance of the system by end users who are accustomed to having complete access to all data records, regardless of their age.

There are different ways of accessing data that has been deleted from the database as a result of data archiving. There are two main types of access:

Direct access versus evaluation

▶ Direct access to individual business objects

▶ Sequential access to multiple business objects

With the first type of access—also referred to as single document or direct access—the desired document is displayed in a view that is essentially identical to the original transaction.

Sequential access to multiple business objects is considered to be an *evaluation*. Its main focus is on totaling or comparative operations, or on creating print lists of the evaluated data.

There are also different ways of displaying archived data, of which the following are the most important:

Displaying data

▶ Displaying data in the application transaction

▶ Displaying data using the Archive Information System

▶ Displaying data using the Document Relationship Browser

Displaying archived data in the application transaction has been implemented for several archiving objects. The user accesses the archived data using the same method and transaction as that used when accessing data in the database. The user is made aware of the origin of the data, that is, a dialog box informs the user that the display program is accessing archived data.

Displaying data in the application transaction

Apart from displaying single documents, it is important to note that you can have a combined display of archived and database data. This display type requires an index, which is built up and maintained in the database once the data has been archived. This display option is found primarily in financial accounting.

Displaying data
in the Archive
Information
System The Archive Information System (AS) enables a generic, application-independent access to archived data (for more information, please refer to Section 4.5). This archive access type is based on an index of archived data—an archive information structure—hereafter referred to as an information structure. Data can only be found in the archive and displayed if this kind of information structure exists, and is filled with elementary information and details concerning the exact position of the individual business objects in the archive file.

The fields contained in an information structure can be freely selected from the field catalog (a collection of table fields belonging to an archiving object) on which it is based. The information structures, now filled with data from the archive, are stored in a separate transparent table in the database.

Using display
variants to reduce
data volumes Creating separate display variants enables you to define different views for an information structure. This prevents the volume of accessible data stored in the database from becoming too large. Figure 1.7 shows an example of an established information structure.

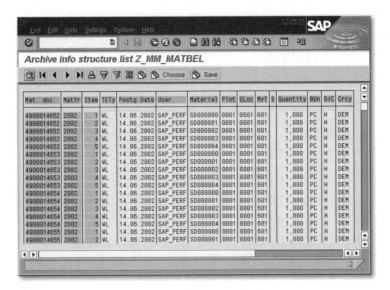

Figure 1.7 Archive Information Structure for Material Documents

The information structure takes you to the individual display of a particular document; the data read from the archive files completes the display window. A dialog window prompts you to select between one technical and at least one business display. With the business display, you can display an original document stored using the ArchiveLink interface. Or, you can use the Document Relationship Browser to display other documents that are linked to the current document.

The *Document Relationship Browser* (DRB) is based on the Archive Information System. The DRB enables you to present a document's relationship hierarchy and to display linked documents—independent of the application from which they originated. This allows you to completely reconstruct a process chain that may have been broken by data archiving. As far as DRB is concerned, the data can be located in the archive files or in the database. The DRB can be used within the Archive Information System, or it can be accessed via the user role SAP_DRB. The most frequently used archiving objects are connected to the DRB.

Displaying data in the Document Relationship Browser

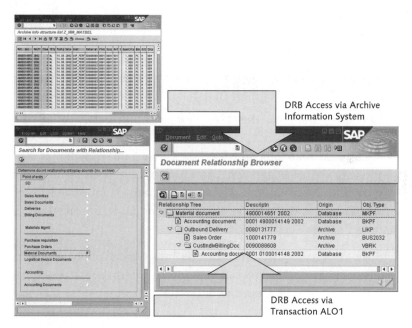

Figure 1.8 Document Relationship Browser

Another type of access that is available for some archiving objects involves reloading archived data into the database; however, you should note that this function is inherently risky. These risks are linked to the fact that a company's structure, and therefore its organizational mapping in the SAP system, are subject to change over

Reload risk

time. The larger the time interval between data archiving and reloading, the greater the probability that the original system has changed.

These changes can be purely technical in nature, for example, a change in the table structure on which a business object is based. Or, they can be organizational, such as a company share purchase or sale, or the introduction of a new local currency. Although the concepts on which data archiving are based support changes in the system environment (see Chapter 5), the software cannot compensate for some of these changes. Consequently, inconsistencies may arise when the data is reloaded into the database.

When reloading is not problematic There are two scenarios that should allow for problem-free reloading:

- ▶ **Reloading Data to the Database of a Test System**
  This is the case when all the test data has been deleted from the system either during data archiving tests or when additioanl archiving objects have been used. Although selection criteria may only allow small volumes of data to be selected, it may make sense to select large areas (one or more fiscal years, for example), in order to assess the runtime of individual processes or objects.

- ▶ **Reloading Data to the Live System Immediately after the Archiving Session**
  Because the time interval between archiving and reloading is usually very short, changes will probably not have been made to the system in the meantime. Therefore, reloading immediately after archiving is usually not problematic. For more information on reloading, see Section 2.3.2.

The above access possibilities can be integrated flexibly, alone or together, in user roles. You can then use an enterprise portal to provide the various user groups with the functions they need for their daily work.

There are two other methods for accessing archived data that have not yet been mentioned:

- ▶ Print list archiving
- ▶ Using SAP NetWeaver BI

Planning and preparation for both these solutions must occur before the data is archived and deleted.

With print list archiving, a print list with corresponding data fields is created—ideally using hyperlinks—and then saved in an optical storage system. Print lists are the end result of evaluation runs in the SAP system, for example, accumulated balance audit trails, batch where-used lists, object service catalogs, balance sheet valuations, or cost center reports. If you access these print lists at a later date, you can use the hyperlink to display the original document to which the corresponding list entry belongs. For more information about print lists, see Chapter 3.

Print list archiving

With SAP NetWeaver Business Intelligence (SAP NetWeaver BI), you can evaluate data from operating SAP applications. You can also evaluate data from any other business applications and external data sources, such as databases, online services, and the Internet. SAP NetWeaver BI provides flexible evaluation and analysis tools for strategic analysis and support in decision-making within the company. If you use extractors to transfer the data you want to archive to SAP NetWeaver BI prior to archiving, you can include this data in future analyses using the available tools.

SAP NetWeaver BI

A specific SAP BW 3.0 infrastructure may allow you to include data from archive files in InfoCubes; however, this may have a negative impact on performance, so it is not recommended. You should only use this option for initial loading, that is, in the event that data was archived without SAP NetWeaver BI. Therefore, you should always try to load data that you want to archive into SAP NetWeaver BI prior to archiving. For more information on data archiving in SAP NetWeaver BI, see Section 6.3.

1.3.2 Storing Archive Files

Although data related to completed business processes is no longer required for day-to-day business, it must usually remain accessible for years after archiving, and must therefore be stored securely. In this sense, secure, long-term storage of archive files is as important for data archiving as writing, deleting, and accessing the data.

Secure long-term storage

The following methods, described in more detail in Chapter 3 (see also Figure 1.9), can be used to store archive data:

► Storage in a certified storage system using ArchiveLink or Web-DAV (see Section 3.2.4.2)

▶ Using a Hierarchical Storage Management system (HSM) or a different storage system with file interface

▶ Using existing storage media

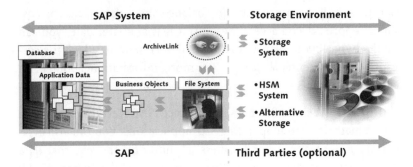

Figure 1.9 Storing Archive Files

External storage systems

Two key elements are involved in storing archive files on a certified external storage system: the storing software, and a hardware component—the archive server. The external storage system is connected to the SAP system using the ArchiveLink interface, and for SAP R/3 4.6C and later, using the HTTP Content Management Service. External storage systems, also referred to as content servers, can be certified by SAP. They can store

▶ Incoming, scanned documents

▶ Outgoing documents

▶ Print lists

HSM system

When an HSM system is used, the data is fully or partially administrated by software. The HSM system integrates several storage systems, and handles storage tasks according to various, individual specifications. This integration could include a network of hard disks, optical storage, and a tape robot. The data from the SAP system is stored via the file interface. If an HSM system is used, the SAP system must be able to access the storage medium with the same ease as a hard disk. Since access times in this scenario are inversely proportional to the cost per storage unit, this system could be managed by transferring files that are not required for a long time to the cheaper, slower access medium. Other useful functions for an SAP environment include reading individual blocks, direct writing from the cache to the storage medium, and simultaneous writing on several media.

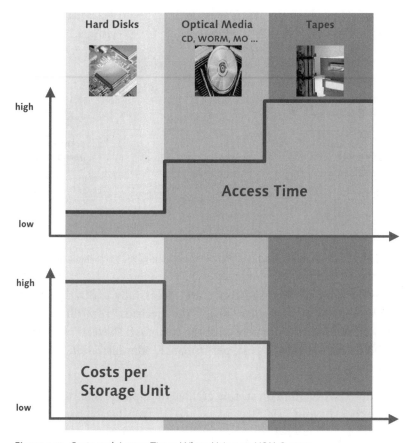

Figure 1.10 Costs and Access Times When Using an HSM System

In contrast to an HSM system, purely magnetic disk-based storage systems use only magnetic disks to store data (the storage process itself also occurs via a file interface). This type of data storage can be specifically optimized for the long-term storage of data that is no longer supposed to be changed (fixed content).

Magnetic disk-based storage systems

Unlike external options, existing storage systems in the company should be (re)used, in order to avoid incurring additional investment costs for hardware or software. (This option is described as "alternative storage" in Figure 1.9.) These storage systems frequently consist of large robot systems or jukeboxes that are already in use within the company. However, with this solution, the customer must take responsibility for the administrative tasks and data security.

Existing storage systems

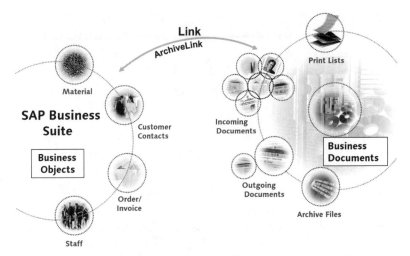

Figure 1.11 Links Between Business Objects and Documents via ArchiveLink

All three options discussed above are successfully and satisfactorily implemented on a regular basis. The decision regarding which method to use lies ultimately with the customer. The choice must be based on factors such as cost, performance, administration, security, and so on.

For more information on storing archive files, please refer to Chapter 3 and to SAP Note 71935.

1.4   Performance Aspects

Data archiving makes an important contribution to stabilizing database performance and administration, by archiving data that pertains to completed business processes. At the same time, however, this puts a considerable additional load on the databases in question, especially during the write and delete phases of data archiving.

High I/O load during data access — Data archiving mainly affects mass data found in large quantities in the system, which other processes generally no longer access. Accordingly, the I/O (input/output) load is usually very high when the data is accessed for processing. This can lead to a situation in the database buffer in which data that may be required by other processes is displaced by data for archiving. Under certain circumstances, this may increase the I/O load of other processes running in parallel with the archiving session.

Data deletion is among the most expensive database operations. This operation is similar to data writing; both the data and the corresponding indexes must be taken into consideration. But in contrast to the writing operation, much more information is copied, so that the state prior to deletion can be reconstructed, when reversing a data change.

Data archiving places a load on the same components in larger systems that limit the maximum possible throughput during normal operation. Therefore, data archiving should not be initiated at the same time as the high-load phase. In any case, should data archiving lead to resource bottlenecks, the system administrator can explicitly interrupt the write phase (see Section 5.4.3), or exclude specific servers from the archiving process by creating server groups.

Avoid archiving during high-load operation if possible

It is also important to consider the effects that the selection criteria applied during data archiving will have on the resource consumption. Data is saved in data blocks in the database, each of which consists of several data records. In general, all records within a block will have been written at around the same time. During read access, all records within a block are read to the database server's working memory. If a block with old data is requested during data archiving, then it would be ideal from the database point of view if all data in this block could be archived, so that the entire block could be released. Whether this actually takes place is primarily dependent on the residence time criteria, as well as archivability checks or other selection conditions applied to the archiving programs.

The contents of a block should be completely archived

Customers often want to archive specific data on certain organizational units, such as plants or company codes. The more restrictions you impose when selecting data for archiving, the greater the probability that the data blocks in question will only be partially emptied. This situation substantially increases resource consumption for data archiving, because the same data block must be read several times, by several archiving processes (each with different selection parameters), before all the data is deleted. Furthermore, the space left in a partially emptied block can only be used for new data under certain conditions. To ensure continued optimal system performance, this may necessitate additional data reorganization tasks, as described in Section 5.2.5.

Influence of the
data age on
system perfor-
mance

Another important aspect with regard to data archiving and performance concerns the age of the data that is stored in the database. For
a better understanding, you should once again be cognizant of the
fact that the data in the database is always selected in the form of
blocks by the hard disk and then loaded to the memory (see above).
The requesting application, such as an evaluation program, for example, then processes a block as one entire unit. The size of the block
depends on the database system being used (in an Oracle database,
for example, the size of a block is 8,192 bytes).

If a block contains a mixture of new and old data ("old" data being
data that pertains to closed business transactions and data that could
be archived), the old data is also loaded to the memory although the
application did not request it. This results in a decrease of the buffer
quality for this query and consequently in a system performance
decrease during the data access (the I/O load increases because the
missing data must be re-read in the database). This applies to tables
that store the actual application data, as well as to the index tables
required for accessing the data.

Chronologically
and non-chrono-
logically sorted
indexes

Experience has shown that this behavior primarily affects indexes,
particularly if the indexes are not sorted chronologically. Note that
the entries in index tables can be sorted in two different ways: chronologically (according to a time factor) and non-chronologically
(according to another factor, such as Globally Unique Identifiers
[GUIDs] or material numbers).

In a chronologically sorted index (including indexes that are sorted
by document numbers, provided these numbers are chronologically
ascending), old and new data is never stored together. This makes it
nearly impossible that a data block is loaded into the memory, which
contains old data records.

This is different in a non-chronologically sorted index. Because this
type of index is not organized in chronologically ascending order,
new data is inserted into the index only according to the values of
the index fields. This means that new data and old data can be stored
in close proximity to each other—a characteristic that is then also
reflected in the data blocks. If those data blocks are loaded into the
memory, the system performance can deteriorate considerably (see
above).

This topic is too complex to be addressed in this book. Therefore, we would like to refer you to the publications, *Performance Aspects of Data Archiving—Factors for Optimal Results in Archiving Projects*, *Data Archiving Improves Performance—Myth or Reality*, and *Data Archiving—The Fastest Access to Your Business Data?* [DAPERF01, DAPERF02, DAPERF03]. In these articles, we examine the relationship between data archiving and system performance in greater detail on the basis of examples that can be easily reproduced. In addition, we also provide detailed solution concepts for performance-based data archiving.

1.5   Archiving Projects

Introducing data archiving within a company often takes much more effort than first envisioned. The data archiving process is not bound by single applications or departments. It also affects a large number of topics and areas with links to data archiving; links that are often not recognized or are underestimated. In many cases, these areas have very different goals, which must be accounted for when establishing the project team that will introduce data archiving.

Working with various departments

The IT department will be concerned primarily with removing as much complete data as possible from the system, so that the system remains easy to manage and offers users the highest possible performance. However, end users or those responsible for the application often see the situation quite differently. They are intent on keeping as much data as possible in the system, in order to have easy access to it at all times. Archiving projects must bridge these opposing viewpoints, by including all affected areas in planning the content and process of the project. The entire project team must develop the best possible solution for the company, which also sufficiently considers tax and legal aspects.

Figure 1.12 illustrates the possible phases of an archiving project, and includes key terms that are relevant for the respective phases. Section 7.3 contains a considerably more extensive example of an archiving project concept, based on the proven ASAP method.

Project phases

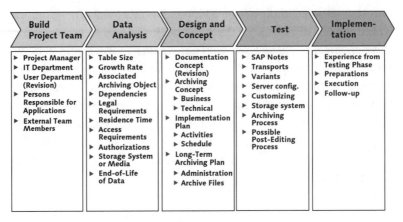

Build Project Team	Data Analysis	Design and Concept	Test	Implementation

▸ Project Manager
▸ IT Department
▸ User Department (Revision)
▸ Persons Responsible for Applications
▸ External Team Members
	▸ Table Size
	▸ Growth Rate
	▸ Associated Archiving Object
	▸ Dependencies
	▸ Legal Requirements
	▸ Residence Time
	▸ Access Requirements
	▸ Authorizations
	▸ Storage System or Media
	▸ End-of-Life of Data
		▸ Documentation Concept (Revision)
		▸ Archiving Concept
		  ▸ Business
		  ▸ Technical
		▸ Implementation Plan
		  ▸ Activities
		  ▸ Schedule
		▸ Long-Term Archiving Plan
		  ▸ Administration
		  ▸ Archive Files
			▸ SAP Notes
			▸ Transports
			▸ Variants
			▸ Server config.
			▸ Customizing
			▸ Storage system
			▸ Archiving Process
			▸ Possible Post-Editing Process
				▸ Experience from Testing Phase
				▸ Preparations
				▸ Execution
				▸ Follow-up

Figure 1.12 Possible Phases of an Archiving Project

1.5.1 The Right Moment

Data archiving is often thought to be worthwhile only once a system has reached a certain size, or has been in live operation for a certain period. However, this statement is inaccurate for two reasons. First, there are numerous archiving objects that can already be used as soon as a business object is business-complete. This only depends on the scenario in which the business object is integrated. Secondly, there are often application areas or tables that grow very quickly. Therefore, they can reach a respectable size in a short period, even if the database as a whole grows only moderately.

Plan data archiving as early as possible

In general, data archiving should be considered in the early stages of system planning; ideally, during the sizing phase, in which the required system size is determined.

Data archiving is primarily a preventive tool that enables the database system to keep performing as intended. Data archiving is not intended to—nor can it—return a database to this high-performance state.

Archiving processes require considerable resources

Because data archiving operates on a very large data volume, archiving processes in large databases require the most resources. The results of a large number of successful archiving projects confirm this fact.

1.5.2 Data Management

Although data archiving is very effective in reducing large data volumes, it is not the only method that should be applied. In principle, data archiving should only take data into account that was previously required in the system. In order to keep database growth under control, there should be alternatives for handling data that does not fit this description. It is always advisable to review whether it is necessary to update certain data , or whether these data volumes could be aggregated. Ultimately, the entire archiving process is faster and simpler if the data volume is small.

The following four-step decision process should be followed prior to archiving, or no later than during an archiving process:

Preventing, aggregating, deleting, or archiving

1. **Prevention**

   There are technical means of discontinuing updates on certain data. If this data is not needed from a business point of view, then updates should be discontinued.

2. **Aggregation**

   Data can be aggregated at a higher level in some cases (e.g., by accumulation or the like). If the aggregated data is sufficiently useful, then it should be aggregated.

3. **Deletion**

   You can delete a lot of data from the system shortly after its creation, if it doesn't need to be archived. Spool data is a good example of this kind of data.

4. **Archiving**

   Data that cannot be prevented or deleted must be archived. Determine how long data must remain in the system from a business point of view. Data should only be archived if it is no longer required for live operation. Therefore, archiving cannot be used to blindly reduce the volume of data.

Note

With regard to establishing an efficient data and information management system it is important to always take legally required retention periods into account, which directly affects the destruction, that is, the permanent deletion of data. For this reason, you should familiarize yourself with the relevant retention periods prior to, or at least during, the archiving project, and structure the archived data with regard to its future deletion via available tools, such as Archive Routing (see Section 5.3).

You can find more information on data management including detailed notes on individual critical tables in the Data Management Guide (DMG).

Data Management Guidelines

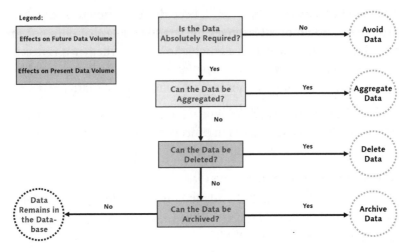

Figure 1.13 Data Management

1.6   Taxation Requirements Placed on Archived Data

GDPdU   In many countries, you can no longer simply file documents to satisfy tax law requirements. Finance authorities want access to the original tax data within a company, either directly in the source system, or in their own offices via external data media (and with the aid of suitable evaluation software). The main focus of these tax audits is usually on reconstructing or replicating certain document relationships.

In Germany, this is regulated by the GDPdU regulations, in effect since January 1, 2002, which prescribe how companies must make their electronic data available to tax authorities during an audit.

It is important that the master data, as well as linkage and Customizing information, be available on the audit date—often many years after the data was created—in addition to the transaction data.

Scope of required information   Another challenge for companies that are subject to paying tax is the extent of information that must be made available for tax audits. Whereas there are exact specifications for this in some countries, other countries remain somewhat vague, by demanding all data that is in any way relevant to taxation. Many companies take the same approach to satisfying this unspecific demand. After processing, they relocate from the database all data that is relevant to taxation to external files. This process takes place periodically, depending on the growth and extent of the data volume. To satisfy these requirements, SAP has developed the tools AIS and DART, which are described in the following sections.

In light of the considerable disparity between the requirements and goals of data archiving and tax audits, it is necessary to preserve separate, appropriate data volumes that suit each purpose in external files.

1.6.1 Audit Information System

Regulations in many countries stipulate that financial accounts must be structured in such a way that an outside specialist could gain an understanding of the system within an appropriate period of time. The Audit Information System (AIS, see Figure 1.14) provides auditors with suitable methods for carrying out internal and external audits, thus improving the process and quality of an audit. The audit can take place in *real time*, that is, directly on the screen in the live environment.

AIS: a tool for auditors

AIS includes an audit report tree, and a number of structured, preset standard SAP programs. Link functions enable access from the level of highly aggregated data to the individual document level. All of the relevant data for the audit period should be available in the database; evaluation of archived data is only supported in a restricted sense.

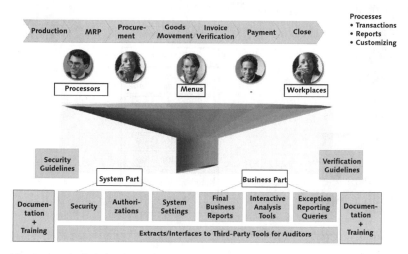

Figure 1.14 Audit Information System

1.6.2 Data Retention Tool

The *Data Retention Tool* (DART) was originally developed to comply with the specific requirements of the U.S. Internal Revenue Service (IRS) regarding data retention and evaluation. DART is used mainly in the North and South American markets. The program is a standard feature of SAP R/3 4.5 and later. Since the release of DART 2.0, the tool contains new functions that also meet the requirements of the German taxation regulation (GDPdU). For example, DART enables you to extract additional data segments that are relevant for German tax auditors.

DART also allows the extraction of data relevant to invoicing from the ERP system and the storage of that data in an external file. This data is sequentially stored in an uncompressed plain text format. It can then be evaluated using external tools, although it can also be displayed using DART tools.

DART can process database data, as well as relocated data (with the help of SAP data archiving). To do this, the program first reads the business objects and then filters the relevant field contents. The data is then saved in temporary database tables. However, these tables are not identical to the actual tables that describe the physical data model of a business object.

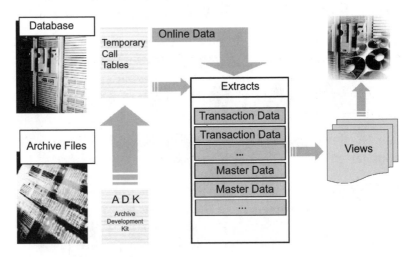

Figure 1.15 Data Retention Tool

This chapter provides a general description of the data archiving procedure in an SAP system. It also contains details about the most important processes that are relevant for data archiving.

2 Data Archiving Processes

by Helmut Stefani

At first glance, data archiving appears to be one continuous process; once started, data is relocated in a single step from the database into archive files. But if we take a closer look, we see that this process consists of several consecutive subprocesses, which together make up the actual data archiving procedure. In fact, the subprocesses or phases run independently, although they can be configured to run as an automated, integrated process (see Section 5.4).

The archiving process as a sum of individual phases

2.1 Checking Archivability

Checking archivability of the business objects precedes the actual archiving process. This should ensure that data is not archived, if it is still needed for business operations by an application. The data in question is checked, prior to archiving, in order to determine whether it meets the archivability criteria.[1]

A business object, such as a sales or material document, is generally considered to be archivable, if it has met the following criteria:

Archivability criteria

- ▶ It is completed.
- ▶ It has reached the predefined *residence time*.

---

[1] In principle, the type of archivability check is determined by the archiving object and cannot be changed by the user. Thus, the information and descriptions provided in this chapter are primarily intended for developers of archiving objects.

Processing status   Almost all applications contain a function that monitors the processing status of a business object. This function indicates if a business object is **In process**, **Completed**, **Reversed**, **Locked**, and so on. There are many such status indications; most of them are application-specific. In SAP ERP, these status indications are often saved using the general status management. With regard to data archiving, the **Completed** status is the most important, since business objects should only be archived if they are no longer needed in the current business processes. Checking archivability always includes checking the status management to determine whether a business object is archivable.

Residence time   The residence time describes the time period that must elapse before a business object can be considered archivable. The residence time is calculated based on different reference times, depending on the application. For a document from a logistics application, this could be the entry date, the change date, or the completion date. Figure 2.1 shows the calculation of the residence time for a sales document. The residence time begins either with the entry date of the document, or if it was changed before the residence time expired, with the last change date. The desired option can be set in the application-specific Customizing section of the associated archiving object SD_VBAK.

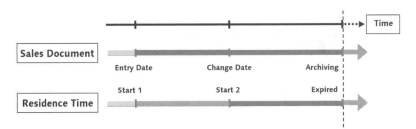

Figure 2.1 Calculation of the Residence Time for a Sales Document

In contrast, financial accounting mostly uses the term *retention period* in this context, wherever other reference bases are involved, such as the document type life, or the account type life for financial accounting documents. For more information, see Section 6.1.1.

Each individual application defines the best point in time for calculating the residence time of a business object. The residence time is set in the application-specific Customizing section for an archiving object, and is usually measured in days.

Because it can be automatically checked (with no user action required), the residence time archivability criterion is used primarily for transaction data. As a rule, however, master data is checked more "actively" for archivability, that is, the user often decides to set a deletion flag or a deletion indicator. For more information regarding the use of deletion or archivability indicators, see Section 2.1.2.

Residence time for transaction data, deletion indicators for master data

Depending on the application, archivability is checked at the header and item levels of a business object. If one of the archivability criteria is not fulfilled, the entire business object is considered to be non-archivable. Similarly, even though the document type life and minimal retention period of a financial accounting document are defined at the header level, you can ensure that the individual items don't contain open items and that the account type life has been reached. In other words, for the document to be archived, all of the archivability criteria at the header and item levels have to be fulfilled.

Checking at header and item levels

2.1.1 Linked Application Data

Besides the aforementioned main criteria (processing status and residence time), other application-specific data archivability criteria may exist. However, due to their many possible variations, we will not describe these criteria in detail here. Suffice it to say that these criteria primarily involve the linking of data in the system.

Very little application data exists as independent business objects in the system. Generally, there are strong dependencies between business objects. For example, a sales document from the SAP ERP subarea, Sales and Services, is integrated into a complex business process that includes other sales-related documents, such as quotation, delivery, and billing documents. There are also links between applications. To use the same example, the sales-related documents are complemented with documents from materials management (key area Procurement and Logistics), financial accounting (key area Financials), and—if goods are manufactured internally—from the key area Product Development and Manufacturing.

Dependencies between data

Because applications are highly integrated, documents that are created in them are also closely linked. Therefore, individual documents cannot just be removed from the system, without taking other linked

Document flow

documents into account. The entire business process document chain, called the *document flow*, would be interrupted and could no longer be reproduced. Even if a document is completed and its set residence time has been reached, it still might not be archivable, because other documents that were created with a reference to this document are themselves not yet archivable.

Preceding and succeeding documents

Figure 2.2 shows a part of the "sales order" business process document flow, and lists the associated archiving objects. This flow represents a typical business process in sales. Starting with a sales document, a delivery is created. Based on the delivery, a billing document is then created, after which the business flow in SD is finished. Finally, the billing document is sent to financial accounting, where documents are also created. These can be archived using the respective archiving objects from financial accounting. Therefore, a business object that is integrated into a business process usually has one or more preceding or succeeding documents.

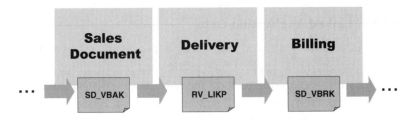

Figure 2.2 Document Flow in the "Sales Order" Business Process

The document flow illustrated in Figure 2.2 above is a simplified diagram. In reality, a document flow can be considerably more complex, with several branches (which usually range across applications). This complexity depends on the individual application and the number of business transactions in the business process.

Archiving sequence

The linearity between document flow and the related archiving objects suggested in Figure 2.2 does not always exist. If several archiving objects are assigned to a common business process, then under certain circumstances, archiving will occur in a particular sequence, depending on the application.

Sequence for a third-party order

For a third-party order (not a simple standard order, like the example above), which includes additional purchase requisitions and purchase orders, you should adhere to the following sequence when archiving:

1. Deliveries

2. Billing documents

3. Purchase requisitions

4. Purchase orders

5. Sales orders

Purchase requisitions are archived using the archiving object MM_EBAN, and purchase orders are archived using MM_EKKO. The fact that sales orders are created at the start of the process chain, but are archived last, shows that accounting needs to keep these in the system, in case credit or debit memos need to be created.

A business process chain in a production system is always customer-specific; therefore, there can be no general guidelines for an archiving sequence. In principle, though, business objects should be only archived, if possible succeeding objects within a business process chain have already been archived. Therefore, the document chain is "cleared" in a reversed order during archiving. Whatever the order, a business object still needs to fulfill the archivability criteria prior to being archived.

Succeeding documents before preceding documents

Note

Before archiving a business object that is part of a longer process chain, you should always consider the effect that this will have on the business process. What will happen, if a linked business object (whether it is a preceding or succeeding object) is changed? Will this also change the business object to be archived (through a status update, perhaps)? If this is the case, then the business object must remain in the system, and cannot be archived. For many archiving objects, this is ensured by the archivability check. Nevertheless, it is recommended, especially for complex or cross-system business processes, that you form an accurate picture of the dependencies between the affected business objects.

A graphical representation of the entire business process, for example, a flow chart or data model, might help you to form this picture. This can help you gain indispensable knowledge of the underlying business processes. After obtaining an overview of the business object links, you can draw up a sequence concept for archiving the business object.

The network graphic, which you can reach from Archive Adminsitration (transaction SARA) via **Goto • Network Graphic**, will show you whether an archiving object is linked to other archiving objects. The archiving objects are listed in the order in which they should be archived. In most cases, this sequence corresponds to the inverted sequence in which business objects were created. Figure 2.3 shows a section of the network graphic for sales documents.

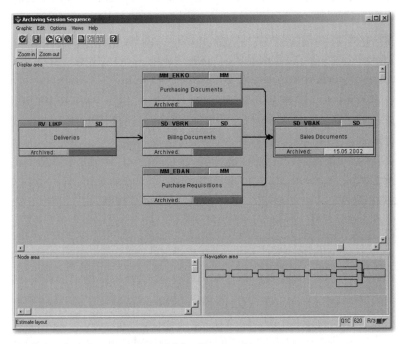

Figure 2.3 Archiving Sequences of Sales Documents

Network graphic as an orientation guide

When using the network graphic, you should remember that this is only an orientation guide to determine possible relations between business objects. Because it does not contain any business logic, but only shows these relations graphically, the network graphic cannot completely depict all of the business object types and their connections. Therefore, you cannot consistently derive the actual archiving sequence from the network graphic. Information concerning the business context into which a business object is integrated can only be supplied by the business object itself or the application.

If you don't adhere to the archiving sequence shown by the network graphic, inconsistencies will not necessarily arise, since this is prevented by the relevant checks at business object level. However, if you use the network graphic to orient yourself, you stand a greater chance of archiving the majority of business objects successfully, than if you didn't follow the archiving sequence.

In conclusion, the archivability check is tied to various criteria, which depend on the data type, and the application in which the data was created. This check is always application-specific, because only the application contains information about which data to archive and which data to retain in the system.

2.1.2 Performing the Archivability Check

The archivability check is either performed directly in the write program, or in a special check program that precedes the write program. For more information about individual archiving programs, see Section 5.1.3.

If the write program is to conduct the archivability check, it must combine all of the technical and business logic of a check program, as well as the write logic itself. Then it can select and write only those business objects into the archive that meet the archivability criteria.

Checking in the write program

Some data will be checked for archivability by a check program, which precedes the write program, and which adds an indicator to the archivable business objects. Depending on the application, this indicator is called a *deletion flag* or a *deletion indicator*. The terms *archiving flag* or *archiving indicator* are also commonly used. This type of check program is scheduled as a preprocessing program in Archive Administration.

Checking in a preprocessing program

When a deletion indicator is set, the tagged data can no longer be changed. The user can only display it as read-only data. Therefore, the deletion indicator works as a change lock that cannot be revoked. Data that is tagged in this way can only be archived. Depending on the application, deletion indicators can be set by the user, or set automatically by the system.

Deletion indicator

For some master data, such as material master data, a user-enabled deletion flag is used instead of a deletion indicator. Material master records are used mainly in industry. Article master records that are used in the SAP for Retail industry solution pertain to material mas-

Deletion flag

ter records, but are archived and deleted according to a different procedure. In order to set deletion flags, the user can use a deletion proposal list, which contains all materials that have no inventory. The user can set the deletion flag to be effective immediately, or schedule it in the system to be set at a later date. The tagged master records are considered to be logically deleted, although the user can clear the deletion flag at any time. After archiving, the master records will be physically deleted.

The residence time concept is not used for material master records. By setting the deletion flag, you ensure that further transaction data that reference the material master record being tagged for archiving and deletion, will not be created. Deletion flags can be set at different organizational levels, such as the client, plant, or sales organization. The material master record is then considered to be logically deleted, and will be physically deleted at this and all other hierarchical sublevels at a later date.

Combined procedure

For some data, a combined deletion flag and deletion indicator procedure is used, instead of the simple concepts described above. This combination enables greater flexibility for tagging business objects for archiving.

With this procedure, tagging involves two steps. First, the preprocessing program, in its first run, sets a deletion flag for all business objects that meet the archivability criteria. Then, if a user calls a business object in the change mode, a message indicates that the data can no longer be changed. However, some applications allow you to manually remove deletion flags. These business objects will no longer be considered by the write program, and can be processed by the user afterwards.

During the second run, the preprocessing program marks all business objects that have deletion flags with deletion indicators. These business objects are then locked against further changes, and will be archived during the next write session of the archiving object.

Deletion flags and deletion indicators are used primarily for archiving master data. As shown above, however, the deletion flag for material master data is not set by a preprocessing program, but by the user. The reason for this is obvious: a program cannot decide if a master record is no longer needed and can therefore be archived and deleted. Only the user can make this decision. Ultimately, the human factor is still the determining factor.

Archivability checks that occur in the write program can have a negative influence on the runtime performance of the program, if they are complex. For example, there are some checks that test for several statuses, which prolongs the overall runtime. However, because the write program performs the archivability check, a preprocessing program is not needed, causing the total duration of the checking and writing phase to remain the same.

Performance aspects

The use of a dedicated check program has a positive influence on the runtime of the write program, because the check logic is completely integrated into the preprocessing program. The write program then simply has to evaluate the indicator, and can write the particular business object into the archive, without further testing.

The choice of combined or separate programs for archiving depends, first, on the data type to be archived, like the material master in our previous example. In some cases, there are technical reasons for separating the check and write logic. For example, if the archivability check is a complex multilevel process, then it should be separated from writing for performance reasons.

2.2 Main Data Archiving Processes

SAP data archiving is divided into the following main processes:

Two mandatory processes and one optional process

1. **Writing to the archive**
   Based on an archiving object, the data to be archived is read in the database and is sequentially written to newly created archive files.

2. **Deleting from the database**
   After the data to be archived is written to the archive files, the delete program removes the data from the database. In order to ensure that the data has been properly archived, the delete program first reads the archive files created during the write phase, and then deletes the corresponding data from the database.

3. **Storing the archive files (optional)**
   Archive files created during the write phase can be transferred to external storage systems. This phase is not a part of the archiving

process itself, but can occur optionally, even before the delete phase.

Complete archiving sessions Both the write and delete phases are essential parts of every complete archiving session, during which data that has been previously written to the archive is completely deleted from the database. This is the only way to ensure that the data exists in only one place—the database or the archive.

Data security due to a two-step procedure In order to avoid data loss due to errors during archiving, a two-step procedure is used. During the first step, the data is written to archive files. The second step, deleting the data from the database only occurs after the archive file has been completely written and at least the file header (see Section 5.2.3) has been read successfully. This procedure detects possible errors that may occur during the transmission of data over the network from the database to the archive file. If there is an error, a new archiving session can be started, because the data still exists in the database.

Archiving during live operation Data can be archived during live operation, that is, the user can continue to work with the system during archiving. However, this can cause performance bottlenecks during large-scale archiving sessions, for example, if tables are accessed during live operation in which records are being deleted. For this reason, data archiving should be carried out during periods of low system load.

Storage Archive files that have been created don't need to be stored on an appropriate storage medium; however, it is often part of the archiving process, because it is not safe and cost-effective in the long run to simply keep the archive files in the file system.

Accessing archived data Access to archived data is very important, especially for research and evaluation (which should also include archived data).

Reloading The reloading of archived data into the database represents a special case. Reloading should only be attempted if the wrong data was falsely archived, and this operation needs to be reversed. Therefore, reloading is not part of the archiving process itself, and should only be carried out by experienced administrators. For more information about reloading, see below in this chapter, or refer to Section 1.3.1.

For some archiving objects, it is necessary to carry out additional jobs by executing preprocessing and postprocessing programs (before or after archiving).

The main phases of the data archiving process are detailed in the following sections, along with other activities that sometimes occur within the framework of data archiving. You can carry out the described processes and activities through Archive Administration, which you can reach via transaction SARA, or from the SAP menu by using the path **Tools · Administration · Administration · Data archiving**. Figure 2.4 shows the initial Archive Administration screen that appears after entering archiving object FI_DOCUMNT for financial accounting documents.

Transaction SARA—entering Archive Administration

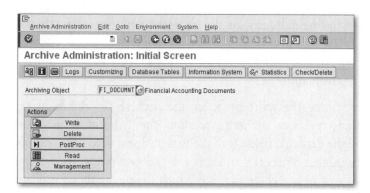

Figure 2.4 Initial Screen of Archive Administration

2.2.1 Writing Data from the Database to the Archive

The write phase is the starting point of the archiving process. This phase starts with the execution of the write program, which you can schedule through Archive Administration. Enter the desired archiving object, select a variant or create a new one, then set the start date, as well as the spool parameters. When entering a variant, make sure that it has not been used in another write session. Otherwise, you run the risk of archiving data multiple times, which can lead to corrupted results when evaluating the archived data volume. If you select a variant that has already been used, Archive Administration will inform you.

Scheduling a write program

In order to estimate the storage space available in the target file system for the archive files, you can determine the current free space

Determining free space

(currently available storage space) using the **Archive Directory** function, prior to the write phase. The function is available in the **Create Archive Files** screen in Archive Administration. The amount of space that the archive files will occupy in the file system is difficult to estimate. Therefore, the detected free space should only be considered as an indication of whether the write phase can conclude without storage space problems. During archiving, data is compressed by up to a factor of 5. Data stored in cluster tables is not compressed further.

You can determine the expected storage space requirements by starting the write job in the test mode, and by analyzing the log created by the test run. In addition to the space requirements, this log also provides additional statistical information, such as the number of processed business objects, or the occupied table space in Mbytes. You can view this information using the log function that you can reach from Archive Administration via **Logs**. See also Section 5.2.5 for more information.

Process flow   When executing the write program, the Archive Development Kit (ADK) first creates an archiving session. Then, the write program selects all the data that belongs to the first business object. As soon as the first business object is written as a data object (see glossary), the ADK creates a new archive file into which the next data objects are written. If the predefined file limit is reached and more data objects have to be written, the ADK closes the current archive file and creates a new archive file. This file switch only occurs between data objects and not within a data object.

This procedure ensures that all the data of a data object is kept together physically in one archive file. A data object can be read either as a whole or not at all, which ensures that no inconsistencies occur during later deletion of data. Figure 2.5 shows the flow of the write process during data archiving.

After the last data object has been written, ADK closes the last archive file. As far as ADK is concerned, writing is just a technical process—data can originate from one or several database tables. This data source information is saved in the respective archiving object.

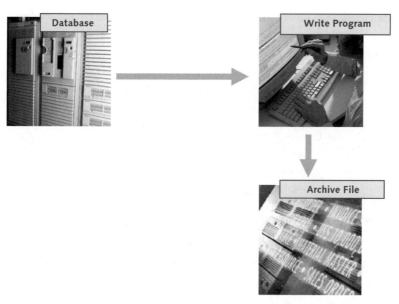

Figure 2.5 Creating the (First) Archive File

Strictly speaking, the write operation continues until one of the following events occurs:

▶ Archiving is completed.

▶ The archive file has reached its maximum size, defined in archiving-object-specific Customizing.

▶ The archive file has reached its maximum number of data objects, defined in archiving-object-specific Customizing.

You don't need to back up your database before archiving. After finishing archiving, however, you should perform a backup of the created archive files, because data might be deleted, if archive files are lost after the delete phase. During the write phase, ADK saves verification data, in addition to the actual data, in the archive file. Verification data can be analyzed when data is deleted, read, or reloaded, in order to ensure that only intact data is processed. For example, you cannot delete data from the database, if the archive file is corrupted. For more information about this function, see Section 5.2.3.

After finishing the write phase, that is, after all the data belonging to one archiving session is completely written into the archive, ADK triggers a system event. By concatenating this event with a certain background job, for example, saving the archive data before the delete phase, you will automate tasks that follow the write phase. You can define new jobs using transaction SM36. For more information about this function, see Section 5.4.4.

Suspending archiving sessions

If necessary, you can interrupt an archiving session that is still in the write phase, and continue it later. This is a useful option, if the predefined timeframe for carrying out archiving was too short, or if you realize that the free storage space for the archive data is too small. However, a interruption can only occur if the archiving object in question supports the suspension.

For more information about interrupting and continuing archiving sessions, please refer to Section 5.4.3.

2.2.2   Deleting Data from the Database

Scheduling a delete program

After the data objects are completely written into the archive during the write phase, they must be deleted from the database during the delete phase. Data is deleted by ADK deletion programs, which you can schedule using Archive Administration. Scheduling requires that you select the archiving sessions that the delete program should process. Usually, this is only the latest created archiving session.

Event-driven scheduling

In addition to supporting the time-dependent scheduling of the delete program, ADK also supports event-driven scheduling. You can define the event that should trigger the start of the delete job in archiving-object-specific Customizing, under **Settings for Delete Program**.

Scheduling delete programs outside Archive Administration

In general, you can also schedule delete programs outside of Archive Administration. This is especially useful when the number of scheduled simultaneous delete jobs needs to be limited, or when you want to have a better overview of all delete jobs during the delete phase. Delete jobs are either directly scheduled using the SAP Job Scheduler (transaction SM36), an external scheduler, or indirectly using the program RSARCHD. For more information about scheduling delete jobs, see Section 5.4.5.

> **Note**
>
> By setting the **Test mode** indicator in the initial delete program screen in Archive Administration, you can execute the write program in test mode, without deleting data from the database.

You can use this functionality to estimate the expected duration of the delete process, and you can check if errors could occur during a delete session in live mode. The relevant information about this process is stored in the associated log that can be accessed from Archive Administration by selecting **Logs**.

If necessary, you can change the sequence of the archiving phases. You can start the storage phase first, so that you only execute the delete phase after the storage phase finishes. For more information on this topic, see Section 2.2.3.

Delete phase after storage phase

The delete phase starts when the delete program opens a specific archive file; the data stored there will then be deleted from the database. Data is always deleted on a per object basis. However, before a data object can be deleted, a corresponding ADK function module ensures that the contents of the data object can be read in the archive. This procedure, called *test reading*, ensures that data objects are only deleted from the database if they were properly stored in the archive file.

Process flow

The test reading and delete processes then continue sequentially, until all of the data objects in the archive file have been read. For other files belonging to the archiving session, additional delete jobs have to be scheduled, because only one archive file is processed with each execution of the delete program. To ensure that the delete program does not access a completely processed archive file a second time, archive management records that the archive file has already been processed.

Depending on the Customizing settings of the delete program and the intended effect, there are two possible scenarios for executing the delete program:

Two possible scenarios

- Deleting after writing
- Deleting during writing

2.2.2.1 Deleting After Writing

With this option, the delete job is scheduled to occur separately after the write phase is completed. The write phase is finished when all data objects have been written into archive files, and the archive file created last has closed correctly. Deleting data from the database will then occur in a second, separate step, as shown in Figure 2.6.

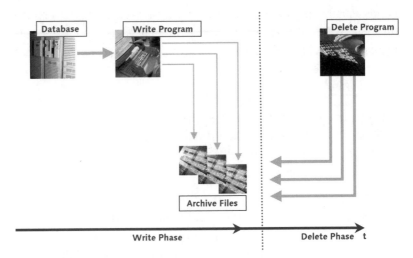

Figure 2.6 Archiving Session with Separate Write and Delete Jobs

Write and delete phases as close as possible to each other

It is very unlikely that archived data will be changed in the application, because data is usually only archived if it is no longer needed for day-to-day business. In order to ensure this, the time lag between the write and delete phases should be as short as possible. Or, deleting should occur directly after writing.

Customizing

You can completely separate the write and delete phases by not setting the **Start Automatically** indicator in the **Settings for Delete Program** section of archiving-object-specific Customizing.

This scenario is especially useful if you want to intervene between the write and delete phases of data archiving. Intervening may be necessary, because you may need to back up archived data before deleting it, or the available timeframe for the resource-intensive delete phase may not be long enough.

2.2.2.2 Deleting During Writing

As soon as the write program has closed the first archive file (and while it is writing the next one), the delete program runs a read verification on the first archive file, and deletes the respective data objects from the database, if the file was successfully read. Then, the ADK runtime system automatically schedules the corresponding delete jobs. Because deleting data in the database generally takes longer than writing the individual archive file, several delete programs usually operate concurrently on the previously created archive files. Figure 2.7 shows that a delete job is started as soon as the corresponding archive file is closed. In this case, three delete jobs are active concurrently.

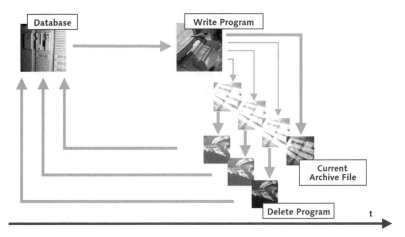

Figure 2.7 Archiving Session with Concurrent Write and Delete Jobs

You can execute the write and delete jobs for a particular archiving object in parallel by ensuring that the **Do Not Start Before End of Write Phase** indicator is not set in transaction AOBJ. In addition, the **Start Automatically** indicator in the **Settings for Delete Program** section of archiving-object-specific Customizing must be set. Because of this parallel process, the data object throughput in the database during deleting is increased, which leads to a shorter archiving runtime.

Customizing

Before using this function, you should first read the documentation concerning the respective archiving object, because some archiving objects don't allow you to clear an indicator that has already been set.

When all the delete jobs of an archiving session have finished, the ADK triggers a system event. By reacting to this event, post-archiving processes, such as updating indexes or the input help, can start. For more information about this function, see Section 5.4.4.

Automating
downstream tasks

2.2.3 Storing Archive Files (Optional)

Storage as an
optional main
process
Technically speaking, storing an archive file outside the file system is not a part of the data archiving process itself. The process is finished when the archive files are created in the file system, and the data is deleted from the database. Therefore, it is the data archiving user who decides what to do with the created archived files.

In general, it is not enough to replicate application data in the archive, and then to remove it from the database. The archive files themselves have to be prepared for potential access to the data saved therein. Usually, this requires the use of a storage system, as well as the introduction of a company-wide concept for managing and safely storing archive files (if they are stored manually).

Figure 2.8 shows the storage concept in the context of SAP data archiving. This figure shows that storage is an additional data archiving process that requires third-party technology.

Figure 2.8 Data Archiving and Storage of Archive Files

Storage options for
archive files
In principle, you can consider the following options for storing and managing archive files, assuming that you don't want to keep the archive files in the same file system in which they were created (which is also possible):

▶ **Storing in a storage system**
Here, the files are stored in a certified, external third-party storage system, which is connected via the ArchiveLink interface (see Chapter 3). Storage systems (usually *jukeboxes* with optical storage media) manage the data on tertiary storage media. The created

archive files are automatically transferred at the end of the write or delete phase (depending on the sequence that is set in archiving-object-specific Customizing), although they can also be transferred manually.

You can use any available storage systems that have been certified for ArchiveLink. You can obtain an overview of certified vendors from the Partner Information Center at *http://www.sap.com/partners/directories/searchpartner.epx* if you select the SAP-defined integration scenario *BC-AL—ArchiveLink Interface for Archive Systems* in the *Search for Solutions* section.

▶ **Transferring to an HSM system**
With this type of storage, archive files are directly transferred to a connected hierarchical storage management system (HSM system), which independently stores and manages archive files. An HSM system consists of hardware and control software that stores and manages data on storage media with varying access characteristics (such as hard disks, magneto-optical disks, tapes, etc.), depending on how often they are accessed.

The HSM system acts as an "unlimited" file system that integrates the file system in which the archive files were created into its storage hierarchy. To enable storage, you only need to update the file path to the target file system in the technical data archiving Customizing section. Communication via ArchiveLink is not necessary.

From the user's point of view, the storage in an HSM system is transparent: You cannot determine on which medium data currently resides. Only access delays to archived data might suggest that the file was provided by a slow data medium.

There is no certification process for using HSM systems with the SAP Business Suite; therefore, any available HSM system can, theoretically, be used for storing archive data. For performance reasons, however, the HSM system should support block-by-block access to archive files. For more information, see SAP Note 71935.

No certification for HSM systems

▶ **Alternative storage**
If you don't want to use a storage or HSM system, you can manually store archived data on company-internal tertiary storage media (magnetic tape, CD-ROM, optical disc, etc.), or you can use standard backup methods (data backup, mirroring, etc.). In this

case, the company's IT department must manage the stored archive files.

In principle, this kind of storage is easier and cheaper to implement, although it requires more maintenance and administration of the data media. It also requires the introduction of a complex company concept, which includes administrative and data security requirements, such as the periodic transfer of data to newer data media, for example.

In order to start the storage phase, one or more archive files, correctly closed by the write program, need to be available. Depending on the desired storage process, the flow is structured as follows:

▶ **External storage system**
When storing archive files in an external storage system via the ArchiveLink interface, the files are automatically transferred to the specified storage system. To do this, the ADK sends a storage command to ArchiveLink, which controls the communication with the storage system. Storage occurs either after the write phase finishes, or after the write and delete phases finish.

▶ **HSM system**
If the archive files are to be transferred to an HSM system for storage, no action is required from the SAP system. Nevertheless, you have to integrate the local file system, in which the archive files were created, into the operating system level of the HSM system storage hierarchy. Because of the technical design of an HSM system, the user can always access the files, as if they reside on a local drive.

▶ **Manual storage**
Archive files can be manually stored on a tertiary storage medium, as long as the archive files were correctly closed during the write phase, and no automatic storage is scheduled. However, manual storage must not be attempted before or during the delete phase, because the delete program needs to access the archived data.

One major disadvantage of manual storage is that the stored archive files must also be manually administrated. This makes subsequent access and provision of archive files more difficult to achieve.

You can set the desired storage sequence in the **Sequence** area of Customizing archiving-object-specific Customizing. The choice of a particular storage sequence is mainly determined by data security aspects. If you choose the **Storage Before Deleting** option, then data in the database will only be deleted after an archive file is stored in the storage system. By setting the **Delete Program Reads from Storage System** indicator, you can further increase data security, albeit at the expense of performance: Data will then be directly read from the storage system and not from the file system during the delete phase. Before deleting the data, you can therefore ensure that the archive files were stored successfully.

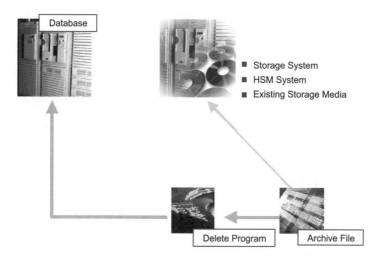

Figure 2.9 Storage of Created Archive Files

You may have to change the settings for the utilized storage system in Customizing. For more information, please refer to the documentation for your storage system.

Figure 2.9 also shows the storage of archive files.

2.3 Other Processes and Tasks

In addition to the central data archiving processes and process flows described in the preceding sections, there are other processes and tasks that must be carried out in the context of data archiving, although they are not part of the actual archiving process.

2.3.1   Accessing Archived Data

Access guaranteed
at any time

The purpose of data archiving is to relocate application data that no longer plays a role in current business processes, and is therefore no longer needed in the system. However, data relocation alone is not enough. Archived data must remain accessible, in case it is needed; otherwise, you may as well have deleted it. SAP data archiving meets this requirement by saving data in such a way that it can be displayed at any time, using the appropriate read program. The read program is provided by the respective archiving object, and is used to select archived data in an appropriate form, according to user-defined selection criteria. In certain cases, you can even reload data back into the database.

SAP data archiving
is platform
and release
independent

Archived data is accessed by using metadata, which ADK writes into the archive file, along with the actual application data, during the write phase. The metadata includes information about the system environment at the time of archiving, such as the codepage used or the number format, as well as relevant database information, such as the data type and table column lengths. When accessing an archive file, this information is also interpreted and is used to display the data. However, the data in the archive files is not changed. This function ensures that SAP data archiving is platform and release independent.

Access types

In principle, you can access archived data in the following ways:

► Evaluating archive files
► Reading individual business objects

2.3.1.1   Evaluating Archive Files

Sequential reading

This access method, which is also referred to as *sequential reading*, is based on the fact that all business objects included in an archive file are read one after the other, and are displayed according to the entered selection criteria. Usually, only the most important basic information of the business objects, such as the sold-to party, order date, or item number, is displayed. This is the simplest way to display archived data, and is used primarily for evaluating the archived data volume. This type of evaluation can be extended to include all documents for a certain posting period or for a certain number range interval. The size and the number of archive files to be read define the speed of the sequential read program. Most archiving objects support this access method.

Figure 2.10 Defining the Data Source for Evaluating Financial Accounting Documents

Furthermore, some applications allow for a combined evaluation, that is, resident data is displayed together with archived data. For example, the document compact journal, (RFBELJ00), and the line item journal, (RFEPOJ00), in financial accounting, both list the most important header and item data for selected financial accounting documents, such as the account, document, and sales type, or the posting period. You can select the data source for both evaluation programs (see Figure 2.10), thereby defining whether each program will evaluate only documents from the database, or from the archive as well.

Combined evaluation of resident and archived data

You can access the functions described above, as well as other evaluation functions for archiving object FI_DOCUMNT, by selecting **Read** in Archive Administration.

2.3.1.2 Displaying Archived Single Objects

This access method is also called *direct or single document access*. This method enables you to display complete single business objects, such as a sales or posting document. Direct access requires an index, which shows the read program the exact storage location of each individual business object in the archive. The storage location is defined by the key of the archive file (where the business object is

Direct or single document access

located), as well as by the exact position within the archive file. Based on this information, the read program can locate and display the desired business object.

Building an index | The *Archive Information System* (AS) is used to assemble an index required for the display of most archiving objects. The index that is built up in this way is referred to as an *archive information structure*. In earlier releases, some archiving objects enabled you to build up and remove an application-specific index via the **Index** function in Archive Administration. For example, for FI_DOCUMNT it was the index ARIX_BKPF. However, compared to an archive information structure, this kind of archive index provided only very limited selection options when searching for archived data. For this reason, most of those archiving objects have been switched to the Archive Information System by now.

For more information about the different ways of accessing archived data, including the available tools, see Chapter 4.

2.3.2 Reloading Archived Data

Application data that has been archived using SAP data archiving can be displayed years later, even by later releases (using appropriate read programs). Therefore, archived data doesn't have to be reloaded to your current database, in most cases. Besides, as will be described later, reloading can be a difficult procedure.

Process flow | During reloading, the archived data objects are inserted into the current database tables. A reload job processes one archiving session at a time. The reload program checks each of the data objects in the archiving session to determine whether it meets the reload criteria, and then loads it into the database. Usually, data objects that are not reloaded will be transferred to a new archiving session. The original archiving session is blocked from further access by ADK via a new status. In this way, you can ensure that after the reload process, a data object is either located in the database or in the archive.

Two possible scenarios | The reloading of archived data usually occurs in two scenarios:

▶ **Reloading after archiving**
This will be the case if you realize after archiving that you have archived data that is still needed online. This can be due to faulty

Customizing, such as selecting a residence time that is too short, or entering the wrong selection criteria.

The reload function was designed for real emergencies. After realizing that you have an emergency situation, you should reload data back into the database immediately after archiving. You should be able to do this without encountering any problems.

Reload only in emergency situations and immediately after archiving

Depending on the archiving object, you may not be able to reconstruct all of the archived data in the database. For example, when reloading a sales document, the reload program cannot reload the linked cost center debits (controlling data). Consequently, data is lost from the database. Furthermore, there are certain tables that are deleted as they are archived. This means that the data from these tables was archived, but it cannot be reloaded. Another limitation involves data from certain archiving classes, which also cannot be reloaded. So, before reloading archived data, you should always consider the possible consequences of reloading.

Reload limitations

▶ **Reloading some time after archiving**
This will be the case, if you want to reload data that was archived a while ago.

With this variant, there is the danger that archived data will no longer "match" the current data in the database; the result is possible data inconsistencies. In other words, you are trying to load data from a historical database context into a current database context. The following problems can occur:

Possible data inconsistencies after reloading

▷ **Overwriting of documents:** In the time that has elapsed between the archiving and reload processes, some number range intervals may have been reset, due to a number range interval overflow. If the reloaded archive files contain documents with identical document numbers as those in the current database, then the documents in the current database are overwritten.

▷ **Inconsistent organizational data:** Reloaded archive files may contain organizational data, such as a sales organization or a division that no longer exists in the current system. This can also lead to inconsistent data.

The longer the time period between data archiving and reloading, the greater the danger of data inconsistency after reloading. You should not reload data if the system has been updated to a more

Do not reload across different releases

recent release. If you attempt to do this, you should note that SAP is not liable for problems that may occur.

Despite the reservations stated here, you may decide that a reload of archived data cannot be avoided. If this is the case, then you should ensure, prior to reloading, that all data that is related to the data about to be reloaded is still in the database, or is reloaded first. This is the only way to avoid data inconsistencies. In addition, before reloading, you should read the documentation for the relevant application, and you should search for all relevant SAP notes.

For the reasons stated above, the reloading of data is not considered to be a standard function of SAP data archiving, but is only an emergency measure. In general, SAP does not support reloading.

2.3.3 Executing Preprocessing and Postprocessing Programs

Tagging business objects to be archived

For some archiving objects, preprocessing programs are used to prepare the business objects for archiving. The main task of a preprocessing program is to check the selected business objects for archivability, and to set an archiving indicator or status for each successfully checked business object (for more information, see Section 2.1). Business objects, once tagged with such an indicator, can no longer be changed. If the user calls such a business object in change mode, a message will appear, indicating that the business object is selected for archiving, and therefore can no longer be changed.

Preprocessing programs can also have other uses. In the case of sales document archiving, the preprocessing program is only used as an analyzing program. It determines the number of archivable documents, but it does not tag them for archiving.

Division of work between the check and write programs

If a preprocessing program is used, then the write program (executed later) only has to select the tagged business objects and write them into the archive without checking further. This concept of work division between the check and write programs has a positive influence on program performance. Furthermore, it enables a better integration of the archiving process into general system operation. Due to its advantages, this concept is increasingly being used in different areas, such as in the data archiving process of SAP Customer Relationship Management (see Section 6.2).

For archiving objects that provide preprocessing programs, you can schedule these programs from Archive Administration via the **Preprocessing** function.

Postprocessing programs are also not intended for all archiving objects. They are used to execute necessary postprocessing tasks in the database, after archiving is finished. This includes removing log entries, clearing index tables, and updating statistical data. In these cases, the postprocessing program acts as a kind of "cleaning program" for the data volume after archiving.

Postprocessing tasks after archiving

For example, after archiving financial accounting documents, it is useful to delete the respective secondary indexes. This task is performed by a postprocessing program that starts automatically after the archiving session and does not require any separate scheduling. The only prerequisite is that you have set the **Start Automatically** indicator in the **Settings for Postprocessing Program** area in archiving-object-specific Customizing. Or, if there is an acute shortage of storage space in the database, you can also start the postprocessing program manually to delete expired secondary indexes. To do this, you can use the **Postprocessing** function from Archive Administration for the archiving object FI_DOCUMNT.

In some applications, postprocessing programs are only used to delete previously archived data records from the database. In Quality Management, for example, the successfully archived database records of inspection lots are deleted from the database using a postprocessing program.

Postprocessing programs only work on database data, and not on archived data. Therefore, you do not need to link to the archive in emergency situations. Postprocessing programs are usually executed after the archiving session, although they can also be used independently.

For archiving objects that offer postprocessing programs, you can schedule those programs from Archive Administration using the **Postprocessing** function.

The functionalities and use of preprocessing or postprocessing depend strongly on the applications in which they are used. Therefore, they cannot be explained here in detail. For more information, please refer to the relevant application documentation.

This chapter presents the various options available for storing and retaining archive files. It describes the main strategies, focusing on security and access options. This chapter is intended to help the IT manager choose the appropriate storage strategy.

3 Storing Archived Data

by Gerhard Scherer

Archived data needs to be safely stored over a long period of time, because it must always remain accessible. Because the data was removed from the database and still exists in the archive files, storage security requirements are very high.

As we described in Chapter 2, the following options for storing archive files are available, which will be considered in detail in this chapter:

▶ Storage in a certified storage system

▶ Using a hierarchical storage management system (HSM)

▶ Using existing storage media

3.1 Criteria for Choosing a Storage Strategy

Before you decide on a certain storage strategy or storage system, you should first look at the most important selection criteria. We would like to emphasize that there is no "perfect" solution that fulfills all the criteria. Therefore, you have to adapt the criteria catalog presented below to your requirements, and then evaluate its performance. This evaluation is especially important, because certain criteria might contradict each other. In some cases, you might even have to prioritize one criterion over the other. For example, security considerations might lead you to store archive files on multiple external media, before the delete phase is initiated. However, this may pre-

Storage strategies are always customer-specific

vent you from lightening the operational database load, i.e., you might also need to remove data as quickly as possible from the database, if it is reaching its full capacity. It makes no sense to make more demands on the storage system than on the leading system—the SAP system. For example, preparing the storage system for an emergency situation is only useful if the SAP system is also prepared.

This chapter first deals with the most important criteria for storage. A number of storage options are then presented, taking into account the criteria described. Because there is no universal storage strategy that meets the needs of all customers and their requirements, this chapter will not attempt to define any one storage strategy as the optimal solution. Just note that all of the strategies described have been successfully implemented at customer sites.

Storage criteria The storage strategy criteria can be grouped according to the following keywords:

▶ **Security**
How secure is the particular storage option?

▶ **Costs**
How much does the selected storage method cost (per use, day-to-day)?

▶ **Integration**
How can the storage option be integrated into the existing IT infrastructure?

▶ **Access options**
How can the stored data be accessed, and how will this affect the system performance?

▶ **Lifecycle of the storage option**
How long can data be safely stored in the storage system?

This list of criteria and the following discussion are not complete, because the criteria depend on each customer's situation and their requirements. However, we have tried to include and discuss all the typical criteria in the following description of storage strategies. Of course, there are customer situations, in which other requirements, and other criteria need to be considered.

3.1.1 Security

You should ask the following questions when considering security:

▶ How secure is the storage path?

▶ How secure is the storage itself?

▶ Which security options does the storage system provide?

3.1.1.1 How Secure is the Storage Path?

This question concerns the entire process—from creating the archive files to the final storage on external media. The archive files that are created must be transferred to final storage without being altered. In particular, you need to verify that the correct data is transferred to the target machine, when transferring archive files from computer to computer. Simply copying over the Network File System (NFS) is not enough to ensure this security, because the NFS first buffers the data in the main memory. Therefore, you cannot be sure that it was really written to the file.

Furthermore, security considerations require that archive files be backed up before the data is deleted from the database tables, ideally before the delete phase. This requires you to be able to control the storage device in order to specify when and how the archive files are transferred to secure media. For example, security requirements are not met if data can be transferred to secure storage, but the leading system cannot determine whether and when the data was transferred to secure media.

Saving archive files before the delete phase

Concerns about storage security can be summarized by the following questions:

▶ **Verification**
Is it possible or intended to integrate a verification process into the storage process?

▶ **Write-through**
Is it possible or intended to control the write process on secure media during storage?

89

3.1.1.2 How Secure is the Storage Itself?

Storage security is closely linked to the media type used. Different media have greatly differing performance and security criteria:

▶ **Hard disks**
For security reasons, only hard disk systems that don't lose data during malfunctions should be used. RAID (redundant array of independent disks) systems are especially suitable because they maintain maximum availability by using redundant disks.

▶ **MO or WORM**
MO (magneto-optical, rewritable medium) and WORM (optical, non-rewritable medium) disks are based on the same technology. If MO disks are used to store archive files, then the system used must ensure that the written archive files are not overwritten. Technically speaking, the process of writing to MO or WORM disks is the same as writing to a hard disk. Files can be written one-by-one, until the disk is full. With optical technology, it is easier (compared to a hard disk) to technically reproduce data, if a MO or WORM disk fails.

▶ **CD**
Typically, archive files are stored on a CD (optically aided writable medium) in two steps. In the first step, data is received and buffered, until a complete CD can be burned. Once this level is reached, the data is then physically transferred to the CD. This also requires that the buffered data be automatically secured (e.g., on RAID disks).

If you have ever burned a CD yourself, you can understand that the burn process itself is more prone to errors than writing data to a hard disk, MO, or WORM disk. To solve this problem, you have to closely monitor the burn process in the storage system.

The same applies to burning a DVD (also an optically aided writable medium) that can also be used for the long-term storage of data. However, at this point, you should note that compared to the CD, the missing standardization of the DVD (there is an almost unmanageable number of DVD formats and technologies) bears certain risks with regard to the long-term support and security of a specific DVD technology.

▶ **Magnetic tapes**
Magnetic tapes are a cost-effective, but slow storage medium. And regarding security, magnetic tapes can only be used for a limited number of re-writes, before they have to be replaced. Magnetic tapes are exposed to great physical stress.

The following general statements can be made concerning the lifecycle of storage media:

Lifecycle of storage media

▶ Because of the physical stress they endure, magnetic tapes have the shortest lifecycle, and therefore have to be replaced regularly.

▶ Hard disks have a definable average lifecycle.

▶ Suppliers of optical storage media like to advertise that these media have a lifecycle of up to 100 years. This statement is meaningless, because it has not been, and cannot be verified.

Irrespective of the lifecycle of storage media, storage security is primarily measured by whether a read access to the once-written data always returns the correct data. This is not the case in the following situations:

Defective systems

▶ The medium that was written on is defective, or can no longer be read.

▶ The hardware in which the medium is located is defective.

▶ The storage system used is defective.

These problems are often due to relatively simple, easy-to-repair defects, for example, a short-term media or software error in the system used. However, you should also take into account catastrophes such as a fire in the archive room. These types of catastrophic failures can only be tolerated if the entire storage system is physically replicated.

Storage security questions can be summarized as follows:

▶ When storing, is it possible to write simultaneously to more than one medium?

▶ Is the automatic writing of backup copies to different media in different locations supported?

▶ Is there continuous (24 hours/7 days a week) support for automatically switching over from the live to the security system, after the live system fails, without losing time and data?

3.1.1.3 Which Security Options Does the Storage System Provide?

The storage system itself has to be able to back up the stored data. You should note here that storage systems often not only consist of media for receiving data; they also have their own databases. The media as well as the databases have to provide backup functions to save the stored data. Besides the security requirements themselves, the backup solutions provided have to fit or be integrated with your existing security systems. Otherwise, additional costs are incurred from maintaining and managing different security systems.

Backup and recovery
When archive files are stored, two separate technical systems exchange data with each other. With this integration scenario, you need to ensure that backup and, in particular, recovery—i.e., restoration of the data—occurs on a mutually consistent data basis. However, with this archiving scenario, both systems don't have equal importance; the SAP system is the leading system. For this reason, the requirements can be reduced in such a way that the storage system must be able to reproduce any data that it has received, at any time (through recovery, for emergency situations).

In addition, the quality of the security options provided by the storage system can be determined by considering the following questions:

▶ What are the backup options for the storage media used to store the archive files?

▶ What backup options are available for the database of the storage system?

▶ Can you integrate the storage system backup function into the current system landscape?

▶ Which strategies are provided that enable you to execute a backup procedure that is consistent with the database of the SAP system?

3.1.2 Costs

The costs of different storage scenarios differ significantly—not only in terms of the purchase costs, but also with regard to the internal follow-up costs within the company.

3.1.2.1 Purchase Costs

Basically, two different price models are used by different vendors of storage systems: a user model and a volume model.

With the user model, a license is purchased for each user. Some suppliers also offer "concurrent user models" or "named user models." In the first case, a license is purchased for each concurrently accessing user, and in the second case, a license must be purchased for each separate user. In contrast to the SAP pricing system, the concurrent user model is the most common type offered by storage system suppliers.

User model

With the volume model, the volume of data managed is the pricing criteria instead of the number of users. You pay for the stored data volume, irrespective of the number of system users. When using an external storage system for your archive files, you should always compare prices closely, because the systems are priced very differently. The purchase price is not the only criterion; it has to be viewed in conjunction with other criteria.

Volume model

3.1.2.2 Operating Costs

When thinking long-term, the one-time purchase price is less important—the day-to-day operating costs soon become the central cost factor. Besides paying fixed support costs for the external storage system, you should definitely consider internal costs that are incurred from building up previously nonexistent knowledge and infrastructure in your company. This will especially be the case, if the selected storage system does not fit into the existing IT infrastructure of your company. A company whose infrastructure is based on a UNIX operating system will incur high costs to introduce a Windows-based storage system, and vice versa.

Besides the clearly definable costs of using an external storage system, you also have to include the quality costs of your external supplier's support organization. When using a mixed scenario with two systems (the SAP system and the storage system), it is more difficult for the supplier's support organization to deliver high-quality support, than if you only used their system. In theory, the supplier's support organization needs to know and understand not only their system, but also parts of the SAP system, in order to handle error

Non-quantifiable costs

messages and requests professionally. If the support team cannot solve problems that arise quickly, because they lack competence, additional costs are incurred — costs that are difficult to quantify.

3.1.3 Integration

When thinking about integrating the storage system with the SAP system, the following two questions, discussed separately below, have to be asked.

3.1.3.1 How Does the Storage System Fit into the Existing IT Landscape?

The selected storage system has to fit into the IT landscape of your company in terms of both technology and administration. If you don't consider this aspect, you may incur increased costs (see above), and you may end up with acceptance and administration problems. The selected system should reflect your company's hardware, operating system, and database strategy. Integration into the security systems of the existing infrastructure is the central security requirement of the system being introduced.

3.1.3.2 Besides Data Archiving, How Does Storage Add Value?

Using storage systems for data archiving and document management

A storage system adds value primarily in the areas of document management and data backup. Besides data archiving support, many suppliers of archive storage systems also offer extensive document management and document storage functions. Even if these functions are considered part of data archiving when a storage system is introduced, you should review whether document management or document integration will be a future need in your company. If this is the case, then it might be helpful to use the same system for archive file storage, document management, and document integration. This will increase the requirements for the system selection process, but it will help you to decrease costs in the long term.

Using the storage system for data backup

Additional value may be added from using the storage system for data backups in other parts of the company. The same selected storage system can be used not only to store archive files, but also to back up company file systems or databases. You should review this aspect individually, because you cannot assume that every storage system provides the necessary interfaces for integrating with the existing backup infrastructure.

3.1.4 Performance

From the SAP system's point of view, it is the storage system's task to supply stored data to accessing programs. This can be either sequential access to the entire archive file, or direct access to an individual business object (the byte position and length of the allocated area specify the storage location in the archive file). Furthermore, you must be able to completely copy archive files from and back into storage. In principle, all storage systems can carry out these operations—a hierarchical storage management (HSM) system utilizes the respective operating system commands, and ArchiveLink-certified storage systems (see Section 3.2.2) use certification requirements to specify functionality.

Irrespective of these existing access options, we would now like to focus on performance, by illustrating this aspect with an example of a typical performance problem during archive file storage.

3.1.4.1 Parallel Job Processing

Many external storage system operations can be sent out in parallel from the SAP system. A known problem is the parallel assignment of external storage systems when several large archive files are to be processed.

An archiving session created in the SAP system can contain several individual files. If the entire archiving session has to be copied back into the file system of the SAP system, the SAP system sends several parallel jobs to external storage. Each job consists of copying an archive file into the SAP file system. To execute these jobs with the best possible performance, a mechanism has to be implemented in the external storage system, which separates communication with the SAP system from the process itself (file provision). If this mechanism does not exist, then each job is sequentially processed from start to end, until the system can accept and process new jobs. This can lead to communication *timeouts* between the two systems.

If you have retrieved copies of archive files that are stored in a storage system into the file system and want to delete these copies, you

Deleting retrieved archive files

can use the RSARCH_LIST_RETRIEVED program. This program also ensures that the associated administration entries in archive management are updated. Please refer to SAP Note 597646 for further details.

3.1.4.2 Block-by-Block Access

A second important performance-critical aspect concerns the way in which the external storage system handles block-by-block access, when the archive file that contains these blocks is located on a slow medium. This medium could be a tape. A Jukebox with optical disks is also pretty slow, if the medium to be accessed has to be transported to the read drive first.

Two possible strategies

In short, the external system has two strategies for reacting to the job. It can read only the requested block from the slow medium, and then process the job with the block. Or, it can copy the entire file to a faster medium, with the expectation that there will be more requests for this file. As a result, write access for the job occurs only on the faster medium.

Both strategies have advantages and disadvantages. The first strategy carries out all the jobs at almost the same speed (except for the one-time reading of the medium into the read drive). With this strategy, you cannot take advantage of the faster medium's speed. The second strategy uses the faster medium for reading, which means better performance if the same file is accessed again. This increase is partially offset by the duration of the first access, in which the entire file has to be buffered to the faster medium.

SAP requires both access types (single read and multiple read) in one archive file. For this reason, you should determine whether the storage system supports an access strategy that combines the advantages of the aforementioned strategies, and suppresses the disadvantages. One possible solution could involve making the first access to the slower medium, while using this access to copy the file in parallel to a faster buffer. Additional accesses will therefore be made to the faster medium.

3.1.5 Long-Term Storage

When archiving files for storage, you must ensure that the storage system used is suitable for long-term storage. The files stored there have to remain accessible for several years.

Like information technology itself, data media evolves at an astonishing pace. You can assume that a new generation of optical storage media emerges every two to three years. The time period over which archived data must remain accessible far exceeds this turnover time. Each new generation of optical storage media is generally distinguished by increased data volume per medium, with decreased access time.

For the new storage media to be used in the existing infrastructure, the storage system must support technologies and strategies for data migration from the old to the new storage media. Automated mechanisms are especially important, because manual copying, which is time consuming, and prone to errors, is not an option.

Automated migration

Statistically, older archive files are accessed less often. If data is less frequently accessed, then access time requirements can be reduced, to the point where data is available offline and can only be accessed through manual administration. Along with this decrease in access frequency, you can decrease data retention costs by using storage hierarchies. Data that is scarcely or never accessed is migrated to slower, cheaper storage media. In order to utilize storage hierarchies, the storage system needs to support this storage technology. Moreover, it needs to contain automated time or data controlled mechanisms for migrating data from faster, more expensive media to slower, cheaper media.

Cutting costs by using storage hierarchies

When using a storage system that is certified for the ArchiveLink interface, another criterion comes into play: The ArchiveLink interface, which is used by SAP data archiving for archive file storage and access, is subject to an evolutionary process, reflected in the different ArchiveLink certification releases. When choosing an external storage system, you should ensure that it is open to future extensions or changes in the ArchiveLink interface. The supplier of the storage system in question can confirm this for you. By looking back at the past development of the respective storage system, you can get an additional sense of security options.

Supporting future ArchiveLink versions

To date there have been four ArchiveLink interface releases, to which storage systems can be certified. You should first check if the system is certified according to the current interface version. If it is not certified, then this usually shows that the supplier is not interested in the ArchiveLink interface in the long run—the current interface version has already been certified for several years. You can obtain an overview of certified vendors from the Partner Information Center at *http://www.sap.com/partners/directories/searchpartner.epx* if you select the SAP-defined integration scenario *BC-AL—ArchiveLink Interface for Archive Systems* in the *Search for Solutions* section.

Migrating to other storage systems

When looking at the long-term storage of data, you should also determine whether the storage system supports the migration of archive files to another storage system. This check is almost unnecessary if an ArchiveLink-certified system is used. Using ArchiveLink, you can migrate all objects known to ArchiveLink (including archive files) from one ArchiveLink-certified system to another certified system. However, this functionality does not mean that this solution will give you the best performance. ArchiveLink cannot migrate known objects according to physical viewpoints, that is, media-oriented object migration.

In summary, the following questions need to be asked regarding long-term storage:

▶ Does the storage system offer automated migration techniques for new storage technologies?

▶ Does the storage system offer automated time or volume-controlled migration mechanisms between different storage technologies?

▶ How long-term is the partnership with SAP (certification) for using an ArchiveLink-certified system?

▶ How open is the architecture of the storage system regarding data migration to another system?

3.2 Storage in a Certified Storage System

Archive file storage in an external storage system occurs through the ArchiveLink interface. For that reason, only ArchiveLink-certified storage systems should be used for storage.

But, before we delve into how archive files are handled when using ArchiveLink, we will discuss the purpose and specifics of ArchiveLink. You should not view the ArchiveLink solution only in the context of data archiving, but rather analyze it in a much broader context. ArchiveLink processes, as they historically relate to data archiving, are then examined in more detail. During this examination of archive file storage and access processes through ArchiveLink, the most important technical questions are discussed, and solutions to known problems are presented.

The section ends with an examination of the advantages of using ArchiveLink-certified storage systems.

3.2.1 Definitions: ArchiveLink, KPro, CMS

In the following sections, we will define the different services used for integrating documents with SAP applications from a historical and functional point of view. We will try to increase your understanding of the terms *ArchiveLink* and *Knowledge Provider* (KPro).

The following components are required to integrate documents into SAP applications:

Components for integrating documents

▶ **External content server**
on which documents are stored. From the SAP point of view, this content server could be a storage system.

▶ **Content server interface**
which allows you to execute functions on documents that are located on the content server. Some important functions include the display of a document, the storage of a file as a document in the external content server, and the retrieval of a document as a file from the content server.

▶ **Application interface**
for SAP applications, which enables you to use the relevant functions on the content server. This application interface actually consists of two interfaces, an application-level and a document-level

interface. The document-level interface encapsulates the content server interface for the applications, while the application interface maps the administration layer functions for the application level. To better understand the roles of the application interface, consider the following ArchiveLink example:

If an application wants to display a document, it can call a function on the application level interface, which could look like the following: "I am application object XY. Show me all documents that are linked to me." At the document-level interface, a comparable call would be the following: "Show me document number 9876 from content repository A1."

▶ **Administration layer**
between the content server interface and the application interface.

With SAP R/3 4.5A and earlier, only ArchiveLink fulfilled most of the functions mentioned for SAP applications. An SAP application integrates ArchiveLink functions; therefore, it can access administrative and interface functions, in order to process documents in the external content server. ArchiveLink is mainly distinguished by its ability to operate with very simple and slim administrative structures and application interfaces. This architecture is especially advantageous because of its integration simplicity for business applications, and because of its "mass" capability, due to its slim management tables.

Knowledge Provider for SAP R/3 4.5B and later

For SAP R/3 4.5B and later, this concept has been functionally expanded at the administration layer through the development of *Knowledge Provider* (KPro). KPro offers an application interface, based on content models, which enables very extensive, flexible document modeling. Applications are available for numerous functions beyond ArchiveLink, such as versioning, variant creation, content model-dependent indexing, and much more. In this way, SAP applications are able to integrate almost any document management function via KPro, or use ArchiveLink for "simple" documents, depending on the actual data process request.

Thus, the primary difference between ArchiveLink and KPro can be found at the application-interface(s) and administration layer levels. The content server interface is the same for both components, because it must be possible to use the same document functions on the same content server.

The components mentioned above are usually referred to as the following terms:

Frequently used terms

▶ **External content server**
In the KPro environment, it is referred to as a content server on which content repositories are set up. In ArchiveLink, these terms are also used since SAP R/3 4.5B. The terms *storage system*, *archive system*, and *external archive system* all have a similar meaning, and are still often used.

▶ **Content server interface**
The terms *ArchiveLink interface* or *ArchiveLink HTTP content server interface* (as of SAP R/3 4.5B) are used as synonyms for content server interface. For the same release and later, the functionally reduced HTTP content server interface also exists.

▶ **Application-level application interface**
In the KPro environment, the application-level application interface is called *KPro DMS interface* (Knowledge Provider Document Management Service). In the ArchiveLink environment, the term *ArchiveLink interface* is commonly used.

▶ **Document-level application interface**
The document-level application interface is called *KPro CMS interface* (Knowledge Provider Content Management Service) in KPro. There is no term in ArchiveLink because this interface is used by only a few applications. If a name is required, the term *ArchiveLink interface* is also used.

▶ **Administration layer**
The administration layer of KPro is usually called *KPro DMS*. In ArchiveLink, no special term is used for the administration layer.

To summarize, the following points regarding the use of the above components and terms should be emphasized:

Summary

▶ All functions used for integrating documents in SAP applications use certified ArchiveLink interfaces to external storage systems for document storage. In this way, the same storage systems can be used for any purpose, regardless of whether the application uses an ArchiveLink or KPro application interface.

▶ The terms *ArchiveLink interface* and *KPro CMS* can be used interchangeably, and refer to the use of document-level application interfaces. This is particularly important for data archiving, because, for reasons of simplicity, the ArchiveLink application interface was changed to the KPro CMS application interface for SAP R/3 4.6C.

From this point on, *ArchiveLink* will be used as the main term. This also corresponds to the term used by customers, because the established name is derived from the certified *ArchiveLink interface*. Whenever greater accuracy is needed, though, we will distinguish among ArchiveLink, KPro and CMS.

3.2.2 What is ArchiveLink?

ArchiveLink must be examined from two sides: from the functional business side, and from the technical side. On the technical side, we can best describe ArchiveLink by its components (see also Figure 3.1).

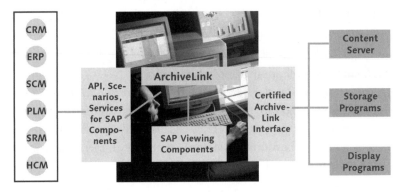

SAP Business Suite

Figure 3.1 Integration and Components of ArchiveLink

ArchiveLink provides a bundle of interfaces, services, and scenarios to SAP applications, which enable documents and business processes to be easily integrated. Furthermore, ArchiveLink contains a certified interface to external storage systems, which is used to supply external system functions to the SAP system. ArchiveLink contains an extensive display concept and a separate document viewer for the central document access function (displaying).

3.2.2.1 The Main Purpose of ArchiveLink

ArchiveLink enables business documents to be automatically integrated into SAP applications. Originals, such as scanned incoming invoices, are linked to the respective business objects (documents), through which they can be directly accessed from the respective business process and application document. In this way, ArchiveLink provides services for optimizing business processes (which include documents, or are based on documents).

Integrating business documents

In addition to the classical business objects (application data), business documents also play an important role in business processes. The smooth exchange and processing of documents is based on providing an electronically prepared form, which ensures access to these documents at any time. Electronic storage and document management play an important role in achieving this functionality—the process of preparing, storing, and providing documents is electronically organized. Figure 3.2 shows an overview of the integration process.

The electronic entry and storage of documents (optical archiving) is an important special case of document management. But the ArchiveLink concept goes further, allowing the integration of documents into business objects, independent of the type of physical document storage in external storage systems.

Integration independent of physical storage

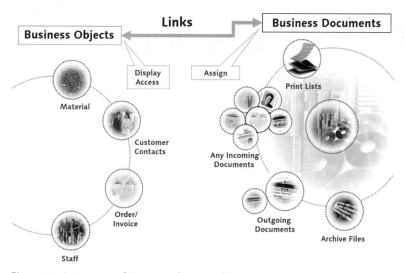

Figure 3.2 Integration of Business Objects and Documents

The central task of ArchiveLink is to integrate all objects and documents that belong to a business process, which provides the following advantages:

► Use of all of SAP's document drilldown possibilities because stored documents are accessed from the SAP application document

► Document integration into the business process by linking to the respective business objects

► Data security by using the SAP authorization concept (application authorizations, ArchiveLink authorizations)

Documents managed in ArchiveLink are physically stored in external storage systems or content servers (for storage of editable documents, see Section 3.2.4.3) via the ArchiveLink interface (developed, defined, and certified by SAP). Therefore, ArchiveLink connects SAP applications with defined external storage systems (see Figure 3.3). Different external storage system components are controlled from SAP application processes via ArchiveLink.

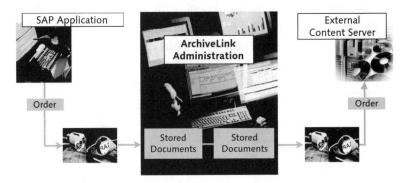

Figure 3.3 Role of the ArchiveLink Administration

A typical ArchiveLink system configuration (see Figure 3.4) consists (apart from the SAP system) of an external storage system for storing read-only documents, and possibly an SAP Content Server for storing editable documents that are currently being processed. The client side has central or decentralized data-entry work centers (e.g., for scanning and document storage), and clients through which documents can be accessed.

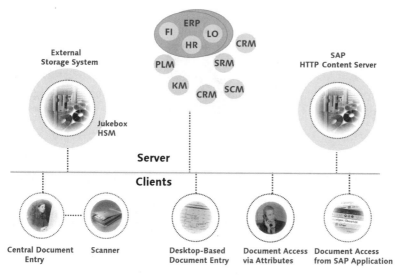

Figure 3.4 Typical Configuration of an ArchiveLink System

3.2.2.2 The Term Document

The term "document" in the ArchiveLink environment has a technical and a business definition.

Technically, ArchiveLink has the task to manage (and grant access to) any objects that are not saved in the SAP system. To do this, ArchiveLink contains an interface for controlling external storage, as well as a bundle of interfaces and services, which are used to conveniently integrate these control features into applications and their technical or business processes.

From the business point of view, ArchiveLink is used to map, as completely as possible, typical business processes with documents in SAP processes (see Figure 3.5).

ArchiveLink differentiates between four document categories: incoming documents, outgoing documents, print lists, and archive files.

Four document categories

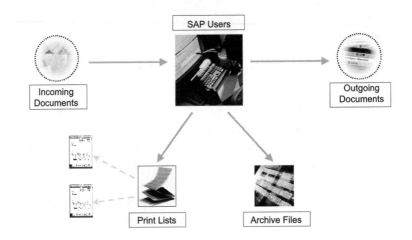

Figure 3.5 Documents in the Business Process

From a business point of view, these documents can be defined as follows:

- **Incoming documents**
  can trigger business processes.

- **Outgoing documents**
  are created as documents within the framework of a business process or as its result.

- **Print lists**
  are documents that are created when business processes are evaluated.

- **Archive files**
  comprise business process information; these files are relocated as data from the SAP system database, and they have to remain accessible.

From a technical point of view, the document categories are defined by the communication path or by the format:

- **Incoming documents**
  An incoming document is any kind of document that is not created by SAP itself. Typical incoming documents are scanned documents or files on a local PC. The format of incoming documents is determined by the creating application (scanned documents are

usually saved as .tif files; PC files remain in the format in which they were created). ArchiveLink transfers the document to the storage system unchanged.

The following three categories of documents are created in the SAP system:

▶ **Outgoing documents**
Outgoing documents are created using the SAP word processing system SAPscript or Smart Forms. These documents can be displayed via different output channels, such as printers, fax machines, or the computer screen. There is a special channel for storage via ArchiveLink — outgoing documents are transferred from the SAP system to storage as .pdf files.

▶ **Print lists**
Technically, a print list is the result of a reporting program. Like outgoing documents, print lists can be displayed via different output channels, and also support ArchiveLink. They are transferred as ASCII files to the storage system. Apart from the actual data records, these ASCII files also usually contain control information for preparing data for display.

▶ **Archive files**
These files are created as database extracts from the SAP system. Contrary to the other categories, archive files cannot be directly displayed as documents.

3.2.2.3 Document Search

Transactional users from different departments usually access stored documents directly from their application transaction. In addition to directly accessing the assigned business object, integrated document searching and display also has the following requirements:

▶ Document-centered integrated access to all documents that belong together operationally (document flow search, record search) Requirements

▶ Document-centered integrated access to SAP documents (documents managed in the SAP system via ArchiveLink) and non-SAP documents (documents managed outside the SAP system)

Documents are linked with business objects. Looking at a simple example (see Figure 3.6), the purchasing process consists of the following business objects: customer inquiry, quotation, contract, purchase order, goods receipt, and invoice. All of these objects can be linked to documents that were stored on an external content server via ArchiveLink.

From the process point of view, several access functions are necessary:

▶ **Single access**
Direct access from the business object "purchase order" to the documents **incoming order confirmation** and **outgoing purchase order**, and direct access from the business object "invoice" to the invoice document sent.

▶ **Overall access**
Direct access to all documents that were created and stored in the process.

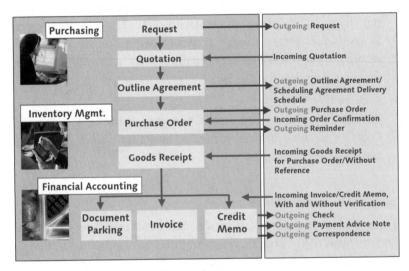

Figure 3.6 Business Process Flow in Purchasing

Frequently used terms

Access to all documents can be viewed from the perspective of business object processing, in which case, the term *document flow* is used. Or, if you look at this access from the document perspective, the terms *document record* or, more generally, *electronic record* are used.

If the mapped process exceeds the limits of the SAP system (i.e., certain parts are not mapped in SAP systems), then the document search faces the problem that documents that are only partly managed by

ArchiveLink in SAP have to be integrated into a record display. In order to complete the view, these SAP documents must be complemented with documents that are managed outside of SAP (non-SAP documents).

To enable an integrated view of all documents, SAP provides two application components:

Application components

▶ **Records Management**
for the complete administration of any process-related information in an electronic record

▶ **Document Finder**
for any desired access to documents

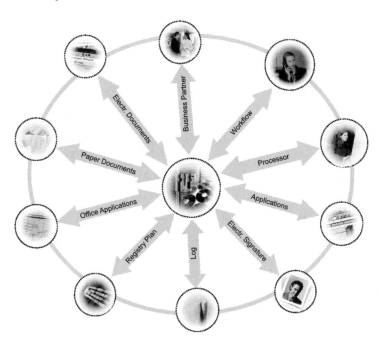

Figure 3.7 Records Management

Records Management

Records Management (see Figure 3.7) goes far beyond simple document creation, by integrating any information in electronic records. It's immaterial whether they are documents, business objects, transactions, programs, or workflows, and they can come from different information units in a single SAP system, or they can be distributed across several SAP systems. Because of its open architecture, Records

Integrating any information objects

Management also enables information objects that are managed by non-SAP systems to be integrated. Because a record is an information object in Records Management, multilevel records can be mapped.

Electronic records

Some examples of electronic records are personnel records, customer records, purchase order records, order records, loan records, and account records. An example of a multilevel record would be the customer record of a bank: It consists of a business partner (a business object), and subrecords for checking accounts (checking record), savings accounts (savings record), loans (loan record), and so on.

Case Management

The technology of Records Management is also used in *Case Management*. This is a component for electronic case processing that enables the responsible person, for instance, to follow up on a customer complaint, a reminder, or a delayed delivery, and to close the case.

Case Management is based on SAP Records Management and enables the aggregation and electronic transfer of all documents related to a case to other processors. In addition to the actual data that it contains, such a case also includes a log of all the steps performed (i.e., who did what and when). This makes it easier for the processor to obtain an overview of the case and to close it as quickly as possible. Case Management is used in several SAP Business Suite applications, such as SAP CRM or SAP ERP Financials.

Document Finder

Searching according to different criteria

The Document Finder (see Figure 3.8) makes it possible to search for documents according to different criteria, and access them. The Document Finder can also look for documents, regardless of whether the search characteristics are managed within or outside of the SAP system. Within SAP, the following strategies are supported for managing search characteristics:

Search strategies

▶ **Searching within document ranges supplied by SAP**

  ▷ Searching for documents that were stored via ArchiveLink, using technical attributes known to ArchiveLink

  ▷ Searching for print lists that were stored via ArchiveLink, using attributes known to ArchiveLink

  ▷ Searching for documents that are managed by the SAP document management system

  ▷ Searching across several SAP systems

- ▶ **Searching within customer-specific document ranges**

  - ▷ Searching for documents using customer-specific attribute tables

  - ▷ Searching for documents using business information, according to customer-specific criteria

- ▶ **Searching for documents using search characteristics that are unknown to SAP**

  - ▷ Searching in external storage locations using the Document Finder interface

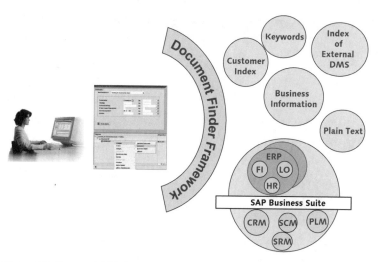

Figure 3.8 Document Finder

The Document Finder provides the end user with a dynamically created attribute search and/or full text search, depending on what the requested *service provider* (who provides integration and element access in Records Management) supports. The full text search is integrated into SAP document management. Therefore, this function is also available via Document Finder. The hit list of found documents is built in a dynamic tree structure, which can be used to display the documents and attribute specifications, as well as attached business objects.

By using the service provider concept, the Document Finder can be extended by special document ranges (with special functions) at any time. The following example from HR is intended to demonstrate this flexibility.

Service provider concept

Example The goal is to search all the archived documents of the HR master records of all employees, as well as to present the list as a personnel folder. The search should target the personnel number, the infotype, and the document's storage date. The hit list should be presented as a tree, grouped by personnel number, infotype, and document type.

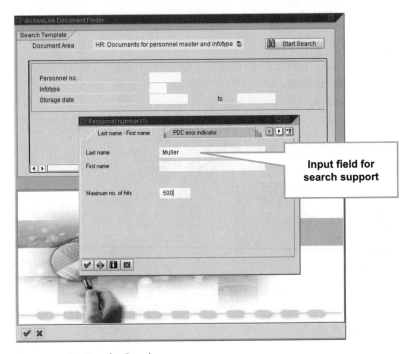

Figure 3.9 Starting the Search

After choosing the document range, you must determine which search criteria exist. These are dynamically presented as active input fields in the search template (see Figure 3.9). Because these are criteria that are managed in the SAP system, all of the SAP system's possible entries for the respective criteria are also available. The successful hits are arranged in a multilevel tree. Technically speaking, the first two levels represent business objects (HR master record and infotype), and the third level lists the documents (see Figure 3.10).

The Document Finder supports the linking of different units in its hit list to different functions. In the present example, the business objects have a function for displaying the business objects (the HR master records and the selected infotypes), while the document units have functions for displaying attributes and documents. These different functions for the different elements can be dynamically accessed via a context menu (see Figure 3.11).

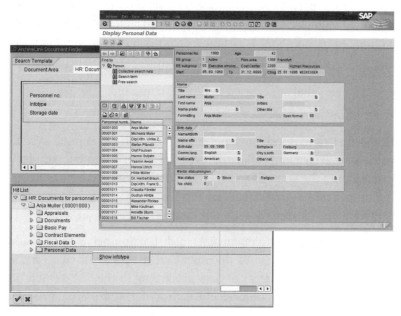

Figure 3.10 Display of the Selected HR Infotype

Figure 3.11 Display of an HR Master Record

3.2.3 Document Scenarios

The main task of ArchiveLink is to integrate documents into the business process. Besides controlling the storage system itself, this also means providing scenarios for integrating document entry and storage processes with the handling of process-relevant data, objects, and transactions. As a first step, we can differentiate between

▸ documents that are created in SAP systems, and

▸ incoming documents

Documents from SAP systems

In the first case, documents are directly created during SAP system processing. For example, the **order confirmation** document is directly created from the entry of an order in the SAP system. This document is automatically stored outside of the process via ArchiveLink. Separate ArchiveLink scenarios are not necessary.

Incoming documents

In the case of incoming documents, a distinction needs to be made between the subprocess of document creation and storage on the one hand, and the process of data processing in the SAP system on the other. This distinction becomes clear if you examine a typical case of paper invoice receipt processing.

Example: Invoice receipt processing

The process starts with an invoice document being received in the company. This invoice must be retained; therefore, it has to be scanned and stored. Furthermore, the invoice has to be posted in the SAP system. Both these steps have to be efficiently linked to each other through a suitable scenario.

The following sections present the most important business scenarios. Because of the many possible variations for these scenarios, we cannot go into all the available options. Therefore, each scenario is shown only in its most important application. Of course, there are also other scenarios available, but they are not discussed here.

3.2.3.1 Workflow-Based Document Scenarios

The document triggers the business process. It is digitized and stored as soon as possible. The following necessary steps (such as posting a document) are automatically carried out using a prepared business workflow template.

With the scenario *Storing for Subsequent Entry*, also known as *Early Archiving* (see Figure 3.12), the incoming document is stored before the resulting application document is entered. After storing the document, a workflow starts, which is sent to the responsible transactional user or users. Based on this electronic document, the transactional user can directly start entering the application document in his inbox, by executing the workflow. After the application document is posted, it is automatically linked in the workflow to the respective document, so that it can be accessed at any time from the business object. For subsequent documents, which are to be stored and linked to the application document at a later time, similar workflow scenarios are available.

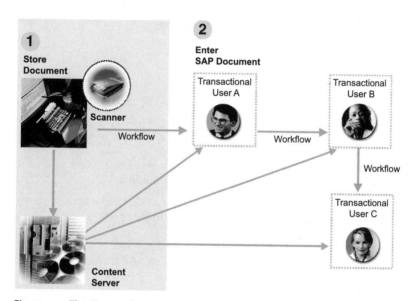

Figure 3.12 The "Storing for Subsequent Entry" Scenario

Document-based workflows can improve and accelerate the document receipt processes.

We will use the example of an incoming invoice to demonstrate the advantages of document-based workflows. An invoice can be paid either during the cash discount period by deducting a cash discount amount, or in full after this period expires. In order to obtain this cash discount, you must post and release invoices for payment as quickly as possible. With a normal financial accounting system, the incoming invoice posting time is several days. In bigger companies,

Storing for subsequent entry

Advantages of document-based workflows

this can take several weeks, because the invoice has to pass through different processing points, which are often physically separated. This process can be considerably accelerated using the described scenario, because the original documents are scanned and stored when they arrive in the mail. From this point on, they are available electronically, and can be processed.

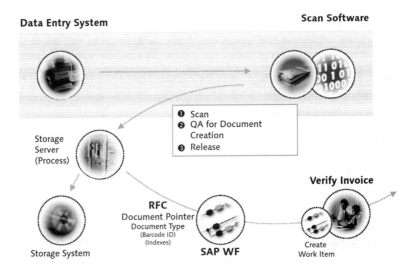

Figure 3.13 Possible Processes in a Workflow-Based Scenario

Three ways for storing

Documents can be stored in this scenario in three ways:

▶ **Control by the SAP system**
In this case, the document is stored via an SAP transaction.

▶ **Incoming fax**
If the document is reported as an incoming fax via the SAP incoming fax interface *SAPconnect*, then the document can also be stored and processed via workflows.

▶ **Storage outside of the system**
You can completely separate the storing process from further processing of the document in the SAP system. To do this, ArchiveLink has an inbound interface, over which an external system can report documents (i.e., unique document IDs) with attributes to the SAP system. These documents are automatically included in the workflow process described above. More complex data-entry systems can be included into the scenario through this route, without losing the aforementioned document workflow advan-

tages. Some examples of data-entry functions are offline scanning, web scanning, Optical Character Recognition (OCR), and classification.

You should note that this inbound interface is not part of the ArchiveLink certification; in other words, the respective storage system supplier should clarify whether this interface is supported.

3.2.3.2 Barcode Scenario

In this scenario, the document remains in paper form as it passes through the company. At the end of the process chain, the document is entered electronically, stored, and linked to the respective business object (see Figure 3.14).

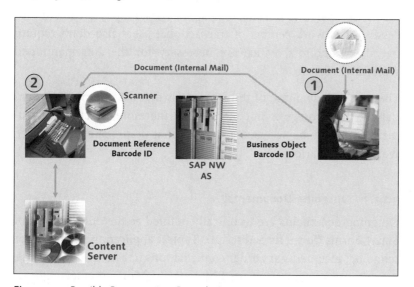

Figure 3.14 Possible Processes in a Barcode Scenario

Upon invoice receipt, the barcode scenario proceeds as follows:

1. The incoming document is manually delivered as incoming mail to the responsible transactional user.

2. The document is labeled with a barcode, either when it arrives in the mail room, or by the transactional user.

3. The transactional user enters and posts the linked SAP document against the paper document. When saving this posting, the user is

The barcode scenario process

prompted to enter a barcode. The barcode from the paper document is either entered manually, or is read with a barcode reader.

4. At the end of the process chain, the document is electronically entered and stored. The data-entry software recognizes the barcode; therefore, the document and the barcode are reported jointly to the SAP system. By matching the barcode, the SAP system automatically links the posted invoice with the stored document. Therefore, the document can now be accessed from the respective SAP transaction at any time in the future.

This scenario is often used to automate the linking process.

Advantages and disadvantages of barcode scenarios

One main advantage of this scenario is that the flow of work and paper is maintained. In this way, less organizational changes are necessary, compared to introducing paperless data input document processing. The work centers of transactional users also don't require oversized monitors, which are necessary for the aforementioned workflow scenario.

The main disadvantage of this scenario is that the optimizing potential of early storage is not utilized. Furthermore, electronic documents can only be accessed at a point that occurs later than in the workflow scenario.

3.2.3.3 Outgoing Documents

Smart Forms

Outgoing documents are technically defined as the output result of Smart Forms (formerly SAPscript). Typical application examples for outgoing documents are order confirmations (created when generating an order), invoices (created by invoicing), or reminders. Outgoing documents have a unique link to an application's business object. An actual order confirmation is created from a unique order. The confirmation is generated by the order, the stored document is automatically linked to this order, and it can be accessed from the order.

Defining the ArchiveLink channel by format, destination, and process

In SAP Smart Forms, documents are created out of the application (see Figure 3.15). These documents can be processed via different output channels (printer, fax, mail, EDI, ALE, etc.). ArchiveLink is a special channel for outgoing documents, which is characterized by a defined format, a defined destination, and a defined processing procedure:

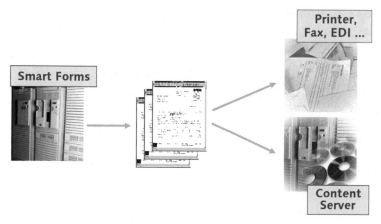

Figure 3.15 Smart Forms—Creating and Processing Documents

▶ **Format**

Outgoing documents are transferred in .pdf format to ArchiveLink. With older system versions, the SAP proprietary format .otf (Output Text Format) was used; it was replaced by .pdf in ArchiveLink 3.0. ArchiveLink allows you to display both .pdf and .otf documents. Documents in .otf format are automatically converted to .pdf format when accessed for display.

▶ **Destination**

The destination for the ArchiveLink channel is an actual, integrated storage system.

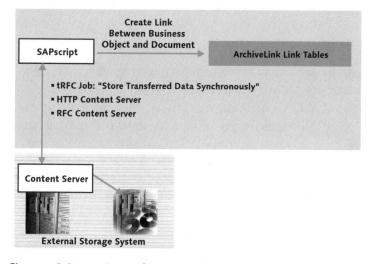

Figure 3.16 Storage Process for Outgoing Documents

▶ **Processing procedure**
The storage process for outgoing documents (see Figure 3.16) occurs per document. Each document is separately placed in an internal SAP queue (transactional RFC), to be transferred to the external storage system via ArchiveLink. For typical outgoing document processing scenarios, this technique places high demands on the systems involved, especially the storage system. In many cases, outgoing documents are not stored separately during the day, but are created in large quantities at defined times. For example, if a large electric utility or telecommunications company invoices their consumers, several hundred thousand documents are created within a short period of time, all of which have to be stored. The ArchiveLink interface is functionally certified by SAP; this certification does not include testing the performance of the systems involved. If the storage system is to be used for outgoing documents, it must be able to carry out the storage process in parallel (with respect to communicating with the SAP system). This performance must be available, regardless of the certification version that is used.

The process presented here is designed to create completely formatted outgoing documents in the SAP system, and to store them as complete documents. Whenever specific formatting or output management systems are to be used for formatting outgoing documents, other scenarios become available. However, they are not discussed here.

3.2.3.4 Print Lists

Results from reporting programs
Print lists are the output result of reporting programs, if they don't use Smart Forms (formerly SAPscript). Print lists don't have the properties of individual documents. Instead, they represent an evaluation based on various types of data, as shown in the following examples:

▶ Accumulated balance audit trail

▶ Document compact journal

▶ Balance sheet valuation

▶ Cost center reports

▶ Journals

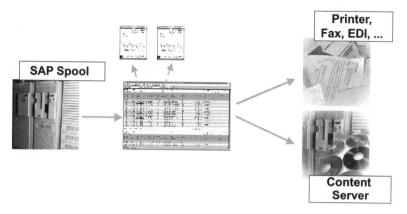

Figure 3.17 Creating and Processing Print Lists

Print lists can be printed on paper or stored via ArchiveLink. Storage via ArchiveLink has the following advantages over paper output:

Advantages of storing via ArchiveLink

▶ More compact storage than voluminous paper storage

▶ Faster (online) availability

▶ Direct access from different work centers

▶ Various possibilities for indexed and free text searches, therefore faster information availability

▶ Integration of links to stored documents in print lists (hyperlinks)

▶ Simple, consistent, and convenient management

Technically speaking, print lists are stored in the SAP Spool system, just like printing. Therefore, any printable SAP standard report can also be stored.

3.2.4 Interface to External Systems

A number of different document scenarios and services are provided by ArchiveLink in the SAP system. In addition, one of the more important aspects of ArchiveLink is that it contains an open, SAP-implemented, defined, and certified interface to external storage systems.

3.2.4.1 Communication

The ArchiveLink interface consists of server and client components. A typical server interface call involves transferring a file provided by the SAP system to the storage system. An example of a client job involves displaying a document.

Certified versions of ArchiveLink

The ArchiveLink interface is currently available in four versions. These are given the same name as the SAP R/3 release in which the function was made available for the first time.[1]

▶ **ArchiveLink 2.1**
First certification. The server communication is based on remote procedure calls, and client integration occurs via the SAP ArchiveLink Viewer.

▶ **ArchiveLink 3.0**
First standardization. The server communication is changed to SAP Remote Function Call (RFC), and the client side supports Object Linking and Embedding (OLE) Automation 2.0.

▶ **ArchiveLink 3.1**
Extended functionality. Some additional functions are added to the interface.

▶ **ArchiveLink 4.5**
The interface is extended for HTTP, RFC-enabling is eliminated, and the SAP ArchiveLink Viewer is no longer provided by SAP.

▶ **ArchiveLink 4.6**
This is not a new certified interface version, but an SAP-internal version that can only be used for SAP Content Server. In contrast to Version 4.5, it contains selected administration commands.

Current SAP systems support the last two versions: ArchiveLink 3.1, and ArchiveLink 4.5.

Server communication

The server communication between the SAP system and the content server is based on the SAP RFC interface. This interface is used to exchange messages between the systems. If these messages refer to data that should be either stored in the storage system or provided by the storage system, then the message contains the file name. Physically, the files are transported by a file system that can be reached by

---

1 However, this does not mean that this functionality can only be used for SAP R/3 or SAP ERP—it is available to all SAP applications.

both systems. ArchiveLink Interface 3.1 (see Figure 3.18) therefore requires remote file access between the SAP application server and the storage server. This communication is used especially for storing print lists, and for storing or providing archive files. Synchronous and asynchronous messages are both defined in the server interface.

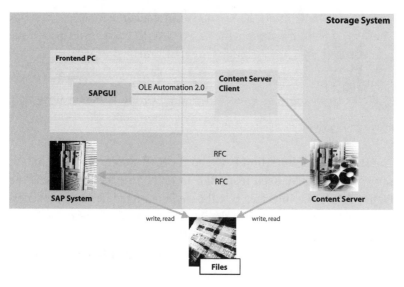

Figure 3.18 ArchiveLink Interface 3.1

On the client side, storage system viewer or data-entry clients (such as a scan client) are integrated from SAPGUI via an open OLE automation interface. Contrary to RFC communication on the server side, messages are not defined syntactically, but semantically. "Semantically" means that a storage system supplier must enable a document to be displayed (via a unique document number) via the OLE automation interface. However, the supplier can choose which OLE automation methods to use. The SAP Document Viewer is not discussed separately here, because it is based on the existing interface, and places no additional requirements on the interface.

Client communication

When comparing ArchiveLink Interfaces 3.1 and 4.5, several differences stand out. Apart from the different communication technique, the two versions are based on different document definitions. In ArchiveLink 3.1, a document is, simply put, an indivisible unit, which can be addressed as a whole via a unique document ID. Document portions, such as remarks or notes, cannot be addressed via the interface.

Comparing ArchiveLink interfaces

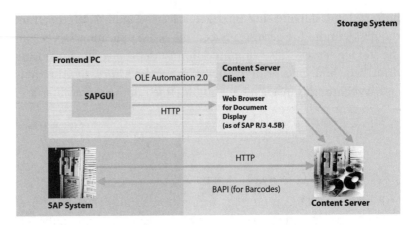

Figure 3.19 ArchiveLink Interface 4.5

The server communication between the SAP system and the content server has been changed from RFC to HTTP in ArchiveLink 4.5 (see Figure 3.19). The interface is still based on a fixed definition of messages to be exchanged. For detected barcode document feedback, ArchiveLink 4.5 contains a barcode BAPI. Files are no longer transmitted by remote file access between the systems; they are transferred directly within the message.

In ArchiveLink 4.5, only synchronous messages are defined between the systems. Asynchronicity was thus transferred from the interface to the systems involved.

Although the client OLE automation interface is still supported, it has been extended to include HTTP so that documents can now be viewed directly in a browser.

In ArchiveLink 4.5, any kind of HTTP communication can be secured by signatures that are activated in Customizing. Signatures ensure that only authorized systems can access documents.

Document definition in ArchiveLink 4.5

The document definition in the interface has been greatly extended with ArchiveLink 4.5. A document consists of *administrative data* and *content* (the entirety of related contents). The content is identified and described by administrative data, and data quantity that is self-contained (a file) is referred to as a *content unit*. This separation between content and content unit in the interface enables several additional interface functions that are helpful for the user. These include the following functions, which can be called directly from the SAP Document Viewer:

▶ Searching within a print list

▶ Entering comments and corrections (redlining)

▶ Text note functions

▶ Storing additional pages as part of the document

3.2.4.2 Certifying Storage Systems

SAP offers an integration and certification service (ICC) for third-party vendors in order to certify their interfaces. In addition, the ICC contains other services, such as the provision of test systems. A new part of the service consists of an extended certification program for optimizing the integration of third-party products into the SAP software. As a prerequisite for using this service, the third-party interface must first be certified.

You can find more information on SAP's integration and certification service at *http://www.sap.com,* quick link *ICC,* and in the SAP Developer Network (*http://www.sdn.sap.com/irj/sdn/sdnservices/icc*).

The certification of storage systems for ArchiveLink is pursued with the following goals in mind:

Goals of certification

▶ Customers can rely on the fact that SAP systems and certified partner systems match each other as products. In this way, introducing a storage system ideally becomes a relatively simple implementation project, instead of an extensive development project. The implementation team can focus on important project components (e.g., data archiving), while storage and access to documents or files is automatically available. In this way, implementation costs can be greatly reduced.

▶ SAP customers can then focus on finding suppliers in the extensive Document Management System (DMS) market that fulfill their requirements in the SAP environment. You can find an overview of certified suppliers in the Partner Information Center at *http://www.sap.com/partners/directories/searchpartner.epx.*

Each system provider who supports the functions of the ArchiveLink interface can be certified by SAP, and each provider of a storage sys-

What does certification mean?

tem that is able to communicate with an SAP system via SAP's ArchiveLink interface (in order to exchange data, for example) can have the system certified by SAP. Thus, each potential buyer knows that the storage system can be used for storing data in an SAP environment. Certification means an extensive technical evaluation of the interface between the SAP system and third-party software. SAP does not certify partner applications. This means, for example, that SAP does not evaluate whether a partner system supports optical, non-rewritable media for data storage, in spite of the fact that this is very important for many applications that use ArchiveLink. Support of these media is part of the partner system's application. It is only analyzed in the customer's selection process, and cannot be a part of the general certification. The certificate refers to a specific combination of a third-party and an SAP application release. The certificate is valid worldwide.

HTTP
Content Server
Interface 4.5

HTTP Content Server Interface 4.5 is closely related to ArchiveLink Interface 4.5. It includes all ArchiveLink Interface 4.5 HTTP components, whereas OLE automation and barcode BAPI are not included. This means that a system that is certified for HTTP Content Server Interface 4.5 cannot be used for all ArchiveLink scenarios. Therefore, most suppliers are certified for ArchiveLink Interface 4.5.

WebDAV for XML
archiving

WebDAV certification represents a new certification module, which—along with the existing certification modules, HTTP Content Server and HTTP Content Server Load Test—completes data archiving certification.

WebDAV[2]—an extension of the HTTP protocol—enables the web-based creation and processing of web content in a specific authoring environment. In addition, WebDAV primarily features a modern communication protocol that contains functions which are not supported by HTTP, such as the creation of hierarchies (collections) or metadata (properties) management.

The purpose of WebDAV certification is to confirm that an external storage system, or rather its interface with the SAP system, fulfills all criteria that are essential in order to communicate with XML DAS, SAP's XML-based archiving technology. The certification exclusively refers to requirements to be met in archiving scenarios.

---

2 WebDAV = Web-based Distributed Authoring and Versioning [WEBDAV].

Storage systems that have been WebDAV certified in addition to the other certifications above are very well suited to meet the needs of data archiving.

3.2.4.3 Certified Systems and SAP Content Server

In addition to the certified partner systems already mentioned, SAP delivers the *SAP Content Server* since Release R/3 4.6B. SAP Content Server also supports HTTP Content Server Interface 4.5 and represents its reference implementation by SAP.

SAP Content Server is a self-contained storage system that is used to manage and store documents in an SAP environment. It uses the integrated MaxDB database (SAP's open source database, formerly known as SAP DB) for data storage, and as of SAP Content Server 6.30, it also uses the file system. You can find further details on the supported platforms, as well as information on the respective supply sources, in SAP Note 622509.

Up until SAP Web AS 6.20, SAP Content Server was not designed for handling large data quantities as they usually occur in data archiving; however, since the introduction of SAP Web AS 6.30, you can use SAP Content Server to store archive files. You should note, however, that SAP Content Server does not contain any drivers that support the integration of optical media; this support is provided only by the file system.

The SAP Content Server is used for documents that are provided by SAP, for instance, through SAP Knowledge Warehouse, and for documents created in defined processes, such as workflow attachments. Furthermore, it is extensively used in SAP DMS for retaining "live" documents that are still being processed.

Since the introduction of SAP Content Server 6.30, which supports file systems, SAP Content Server has been increasingly used as a storage system in the ArchiveLink environment. The main reasons for this are as follows:

▶ There are storage solutions available in the market today, such as EMC Centera, which have been certified by public accountants. Those solutions do not require any optical media.

SAP Content Server

SAP Content Server as an ArchiveLink storage system

▶ Many SAP customers have changed their minds regarding whether they should use complex document management and archiving systems outside of the SAP system. SAP itself offers numerous DMS functions as a result of the continuous advancement of applications such as SAP Records Management. Due to the profound integration of these DMS functions with SAP applications, using these functions has proven so advantageous that it doesn't make sense to use an independent DMS system. Customers who have arrived at the same conclusion only have to face the problem of how they can integrate external storage space with the SAP system. To solve this problem, they are no longer willing to pay the sometimes very high prices of certified archiving systems.

▶ Because the file system interface is supported, it is relatively easy to connect optical media to SAP Content Server. At this point, we should mention that most providers of storage systems also support the integration of optical media via a file system interface.

3.2.5 Storing Archive Files

Communication between the SAP system and the storage system during archive file storage can be either synchronous or asynchronous, depending on the release and ArchiveLink interface that are used. The separation of asynchronous and synchronous methods only refers to the interface. In the SAP system, the storage of archive files always occurs asynchronously, either via a background job or by asynchronous job management. The following table provides an overview of the different storage possibilities.

SAP R/3 Release	ArchiveLink Interface Version	
	3.1 (RFC)	4.5 (HTTP)
4.0	asynchronous	not available
4.5	asynchronous	synchronous
4.6	asynchronous	synchronous
4.6C	synchronous	synchronous
Application systems based on SAP NetWeaver Application Server (e.g., SAP ERP)	synchronous	synchronous

Table 3.1 Storage Methods via ArchiveLink

The HTTP interface only supports synchronous communication; therefore, storage of archive files also occurs synchronously. The RFC interface (ArchiveLink 3.1) generally supports synchronous and asynchronous methods. In SAP R/3 Release 4.6 and earlier, the asynchronous method is used for storing and retrieving archive files. For SAP R/3 4.6C and later, synchronous, HTTP-style communication is used.

3.2.5.1 Asynchronous Storage

The asynchronous storage process (see Figure 3.20) is executed in the following steps (assuming that archive files exist in the SAP system's file system):

Asynchronous storage process

1. For each archive file, a request is sent to the storage system to store this file (**❶**).

2. The storage system verifies the file's existence and accessibility, and confirms receipt of the request in its reply. With this, the first communication is finished (**❷** and **❸**).

3. The storage system then accesses the archive file and transfers it to the storage area (**❹**).

4. When this is successfully done, the storage system reports this back to ArchiveLink (**❺**).

5. ArchiveLink then informs the data archiving process regarding the successful storage (**❻**).

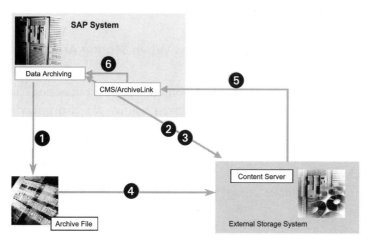

Figure 3.20 Asynchronous Storage via ArchiveLink

Synchronous stor-
age process

3.2.5.2 Synchronous Storage

The synchronous storage process (see Figure 3.21) involves the following steps (assuming that archive files exist in the SAP system's file system):

1. Data archiving sends a storage request to CMS, KPro, or ArchiveLink for each archive file (❶ and ❷).

2. The SAP HTTP client generates the HTTP request, which contains the content of the file to be stored in the body of the request (❸).

3. This HTTP request is sent to the content server, which stores the content and confirms the successful storage (❹).

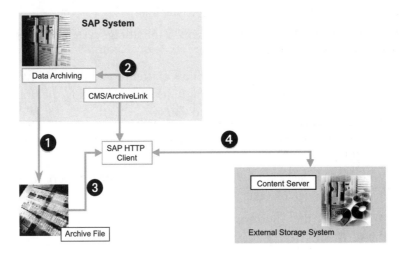

Figure 3.21 Synchronous Storage via ArchiveLink

3.2.6 Known Technical Problems When Storing Archive Files

During the storage of archive files, technical problems can occur. The best known error scenarios are discussed below. We also provide advice on what to do if they occur. The following error scenarios occur most often:

▶ **Synchronous problem**
During synchronous storage of several archive files, a timeout can occur.

▶ **Security gap**
There is a potential security risk if the store phase occurs *after* the delete phase.

▶ **Performance problem**
There is a potential performance problem if the delete phase occurs *after* the store phase.

3.2.6.1 Synchronous Problem

This problem occurs when the SAP system is able to send several parallel synchronous storage requests to the storage system. If the storage system did not consider this in its job processing architecture, a forced sequencing occurs in storage, which appears as a timeout to the SAP system. Because this problem has occurred in several cases with different storage system suppliers, we recommend that you include this in your selection process for purchasing a storage system. From a technical point of view, this same problem could occur in storing outgoing documents. The main difference is that, for outgoing documents, the amount of documents to be stored is greater, while for archive files, the individual files to be stored are larger.

3.2.6.2 Security Gap

As we know, the data archiving process consists of three different phases: the write phase, during which archive files are created; the delete phase, during which the database entries are deleted; and the store phase, during which the archive files are stored on a secure medium.

This process always starts with the write phase, and results in at least one archive file. If this phase is followed by the delete phase, then the archived database entries are deleted in the SAP system. After the delete phase, the entries only exist in the archive file. During the period between the delete and store phases, a security gap is created. If the archive file is lost after deletion, but before storage, the data is irretrievably lost.

In order to close this potential security gap, there are two options:

- **Storing the archive file before the delete phase**
  In this way, the file cannot be lost, and the process is secure. This flexibility in the respective process steps is available in SAP data archiving for SAP R/3 4.6C and later.

- **Backing up the archive file**
  You can do this either by creating archive files directly in a highly secure file system (RAID), or by creating a manual backup before the delete phase.

3.2.6.3 Performance Problem

If you selected the data archiving sequence to be such that storage occurs after writing (with deletion only occurring afterwards), then you can set the system to read the data volumes to be deleted not from the SAP system's hard disk, but from the storage system. This read access is potentially slower than direct access, which might lead to a longer delete phase.

You will have to test whether this problem really occurs in the existing configuration. If there are massive performance problems during the delete phase, you can set the SAP system in such a way that the delete program reads from the still existing, original archive file. Section 5.2.3. provides you with a detailed description of how to configure archive phase and read access sequences. In certain cases, it might be necessary to weigh security and performance aspects against each other.

3.2.7 Accessing Archive Files

Access to archive files stored via ArchiveLink occurs either directly from storage, or by first copying the archive file back from storage to the SAP system's file system. You can then access the archive file information using this local archive file copy.

In principle, there are two different types of access:

- **Access to a block of an archive file specified by position and offset**
  This applies to single document accesses and evaluations that are carried out directly in the storage. A single document access requires less block access to storage. In contrast, an evaluation can

occur in a block-by-block sequential fashion over the entire archive file, i.e., a high amount of requests are issued, although they relate to only a small data volume.

► **Access to the entire file**
This occurs, for example, if the file is copied as a local copy into the SAP file system. This function is executed manually by administration at the administration session level, i.e., you can assume that less retrieval requests are sent "in parallel" to storage, but that each relates to a large amount of data.

As shown in the table in Section 3.2.5, archive file access can involve synchronous or asynchronous processes, depending on the releases and interfaces that are involved. This table only refers to copying entire archive files to the SAP file system. It does not cover block-by-block access to data from storage. Block access to a data range that is specified by a position and offset is always synchronous.

The requirements regarding the utilized storage system can be summarized as follows:

► The system should support many synchronous, parallel requests.

► These requests should cover small, as well as large data ranges.

3.2.8 Known Technical Problems Accessing Archive Files via ArchiveLink

If the storage system does not support access parallelization for small or large data objects, then this might lead to synchronizing problems during access, as described for storage.

For performance reasons, you need to check the actual installation to determine whether access to archive file information occurs in one step (directly from storage), or in two steps (via a local archive file copy). When selecting the second option, you have to partition the file system to be the right size for local copies.

3.2.9 Advantages of Using ArchiveLink

Using ArchiveLink has the following advantages:

► **Added value**
A main advantage of using ArchiveLink systems for storing archive files is the added value of this storage system. ArchiveLink

offers close integration of document functions with SAP systems, as described previously. This integration, with all its advantages, can be used with the certified storage system.

▸ **Certification of ArchiveLink storage systems**
An advantage, which should not be underestimated, lies in storage system certification. Certification ensures that the utilized system can be used with SAP systems, without extensive implementation expenses. This reduces implementation costs in the development project, and also ensures that storage is "automatically" used in all the ArchiveLink scenarios that are used by SAP applications.

▸ **Broad implementation know-how**
Many suppliers of certified storage systems also offer their own solution packages for typical customer situations involving ArchiveLink (e.g., data archiving). With the growing use of ArchiveLink, implementation knowledge gained by consulting companies in this area has significantly increased in the last several years. For end customers, this means increased security and reasonable implementation periods for solutions using ArchiveLink.

▸ **Solution to problems**
In the previous few pages, we have described possible implementation problems for ArchiveLink systems. Without dismissing these problems, we would like to emphasize that you should keep an eye on a particular problem if it arises—it can be solved with a reasonable amount of effort.

3.3   Storage via HSM Systems

In addition to storing data in a certified storage system, as described up until now, HSM systems are also widely used for the storage of data.

3.3.1   What is HSM?

Rule-based data organization

The acronym HSM stands for *Hierarchical Storage Management system*. HSM systems integrate several different storage systems, and organize the physical distribution of files to media, according to different, individually set rules. A simple rule could consist of automatic file displacement from faster to slower media, depending on the frequency at which these files are accessed.

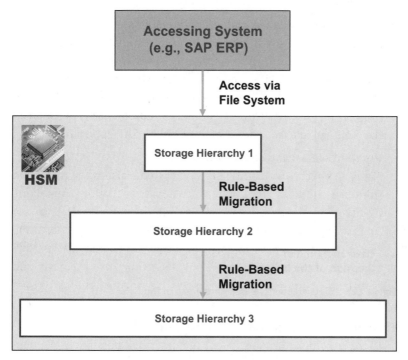

Figure 3.22 Hierarchical Storage Management System (HSM)

HSM systems can be accessed from the outside as if they are file systems. In other words, you don't need a special interface to use such a system for reading or writing. During access, the HSM software handles the automatic conversion of file and directory paths, according to defined rules. Therefore, these systems can be directly addressed by any system as "infinitely large" hard disks. Due to the transparent integration of different storage media and architectures, an HSM system presents itself as a single file system to the accessing system.

HSM presents itself as a file system

The HSM concept has two main goals:

HSM goals

▶ To provide direct standardized access to a continually expandable storage pool. The expansion only occurs in the HSM system. The accessing application is totally unaffected, and does not have to be configured to another file system or interface.

▶ To provide intelligent storage through the intelligent use of various media, thus saving the customer money.

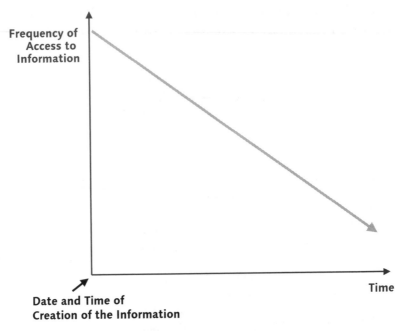

Figure 3.23 Access Frequency Based on the Age of Data

The cost saving aspects can be shown best with an example.

Access frequency
decreases with
increasing data age

In an application, data is created that is relatively frequently accessed, along with data that only requires infrequent access. Information is usually more frequently needed closer to the time it was created, as opposed to later in time (see Figure 3.23). For example, an invoice posted in SAP ERP is most often accessed during the year in which it was entered. At the end of that year, the information is needed again for evaluation purposes, while in subsequent years, it will only be used occasionally, for example, for auditing purposes (see also the section on the lifecycle of data in Section 1.1).

Higher access
frequency
requires faster
data retrieval

During the period when the information is frequently accessed, it has to be available online—in the database, or in fast and directly accessible archive files. Data that is infrequently accessed can instead be stored on cheaper media that may be only available offline (see Figure 3.24). The HSM system bears this in mind, by integrating different storage systems, and by using definable migration rules. The result is automatic, completely user-transparent data migration; manual copying of data between media is unnecessary.

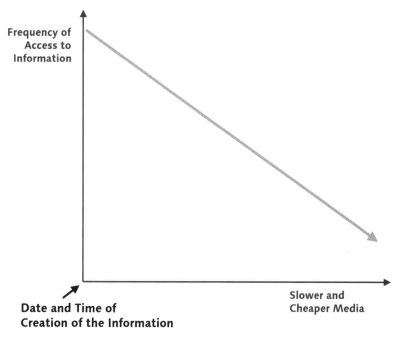

Figure 3.24 Media Used Based on Access Frequency

A commonly used architecture consists of a network of hard disks, jukeboxes with optical disks, and tape robots. A rule for implementing the aforementioned scenario in this network could be the following: data that is regularly accessed is stored directly on hard disks. If the access frequency falls below a certain threshold value, the files are automatically transferred to optical disks. If another threshold value is passed, the files are migrated to magnetic tapes.

A sample HSM scenario

3.3.2   Storing Archive Files

Archive files are stored in an HSM system in such a way that the write program creates the files directly in the HSM system during the write phase (see Figure 3.25).

To ensure the security of the entire archiving process, it is extremely important that the archive files are located on a secure medium before the delete phase (*write through*), so that the data is reproducible at any time after the delete process. The term *secure medium* is not only limited to technically secure media, such as optical disks, but can also apply to secured hard disk systems (e.g., RAID).

Secure medium

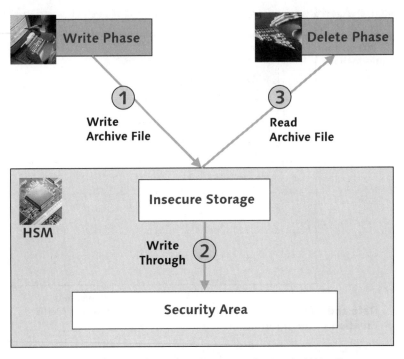

Figure 3.25 Storing Archive Files in the HSM System During the Write Phase

3.3.3 Accessing Archive Files

Read access to an HSM system occurs directly via file access (see Figure 3.26). The HSM system determines where the particular files are physically located, and fulfills the request from this medium. This can occur from a fast hard disk cache, or from slower storage media.

Block-by-block access Block-by-block access to an archive file should be examined a little closer at this point. If the archive file to be accessed is located in the hard disk cache of the HSM system, the request is fulfilled directly. But if the file can only be accessed from a lower-level storage hierarchy, then the system should enable access to the first block directly from the storage hierarchy, and at the same time, offer to copy the entire file from the slower area to the cache.

This function has to be flexible in use, because

► with single document access, only the first accessed block may be needed. The file may not need to be copied to the cache, because it is no longer needed.

▶ for reports, subsequent accesses follow the first one, until the entire file is requested.

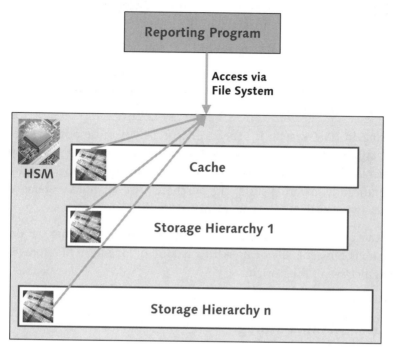

Figure 3.26 Read Access to the HSM System

3.3.4 Typical Technical Problems

When using an HSM system, general data archiving problems occur if the system does not support any write-through mechanism during writing, or if it cannot implement real block access during reading.

No write-through support

Further problems arise from the loose coupling between data archiving and the HSM system. Because they only communicate with each other via the file system, it can be very difficult to properly implement write-through and block-by block access requirements:

Loose coupling of HSM and archiving

▶ **Write through**
If the HSM system is also used for data that has lower security requirements, it is difficult to define useful criteria that determines whether a file should be migrated directly to a secure media. In comparison, a system that is requested to store a file via ArchiveLink can always assume that this data has to be directly transferred to a secure area.

▸ **Block-by-block access**
With the first read access, the HSM system has no secure criterion that it can use to determine whether other read accesses to the file will follow, that is, if it should copy the file to the cache.

There are further disadvantages to HSM solutions, if the advantages of ArchiveLink systems cannot be used.

3.3.5   Advantages of Using HSM Systems

Automatic migration saves money

Using an HSM system is beneficial, especially because of the aforementioned functions. With HSM systems, you can automatically migrate data that is used less often to slower, cheaper media, thereby significantly lowering costs. The purchase price for HSM systems is usually lower than for ArchiveLink-certified storage systems.

Open access interface

Because of the open access interface (file system operations), HSM systems can generally be used for any kind of long-term file storage, irrespective of their origin.

3.4   Manual Storage

When manually storing archive files, it makes sense to (re)use existing storage systems that are already available in the company. In this way, no additional hardware or software costs are incurred. The main storage systems that are envisioned for manual storage include large robot systems or jukeboxes that are already used in the company. These storage systems can be integrated either directly or indirectly into the data archiving process.

3.4.1   Direct Integration

Most jukeboxes have a separate file system interface for transferring archive files to jukebox media. This interface can be used for data archiving just like an HSM system, that is, the jukebox file system is directly written to during the write phase.

Only when using a secure medium

If you want to use this scenario, you have to ensure that archive file writing occurs directly onto the secure medium. The request to close the file at the end of the write program must be the latest point at which file saving is initiated, so that the file does not remain in a cache area. If the jukebox file system driver does not support this function, then you should not use this scenario without further backup.

3.4.2 Indirect Integration

With indirect integration, the storage system is used as a backup medium after archiving. The archive file is created in the SAP file system, and is saved by administration before the delete phase.

3.4.3 Advantages and Disadvantages of Manual Storage

The main advantage of manual storage can be found in the cost savings, because no additional purchase costs are incurred.

Cost saving

Another strength lies in the re-using of existing processes. Existing storage systems in the company are already used in defined and implemented data security processes (otherwise, the systems would not be there). These processes could probably be easily extended for additional archive file backup.

Re-using existing processes

The central weakness of the manual process, in contrast to automated procedures like ArchiveLink or HSM, is that it entails more administrative work. Each individual case has to be analyzed, to determine whether operating costs can be kept sufficiently low in relation to using ArchiveLink or HSM systems.

Administrative expense

The previously described advantages of ArchiveLink and HSM are lost here; they can only be regained through great individual effort, if they can be regained at all. Each company has to determine whether the requirements placed on the utilized solution—like security, performance, cost, and long-term usage—can be achieved. The responsibility for the solution lies exclusively with the company; no system supplier can be held liable for future problems.

3.5 Summary

In this chapter, we presented some important criteria that you should definitely consider when choosing a storage strategy. All the solutions—ArchiveLink, HSM, or manual storage—have their advantages and disadvantages. Therefore, there is no "optimal" storage strategy that could meet each company's requirements.

Deciding which storage strategy is optimal for your particular situation, and then determining which storage system to select, should be considered in a separate data archiving subproject. Time and money spent on these decisions should be taken into account when planning your data archiving project.

This chapter describes the options available for accessing archived data for display or evaluation purposes. It focuses on how to use and optimize the Archive Information System and Document Relationship Browser tools. This chapter is intended primarily for administrators who implement and use these tools.

4   Accessing Archived Data

by Dr. Martin Fischer and Thorsten Pferdekämper

Even after the data has been archived and therefore removed from the database, the system can still access it.

If you were not able to display archived data, you would have to reload the data back into the database (see also Section 2.3.2), which would make the process of archiving data meaningless. The purpose of archiving data is ultimately to remove application data that is no longer required in order to reduce the workload on the database, but also to save this data in such a way that read access is still always possible.

However, the archived data is then no longer controlled by the database. This means that (at least on a purely technical level) you must use different access concepts from those used for data that is still available in the database (the SELECT statement cannot access archived data). Whether this situation will affect the end user depends on how the archive is accessed in each specific case.

4.1   Introduction

There are many options available for accessing archived data. In principle, each archive file created in the same system and client can be

Access options

read. The way in which access to an archive for a certain archiving object is defined in terms of handling, logging, formatting of the results, and so on, depends on the programs of the particular application. The range of options here is very broad. At the low end of the spectrum, there are applications that don't offer any special programs. In this case, you can only display the archived data in the Archive Information System. This type of display, however, is more technical in nature; similar to the way data from the database is displayed in the Data Browser (transaction SE16). At the high end of the spectrum, archive access is integrated into the application so well that the end user cannot tell whether the displayed data originates from the database or from the archive.

In this chapter, we describe the different access concepts using archiving objects from Accounting as examples. However, the scenarios presented here don't necessarily apply to all situations, because hardly any one archiving object can provide every one of the described access options. Nevertheless, almost all archiving objects have at least one of the identified options.

What is not covered in this chapter The following terms and concepts are frequently used in the context of access to archived data, but they only relate loosely to this topic and will therefore not be described in detail in this chapter. Nevertheless, we will discuss these topics briefly to clearly distinguish them from the context of archive access.

▶ **Storing print lists**
If, before you start archiving data, you already know precisely how you want the subsequent archive accesses to appear, you can perform this type of evaluation before you archive the data and store the resulting print lists on suitable storage media. If you want to access data at a later stage, you can find and display the corresponding list. However, you would not actually be accessing the archive in this case. For more information on print lists, refer to Section 3.2.3.4.

▶ **Storing documents**
You can use the document storage option, often also called optical archiving, to store scanned orginal documents or other files that belong to a business object (e.g., a financial accounting docu-

ment). You can then link them to the corresponding object and display them again later. However, access to these documents has little to do with data archiving.

▸ **Reloading**

You could, in principle, restore the status of archived data prior to its archiving by reloading it into the database. You could then perform the usual evaluations using this data. For different reasons already explained in Section 2.3.2, however, you should view the reloading of archived data as a means of correcting an incorrect archiving process, and not as an alternative for evaluating archived data.

▸ **DART**

Although the *Data Retention Tool* (DART) was originally developed to comply with the requirements of the U.S. Internal Revenue Service for evaluating electronic data, it is now also gaining importance in Europe. DART allows you to extract tax-relevant data from the system and to save this data in simple text files known as *flat files*. This tool also contains functions for finding and displaying the saved data. When you view data that has been extracted and stored using DART, it does not matter if the source data was archived in the meantime. However, you can only use DART to access a narrowly defined range of tax-related data. For more information on DART, see Section 1.6.2.

▸ **Audit trails in Financial Accounting**

Similar to the process used in DART, files are exported during audit trails in the financial accounting. These files represent a certain view of the documents in the system. The documents in this case, however, are accounting documents only.

▸ **Accessing stored archive files**

In this chapter, we assume that the Archive Development Kit (ADK) can access the archive files. This means that either the files are located directly in the file system or the storage is configured in such a way that ADK functions can access the storage medium. For more information on storing archive files, see Chapter 3.

4.2 Basic Principles

Basic steps
Irrespective of the type of access, you need to implement the following basic steps to identify and display archived data. It is mainly in the implementation of these steps that the various access options differ.

Selection
1. **Selecting the archive files and business objects to be read in an archive file**
Two different techniques are used here: The first technique involves the user selecting the data manually. The user selects the required archive files in a selection screen of the system, as shown in Figure 4.1.

The second technique involves the system determining the archive files to be read without any further user interaction. To do this, the system uses an *archive index* that it reads based on the selection criteria entered by the user. An archive index is a database table that, in addition to containing application-specific selection fields such as a document number, for example, also contains the key of the archive file where the corresponding data is located.

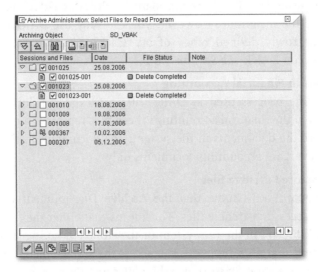

Figure 4.1 Selection Screen for Selecting Archive Files

Opening
2. **Opening the archive files and reading the content**
Again, there are two options available here. The first option is to open the archive file and read its contents sequentially. The sec-

ond option is to access the data directly: To do this, you place the file pointer directly in the location in the archive file where the business object that is to be read begins. This location is called the *offset*.

3. **Filtering the required data**

Filtering

The selection with which the data is to be read from the archive does not generally correspond to the selection that was used to start the archiving session. This means that, by selecting the archive files, more than the required data range is read in the archive. The program must therefore filter the data that is actually required by the user in an additional step, even if it has already read only the relevant business objects.

4. **Displaying the required data**

Preparing data for display

There are different ways in which you can format the display of data read from the archive. The range of options extends from a purely technical display that corresponds to the Data Browser (transaction SE16) to a typical business display for data from the database. You can find the first option in the Archive Information System, while the second option is available in applications that have archive access fully integrated into their display functions. In this case, you can no longer tell whether the data originates from the archive or from the database.

4.3 Sequential Read Programs

The **Read** pushbutton in Archive Administration (transaction SARA) is usually the first contact that users dealing with data archiving have with the subject of archive access. This pushbutton links the user to programs that are used to sequentially read the archive files selected by the user. These programs were specifically written for evaluating archive files and typically only operate on archived data. In most cases, the data is displayed in a format that meets the requirements of the end user. These programs are particularly suitable for checking archived data.

One example of such a sequential read program is the RKAARCS1 program, which is part of the CO_ORDER archiving object (internal orders), and which is also available when you select the aforementioned **Read** pushbutton. After you enter your selection criteria, you

Example

can execute the program. The dialog box shown in Figure 4.1 opens allowing you to select the archive files. In this case, however, note that the selection criteria does not influence which archive files are offered for selection. All accessible files are always offered for evaluation, irrespective of the selection criteria. You should therefore ensure that selection of archive files matches the chosen selection criteria. If you don't select all the relevant files, not all the required data can be displayed. Since the program reads all files sequentially, you should not select too many archive files as this will lead to longer response times.

The read program now reads through the selected archive files sequentially and filters the data according to the specified selection criteria. The selection criteria has very little effect on the runtime of the program. The important factor here is the selection of the archive files. After you have selected an archive file, its content is usually displayed as a list. In the previous example for internal orders, you can navigate further from the generated list, although this is quite unusual for this type of evaluation.

Scheduling in the background In addition to executing the read archive program in dialog mode, you can also schedule it to run in the background. Scheduling basically corresponds to scheduling a delete program manually. The difference here is that the read program requires a variant for transferring the selection criteria.

Programs with subsequently enhanced archive read function While the programs available in Archive Administration are usually dedicated programs for reading archives, there are also programs that were originally developed to read normal evaluations of data from the database, however these programs were then enhanced with additional functions for accessing archives. One particular disadvantage of these programs is that users must know whether the data is located in the archive and, if so, in which archive file it has been saved. The advantage here, however, is that the data is displayed in a familiar format. An example of this type of data is the totals reports (Report Writer reports) in Overhead Cost Controlling.

By clicking on the **Data Source** pushbutton on the selection screen of this type of program, you can specify that the data should be read from the archive (**Read from archive** option) rather than from the database (see Figure 4.2). You can also select the archive files here.

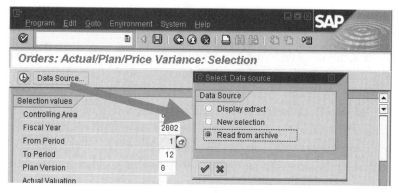

Figure 4.2 Selecting the Data Source in Report Writer Reports

From a technical point of view, the data source selection (database or archive), as well as the archive files to be read are part of the selection screen, even though the corresponding information is not displayed directly on this screen. When you save a selection variant, this means that the data source is also saved along with it. This enables you to create a variant for evaluating specific archives in the background, for example. After you execute the program, you can no longer distinguish from the list displayed whether the data originates from the database or from the archive.

4.4 Direct Access

If you want a large part of the data to be read in the archive file and you know which files contain this data, it is particularly useful for entire archive files to be read sequentially using the manual file selection that you made previously. This can be the case, for example, if you want to check the contents of an archive file. For most end users, however, those functions that require the least amount of archiving knowledge are more suitable. The best option here is automatic archive access. Although some configuration and administration effort is required, the end user has very little to do.

An example of this type of function is the display for accounting documents (transaction FB03). This function also always accesses archived FI documents automatically, so that the user may no longer notice that the displayed data was already archived. In particular, the

Example

user doesn't have to worry about whether the data could already have been archived before she executes the transaction.

Data source With some display transactions, such as KE5Z for evaluating actual line items (see Figure 4.3) or KE5Y for evaluating planned line items in the profit center, before you execute the transaction you can use the **Extras • Data Source...** function to specify whether you want the data to be read in the database, the archive, or in both sources. When selecting the archive, you can also determine whether you want the archive to be accessed automatically from the Archive Information System or manually by selecting the corresponding archive files.

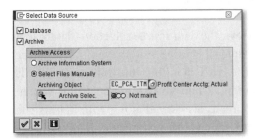

Figure 4.3 Selecting the Data Source in Display Transactions

Archive index for locating data Information on whether the document you want to find has been archived and where you can locate it in the archive is usually saved in an archive information structure of the Archive Information System, or it may be saved in an application-specific archive index. Using the selection criteria of the corresponding program, the archive index can determine the location in the archive (i.e., the archive file and the offset) where the data is contained. In the example shown here, the application-specific archive index is only supported for read accesses but is no longer updated.[1] The database table here is ARIX_BKPF. Table 4.1 below contains the relevant fields for this example.

---

1 This is the case as of SAP ERP 6.0. As of this release, only the Archive Information System is still supported for indexing archived FI documents. However, if you have created old application-specific indexes based on ARIX_BKPF, you will still be able to read these indexes. For more information, refer to SAP Notes 807726 and 596865.

Field	Description
BUKRS	Company code
BELNR	Document number
GJAHR	Fiscal year
ARCHIV_KEY	Key for archive file
OFFST	Offset of business object

Table 4.1 Table ARIX_BKPF

When the document display looks for a document in the archive using the application-specific archive index, it accesses this database table first. The document display uses the **Company code**, **Document number**, and **Fiscal year** fields to determine the archive file and the offset of the business object where the required document is located. The data in the archive is then read by direct access. The program therefore does not read through the entire archive file sequentially, but places the pointer directly on the required offset when the file is opened and only reads the relevant business object. This type of archive access is much more efficient than the sequential reading of archived data if you only want one or a few business objects to be read.

However, this method is not appropriate for fast access to data using fields other than those contained in the archive index. In our example, the archive can only be accessed through the application-specific archive index if you know the company code, document number, and fiscal year. You cannot search for data using other fields from the document. For example, you cannot use the account field, since this field is not contained in the archive index. In this case, the archive indexes of the Archive Information System are vastly superior to the rigid concept of the application-specific archive index.

Run a search only using fields contained in the archive index

The archive index is built automatically during the delete phase for archiving objects that support this concept. You can also build and delete this index information manually at a later stage. You can do this using the **Index** pushbutton that appears in the initial screen of Archive Administration for archiving objects that support this function.

Building the archive index

The archive index is only built automatically during the delete phase if the index build option was activated in the specific Customizing for the archiving object by selecting the **Build Index** indicator. However, this indicator is only available if the archiving object supports the index function. Setting this indicator means that the archive index will automatically be built for future deletion runs.

An archive index is not built for archive files that were processed by the delete program before you set this indicator. This is evident from the information for the relevant archive file, which you can refer to in archive management. You can start the subsequent index build for these types of archive files. This is primarily a sequential read program that does not display the read data, but simply creates an extract of this data and writes it, together with the archive file key and the offset, into the database table of the archive index.

4.5   Archive Information System

Disadvantages of conventional access methods

Despite many advantages, the conventional access methods described so far have several disadvantages, mainly due to technical restrictions and the application dependency of the methods:

▶ For sequential access, the user must know the correct archive files.

▶ Sequential access takes too long if you only want individual documents to be displayed from the archive.

▶ Direct access using application-specific archive indexes are not implemented in all cases.

▶ Application-specific direct access only works using the fields provided by the developer.

▶ The building and deletion of archive indexes is application-specific. Although there is a general procedure for building and deleting archive indexes in Archive Administration, the programs that actually build and delete the indexes are application-specific.

Advantages of the Archive Information System

These disadvantages don't apply when you use the *Archive Information System* (AS). This tool, developed specifically for accessing archives, enables you to configure your own archive indexes, fill them with data from the archive, and search for archived data. As is the case with an application-specific archive index, the archive file and offset are also updated here, which allows you to access the archived data directly. The Archive Information System also offers a generic (rather than application-specific) display of all contents of a business object from the archive. This system works with all archiving objects, including user-defined objects, and requires no application-specific programs or modifications.

The Archive Information System is therefore the tool of choice for accessing archived data quickly. However, you need to pay special attention to the term *tool* here. Due to the generic nature of the Archive Information System, application-specific features cannot, or can only partially, be considered. This is therefore more of a technical tool, which cannot always meet the requirements of the end user in every respect.

Tool of choice for accessing archives

The key term in the environment of the Archive Information System is the *archive information structure*.[2] This term effectively replaces the term for archive index introduced above. Each archive access based on the Archive Information System is performed via an infostructure. Infostructures are created using the *Archive Retrieval Configurator* (transaction SARJ), which is the Customizing component of the Archive Information System. Similar to archive indexes, the data is filled in the infostructure either directly during the delete phase or subsequently by the user. As is also the case with an archive index, data for an infostructure is maintained in a database table. Another component of the Archive Information System, the *Archive Explorer*, supports data mining within an infostructure and allows you to directly access and subsequently display archived data.

Archive information structure

Each infostructure not only belongs uniquely to an archiving object, it also refers exclusively to a specific *field catalog*. A field catalog is basically a collection of fields suitable for indexing the archived files of the archiving object in question. The fields of an infostructure are always a selection of the fields of the corresponding field catalog. The field catalog also contains a number of technical properties that are transferred to the infostructure. Due to the design of field catalogs, you don't need to know the technical details of the archiving object in order to create an infostructure, since this information is

Field catalog

---

2 To improve readability, the short form of this term "infostructure" will be used from now on.

already stored in the field catalog. To create an infostructure, you simply have to select the fields.

In the following sections, we describe how to use the Archive Information System and provide some related background information. The individual steps are listed in the order in which they are normally performed by the user or administrator if the Archive InformationInformation System is used for an archiving object for the first time. You can access all the functions listed here through the central administration of the Archive Information System (transaction SARI). The help function of the application provides more detailed information detailed.

4.5.1 Creating an Infostructure

Do not change standard infostructures

Before you create your own infostructure, you should check whether an infostructure already exists that you can use to evaluate the archived data. If necessary, you can copy this infostructure and change it to meet your own requirements; however, you should not change any infostructures supplied by SAP. If you do make such a change, this modification may be undone with the next upgrade or if Support Packages are installed.

Transferring fields

When you create an infostructure, you define which fields must be transferred from the archive into the infostructure. To do this, you select the required fields from a field catalog and transfer them into the infostructure (see Figure 4.4). The standard SAP delivery already contains field catalogs for many archiving objects. If you cannot find a field catalog that meets your requirements, you can create your own. For more information, see Section 4.5.7.

Key fields

For technical reasons, some fields of the field catalog are transferred immediately into the infostructure and cannot be removed. These fields are usually key fields. However, most fields of a field catalog belong to the list of selectable fields that you can transfer into the infostructure. You can use all the fields of the infostructure to run subsequent searches for archived data. However, you should note that infostructures are stored in the database, and therefore each additional field that is transferred into the infostructure requires additional space in the database.

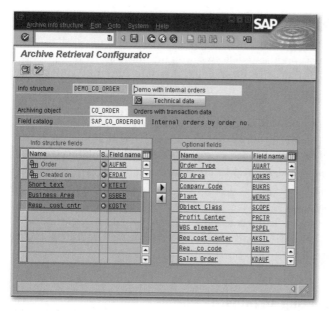

Figure 4.4 Creating an Infostructure in the Archive Retrieval Configurator

4.5.2   Partitioning an Infostructure

To be able to handle very large amounts of data in the infostructures, you can partition the infostructures, that is, you can distribute the data of the infostructure onto several database tables. Consequently, not all the data is written to one single table, but is instead distributed to several tables. The partitioning criterion here is the creation date of the archiving session. For example, the partitioning could be configured in such a way that the records of the infostructure for the sessions of each calendar year would be written into a different table. The basic concept here is so flexible that you don't have to define the partitioning at the start and you can change it at any time.

Improved handling of tables for infostructures

As part of the partitioning process, you could also set the table (or tables) by default for an infostructure. This means that you can freely select the table names and the required technical settings and transport the tables yourself. The advantage here is that the tables for an infostructure in a system landscape have the same name and same properties overall and are easier to manage.

Defining your own table names

The configuration of the partititioning is part of the infostructure itself and is therefore transported and delivered with the infostructure. A partitioning change to SAP infostructures would therefore constitute a modification, so you could practically use the partitioning for user-defined infostructures only.

If an SAP infostructure already contains a very large amount of data, you can transfer this directly into a separate infostructure with suitable partitioning by selecting the **Utilities • Copy Data** menu option. In this case, you don't have to delete the SAP infostructure and build your new infostructure.

It usually only takes a few seconds to execute this function. Make sure that your own infostructure is based on the same field catalog as the SAP infostructure; otherwise, read access processes in the application could behave differently.

4.5.3   Activating an Infostructure

To be able to use an infostructure, you must activate it. An infostructure can only be filled with data from the archive and evaluated once it has been activated. But, you can no longer change an activated infostructure.

Database table for index data

As is already the case with the concept of application-specific archive indexes, the Archive Information System also requires a database table to save the index data. This table is not set by default, however; it is generated using the available information when the infostructure is activated. This table contains the following fields:

▶ The client

▶ The fields of the infostructure

▶ The key of the archive file

▶ The offset of the business object in the archive file

For the above example, the generated database table looks like the one shown in Figure 4.5.

Reporting program

A reporting program is also generated to evaluate this table and to access the archive to display the archived data. After the database table and the reporting program are generated, the system sets an active indicator for the infostructure in question. This indicator means that the infostructure can now be used for evaluations and that it should be built automatically while the corresponding delete program is running.

Field	Key	Length	Short Description
MANDT	☑	3	Client
AUFNR	☑	12	Order Number
ERDAT	☑	8	Created on
ARCHIVEKEY	☐	20	Key for Archive File
ARCHIVEOFS	☐	10	Archive file data object offset
KTEXT	☐	40	Short text
GSBER	☐	4	Business Area
KOSTV	☐	10	Responsible Cost Center

Figure 4.5 Database Table for the Infostructure

4.5.4 Building an Infostructure

During the delete phase of data archiving, all active infostructures belonging to an archiving object are automatically filled with data from the relevant archive file. Based on the defined infostructure, the Archive Information System filters the data from the data records in the archive and inserts it into the generated database tables together with the archive file key and the offset of the business object. These entries are then used as the basis of later searches.

In addition to being built automatically by the delete program, an infostructure can also be built at a later stage for archives that already exist. You can therefore build infostructures when required, for example, to evaluate data that was already archived before the Archive Information System was introduced or to change the fields of an infostructure.

Subsequent build

Besides the generated database table being filled with data from the archive when you build an infostructure, a build status is also recorded. You can use this status in the status management area of the Archive Information System to identify for which archive files the relevant infostructures were built.

Build status

4.5.5 Evaluating an Infostructure

The search for archived data in the Archive Explorer is always conducted using the evaluation program created when you activated the infostructure. The selection screen of the evaluation program contains all the fields of the infostructure, except for the **Client**, **Archive File Key,** and **Offset** fields. When you execute the program, you get a list of all the entries in the infostructure that match your selection

Evaluation program as a basis

criteria. Up to this point in the evaluation process, the archive has not yet been accessed; the system has only read the index data saved in the infostructure. By double-clicking on a list entry, you can now access the archive directly and drill down as far as the field level in the data hierarchy.

Technical and business view

The way the data is displayed in the Archive Explorer is very technical and therefore less suitable for end users. The Archive Information System provides this type of technical display for each archiving object. To adapt the display to best meet the needs of the end user, SAP has introduced the concept of *business views*. This concept means that the archived data is displayed in a format that the end user would expect to see, or that the end user is familiar with from the display of corresponding data in the database. The extent to which this type of display is supported depends on the archiving object. Some archiving objects don't have any business views in the Archive Information System, whereas some objects, such as CO_ORDER, for example, are actually provided with several business views. When you double-click on an infostructure entry, you are first prompted to select the view you require, as shown in Figure 4.6.

Figure 4.6 Selecting a View for Archived CO Orders

Ad-hoc evaluations

An infostructure usually has to have been built already for the Archive Explorer in order to be able to evaluate it. This means that only files with the **Deletion Completed** status can be evaluated. This makes sense, since all the other data is essentially still in the database and therefore there is no reason to search for this data in the archive. However, you may want to simply check the archived data before the start of the delete phase. You can use the **Ad-hoc Evaluation** function for this purpose. In an ad-hoc evaluation, rather than accessing the generated database table, the system instead performs a sequential read access on the selected archive files. The volume of data that would otherwise accumulate when you build an infostructure is only saved internally. The subsequent display of data and the navigation options then correspond to those of a normal infostructure evaluation.

Note
The evaluation of built infostructures with the Archive Explorer or other types of access to the Archive Information System is particularly fast (see Section 4.6) if the system can access the required data using the primary index of the relevant database table.

Database indexes for infostructures

Additional database indexes may be required to access data through fields other than those of the primary index. Because the tables of the Archive Information System are generated in the live system, in most cases, it is not feasible to create this type of index through the ABAP Dictionary. Moreover, if the database table is regenerated, this could result in the index being deleted again.

In this case, the Archive Information System gives you the option of adding information on the required database indexes into the definition of an infostructure. This option also allows you to create user-defined indexes for standard SAP infostructures where you enter the index ID and the corresponding fields into the AIND_STR8 table. For more information, see SAP Note 164704.

4.5.6 Deleting an Infostructure

Like data in other database tables, the data saved in a generated database table needs disk space. For this reason, it generally makes sense to delete data for other archive files again after a certain time. Since the source data has already been archived, you no longer need to consider archiving this data. However, you can generally delete infostructures again manually. This function gives you added flexibility for building or deleting infostructures as required, for example, if you don't need to access archives regularly.

Contrary to when you build infostructures, there is no integration with the Archiving Data Kit (ADK) for deleting infostructures. This means that the deletion must always be activated explicitly. You must take this into account especially when reloading archives. When you reload archived data, you must explicitly delete active infostructures for the corresponding files and build the infostructures for any archive files that may have been created during the reloading process.

Explicit deletion

4.5.7 Creating a Field Catalog

Do not change standard field catalogs

SAP provides standard field catalogs for many applications. You can identify these standard field catalogs by their name, which begins with "SAP_". Therefore, before you create your own field catalogs, you should always check whether you cannot actually use a standard field catalog instead. You should never modify a standard field catalog, not even by adding new fields. Standard field catalogs may be overwritten when you upgrade a release, or when you install Support Packages. Furthermore, some programs assume that the field catalogs look exactly the way they did when they were delivered.

Still, you can copy a standard field catalog into your own namespace and make the changes you require to this copy. Nevertheless, you should keep in mind that standard programs generally ignore infostructures that were created based on user-defined field catalogs. You can therefore usually only use these types of infostructures in the Archive Explorer and in your own programs.

Expertise required

Creating a field catalog requires specific expertise; for example, you must know which tables are archived with a particular archiving object and which of these tables' entries have been used in a business object. You should know this information before you create a new field catalog for an archiving object. This is particularly important for estimating the expected volume of data and for field catalogs with several source tables.

Example for financial accounting documents

A typical procedure that you can apply in most cases is described below. We make a distinction here between field catalogs with one source table and those field catalogs with several source tables. For more detailed information on how to proceed when creating a field catalog and on the significance of relevant fields and indicators, you can refer to the application help function as well as to the field help function. In the procedure described below, we will therefore assume that you know the significance of the individual fields and know how to make entries.

For our example, we will use a field catalog for financial accounting documents that are archived using the FI_DOCUMNT archiving object. A financial accounting document consists of, among other things, a document header and several items. The document header is saved in the BKPF table and the items are located in the BSEG table.

4.5.7.1 Creating a Field Catalog with One Source Table

To create a field catalog with one source table, you proceed as follows:

1. **Selecting the source table**

   To fill an infostructure, the Archive Information System can use each table and structure saved in the corresponding archive files. Which of the tables of an archiving object is used depends on which fields you want to use to search for archived objects. However, note that searching for archived objects using the fields of an item table generally requires more space in the database than searching in a header table. This is because an item table usually has more entries than a header table. In addition, after you create the infostructure, the generated database table usually contains just as many entries as those in the main table of the field catalog in the archive files.

   In our example, the BKPF table of the FI_DOCUMNT archiving object was selected. You should be able to search for the **Document number**, **Fiscal year**, and **Posting date**.

2. **Naming the field catalog**

   The name of a field catalog is subject to the same restrictions as the name of other systems objects, for example, database tables. You should only use letters, numbers, and the underscore symbol. The name should begin with a letter, but not with the abbreviation "SAP." We recommend that you use a name in your own namespace.

   In our example, we have selected "ZDEMO_BKPF" as the name.

3. **Header entry of the field catalog**

   Enter the name, description, and archiving object of the new field catalog. Enter "K" (key field) in the **File in index** column and "D" (data field) in the **Offset in index** column.

4. **Key fields of the field catalog**

   In most cases, it makes sense to use all key fields of the reference table (with the exception of the client) as key fields of the field catalog. We recommend that you choose the numbers 10, 20, 30, and so on as field numbers. Always ensure that the key field numbers are smaller than the data field numbers. As field names, we also recommend that you use the same field names as those used in the reference table.

Make sure that the **Obligatory key field** and **Optional field** indicators are not set for key fields. You must set the **Key** indicator for the key fields.

In the example here, all key fields (except the client) of the BKPF table were added to the field catalog as key fields.

5. **Data fields of the field catalog**
In most cases, it is a advisable to make all the data fields of the reference table data fields of the field catalog too. We also recommend that you use the numbers 100, 110, 120, and so on to number the data fields. Make sure that the **Key indicator** and the **Obligatory key field** indicator are not set for data fields. The **Optional field** indicator should be activated for data fields.

With data fields, it usually makes sense to add as many fields of the reference table as possible to the field catalog. In contrast to adding a field to an infostructure, inserting an additional data field into a field catalog does not require much storage place or runtime. Nevertheless, you should only add fields to the field catalog that also work as the selection criteria of programs. You should therefore not use any fields for the FLTP (floating point number) in particular. You should also avoid using the CURR and QUAN data types, since these are usually formatted incorrectly. For more information on these data types, refer to SAP Note 309384.

4.5.7.2 Creating a Field Catalog with Several Source Tables

To create a field catalog with several source tables, you proceed according to the following example:

1. **Selecting the source tables**
The procedure for selecting several source tables is the same as the one used to select one source table. However note that the source tables must fulfill certain dependency conditions in this case. In addition, unrelated tables cannot be used together in a field catalog. You should generally select tables that belong to a combined document, such as the document header and document item, for example, or tables that can at least be linked through common fields.

Based on our example for the FI_DOCUMNT archiving object, these are the BKPF and BSEG tables.

2. **Determining dependencies**

   The Archive Information System can only use several source tables if the tables are in a hierarchical dependency relationship. Key fields with the same semantics determine which table depends on which table. These fields usually have the same name in the different tables. To define a field catalog, you must be able to arrange all source tables so that each table that depends on another table also has the same key fields as that table.

   In the example for the financial accounting documents, the BKPF and BSEG tables are linked by the **Company code, Document number,** and **Fiscal year** fields. Entries from BKPF and BSEG that are the same in these fields belong together. The BSEG table depends on the higher-level BKPF table and contains the key fields of this higher-level table as its key fields.

3. **Determining the main table**

   After you determine any possible relationships between the tables involved, you will notice that there is at least one table whose fields are the same as the key fields of the field catalog. There may also be several other tables with this feature. This is the case if there are at least two tables with the same number of key fields in the field catalog. In such a case, you can select any of the tables in question as the main table.

   However, if there is no table that has all the same key fields of the field catalog, you cannot create the field catalog in this way. In this case, you must select other source tables or check the relationships between the tables. This is the BSEG table in our example.

4. **Creating the field catalog for the main table**

   Ignore all tables except the main table for the time being. Create the field catalog as described in Section 4.5.6.2. In the example, a field catalog is created for the BSEG source table first.

5. **Enhancing the other table(s) progressively**

   At this point, all the key fields should already be in the field catalog for all other tables. If this is not the case, either an error occurred when you determined the table dependencies, or you didn't select the correct table in the last step.

Now select any of the remaining tables and enter their key fields as additional source fields for the corresponding key field of the field catalog. For our example, this means that the BUKRS field of the BKPF table is entered as an additional source field for the BUKRS field; BKPF-BELNR is entered as an additional source field for BELNR; and BKPF-GJAHR is entered as an additional source field for GJAHR. (There is no corresponding field in the BKPF table for the BUZEI field.)

Then enter each data field of the table into the field catalog as a new data field. Note that the same restrictions for fields of the field catalog also apply for field catalogs with only one source table.

Repeat this step for each table that still has to be added.

4.5.7.3 Typical Pitfalls When Creating Field Catalogs

If you create a field catalog following the steps described above, errors should not normally occur when you build the corresponding infostructures. In some cases, however, problems that were not previously discussed may occur. We will address these problems below using two typical error scenarios.

Error scenario 1: "Records not inserted in infostructure"

During the delete phase or when you subsequently build an infostructure, the error message "Records not inserted in infostructure" (Q6330) may appear. In addition to the other causes for this error mentioned in the long text of this error message, an incorrect field catalog may also be responsible for the error. This is due to the fact that the field catalog key was not defined completely, or did not match the structure of the archive file. The procedure described above is based on the assumption that the table entries defined by the key specified in the field catalog are no longer found in an archive file. If this is the case, however, the error described above occurs when you try to insert the corresponding records into the generated database table.

Solution There are essentially two strategies to solve this problem: On the one hand, you can try to make the key of the field catalog unique by adding other key fields. On the other hand, you can make the business object itself (i.e., the offset in the archive file) the key field. You can do this by entering "K" in the **Offset in Index** column in the header entry of the field catalog. The offset then becomes the key field for the generated database table.

Error scenario 2: "Infostructure is inconsistent"

If the error message "Infostructure is inconsistent" (Q6234) appears during the delete phase or when you subsequently build an infostructure, this is usually caused by the definition of the field catalog rather than by the infostructure itself. As already mentioned above, field catalogs with several source tables must satisfy certain consistency conditions.The source tables must therefore be sorted in such a way that the key fields of each source table are a subset of the key fields of the previous source table in the sorting sequence.

You should therefore check whether the other source fields for all key fields were entered correctly, and whether the field catalog was created following the procedure described above. You may have to delete a source table from the field catalog to ensure the consistency of the field catalog.

Solution

4.6 Archive Access Based on the Archive Information System

In the section about accessing archives directly, an option was described where an end user can access archived data without having to know anything about archiving or without having to know whether the data is in the archive or is still in the database. With this type of access, the system automatically determines whether the data is in the archive and in which archive file it is saved. The system then usually accesses the archives automatically without any interaction from the user. The advantage of this type of access is the consistent integration of archived data into the familiar display transaction. However, an application-specific concept for indexing archived data is required for the solution mentioned above.

With the Archive Information System, the behavior is exactly the reverse. There is a uniform procedure for indexing archived data, but data cannot be integrated sufficiently into the usual display transactions.

You can use the programming interface of the Archive Information System to access the data of an infostructure from a program and to use this data as an application-specific archive index. This means that archived data can be integrated into the normal application transaction without the disadvantage of dealing with different solutions for an application-specific index.

Example The line item reports of Cost Accounting in SAP ERP are an example of this type of function. Figure 4.6 shows the line item report for internal orders (transaction KOB1) with the line items of an archived internal order. It is no longer clear from this report whether the data originates from the database or from the archive. To display the line items, the user does not need to know from where this data originated.

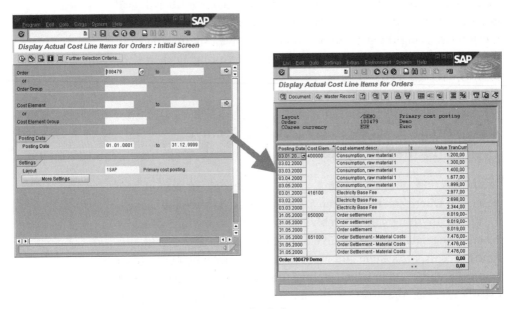

Figure 4.7 Line Item Report for Orders

The line item reports of cost accounting do not automatically access archived data by default. The system must first be notified of this requirement for access through the ASACCESS01 table. In this table, you can specify whether the report should only be read from the database, or whether the archived data should also be included automatically through the Archive Information System.

Corresponding infostructures must be created for the reports to be able to find archived data in the Archive Information System. What is important here is that an infostructure for a specific standard field catalog provided by SAP was activated and built.

In the example shown above, the line items were archived with the CO_ITEM archiving object. For this reason, an infostructure is required for one of the SAP_CO_ITEM_001 or SAP_CO_ITEM_002 field catalogs. In our example, an infostructure was used for the SAP_CO_ITEM_001 field catalog. The important factor in this case is not the use of an infostructure provided by SAP, but the use of a suitable field catalog provided by SAP. Infostructures that were created with reference to user-defined field catalogs are ignored by the line item reports. One reason for this is that the application (in this case, the line item report) requires that specific fields with a specific significance exist in the field catalog. When using user-defined field catalogs, this requirement would not be given with sufficient certainty. However, in addition to the infostructure required for the line item reports, you can use a different infostructure that refers to another field catalog. This does not present a problem for the line item report, but it does consume additional storage space in the database.

Using the standard field catalog

This type of archive access primarily runs in the same way that an application-specific index is read. The difference here is that data is read for a suitable infostructure, rather than from the application-specific index table. Although the infostructure also includes a database table, the fields for this table are not set by default; they are only selected when you configure the infostructure.

Another difference between the line item report described above and direct access to data, for example, for displaying accounting documents (transaction FB03), is the fact that, with the line item report, several business objects are frequently read from the archive and then filtered again using the selection criteria. To a certain extent, this is an indexed sequential access method.

4.7   Document Relationship Browser

Data from the archive and from the database

The Document Relationship Browser (DRB) is used to display linked business objects. These are usually documents that were created during a shared business transaction or that belong to a common process. DRB in this case is not restricted to a specific application but instead supplies linked documents from different application areas. DRB also enables the end user to integrate data easily outside the boundary of the system, for instance, when using different *Application Link Enabling* (ALE) scenario.

Although it is useful for displaying data that has not yet been archived, another advantage of DRB is that you can use it to display archived objects. In this chapter, we mainly want to discuss the capabilities of DRB in relation to archived data. For more information on DRB, see SAP Note 492938.

Archive Information System as the basis

The archive accesses made through DRB are always automatic accesses that are almost always based on the Archive Information System. You therefore do not need to know whether the data is in the archive, although you can use DRB to determine whether it is.

DRB is a service

DRB is not an independent application; it is simply a service that you can call at any time for an entry object. The applications contain different transactions and reports from where you can branch to DRB for each entry object. Most of these functions are summarized in the **Document Relationship Browser** role (SAP_DRB). In addition to some simple lists for finding documents, these functions also include the document display in financial accounting (transaction FB03) and the line item reports for overhead cost controlling.

After you enter DRB using the business object of a particular type, such as a sales order, the program displays which business objects are linked to the entry object (see Figure 4.7). The applications provide the business objects that are directly linked to the entry objects in each case. The relevant application determines what this actually signifies in detail. The links between the business objects do not have any other significant features; therefore, you cannot discern whether an object is the predecessor or successor of a different object. The display in DRB only indicates that there is a link between the objects.

To avoid a cyclical and therefore unnecessarily complicated display of linked business objects, each object within the business process in question is only displayed once. This is also the case if an object is linked directly to several objects. Consequently, not all the direct links are actually displayed. The display can also vary, depending on which entry object you have selected and in which sequence you navigate through the link tree. However, the total number of objects displayed remains the same, irrespective of the sequence of individual navigation steps. In the first step of the DRB display, only the objects that are directly linked to the entry object are displayed. If other objects are linked to these objects, you can also display them by navigating into the displayed link tree. In Figure 4.7, sales order 4972 was selected as the entry object. In the link tree, you can see all the business objects that are linked to this sales order.

Multiply-linked objects are displayed only once

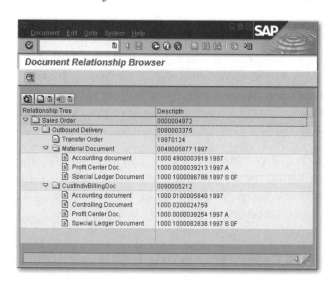

Figure 4.8 Business Objects Linked to a Sales Order

You can branch to the object display by double-clicking on an object key (this is usually the document number). The way this display appears depends in particular on the application in question and on the type of business object.

DRB is divided into a general *Basis core* and other *application-specific components*, such as Sales and Distribution, Materials Management, and Accounting. The Basis core is responsible for displaying links as shown above and for forwarding the functions that depend on the

DRB components

object type to the relevant application. The application components are responsible for determining the links and for displaying the individual business objects.

The specific functions that are performed by the application components require access to archives. Therefore, the corresponding application, rather than the Basis core of DRB, accesses the archived data. The way in which an archive is accessed and the prerequisites required to do this therefore depend on the type of business object.

In order for DRB to access archived data, however, you must select appropriate settings for all object types in the Archive Information System. In most cases, this includes building infostructures for certain standard field catalogs ("SAP_..."). A considerable part of the documentation on DRB deals with the specific details of these settings.

Accessing DRB
using the
SAP_DRB role As already mentioned, DRB cannot independently perform all the tasks for determining and displaying linked business objects. In fact, DRB requires support from the applications, for example, to find the entry object selected by the user. However, the functions from the **Document Relationship Browser** role (SAP_DRB) mentioned earlier can deal with this task. All the functions contained in this role have automatic access to archives.

The way in which a certain business object is displayed in the DRB view is also application-specific. Whether an archived object is displayed differently to a corresponding object from the database also depends on the application or the object type.

4.7.1 Connected Object Types in Detail

In this chapter, we want to focus on some important object types connected to DRB and explore these in more detail. We will address the prerequisites that must be fulfilled to ensure that DRB can find and display archived data for these object types. We will also discuss the links between these object types and how they are displayed in DRB. Information on other object types is available in the documentation for the Document Relationship Browser.

Overview   Table 4.2 gives you an overview of which object types in SAP ERP are connected to DRB.

Application	Object types
SAP NetWeaver Application Server	► Intermediate document (IDoc) ► Workflow work items
Accounting	► Settlement document ► Accounting document ► Direct input accounting document ► Cost accounting document ► Profit center document ► Account statement line items ► Profit and loss statement ► Special ledger documents ► Electronic account statements
Sales and Distribution	► Customer inquiry ► Customer quotation ► Sales order ► Customer complaints order ► Customer contract ► Customer scheduling agreement ► Customer outline agreement ► Credit memo request ► Group master contract ► Returns ► Subsequent delivery free of charge ► Customer delivery ► Sales support document ► Individual customer billing document ► Invoice list ► Handling units ► Shipments ► Inbound deliveries ► Rough goods receipt ► Shipment requirements ► Shipment orders
Materials Management	► Document line invoice ► Incoming invoice ► Purchase requisition ► Purchase order ► Goods receipt

Table 4.2 Object Types Connected to DRB

Application	Object types
Plant Maintenance and Service	▶ Maintenance order
	▶ Maintenance order confirmation
	▶ Maintenance notification
	▶ Service notification
	▶ Service order confirmation
Production Planning and Control	▶ Production order
	▶ Production order completion confirmation

Table 4.2 Object Types Connected to DRB (cont.)

Note that not all the object types listed here are connected to DRB in the same way. For example, not every object type has a function in the system for calling the relevant object as an entry object in DRB.

Object types not listed in the table above can also appear in DRB, because some functions for determining relationships are based on generic properties of the relationship in question. For example, the system always uses the same method to find the source document (see Section 4.7.1.1) for an accounting document, regardless of the object type of the source document. Consequently, source documents can be found, even if their object types are not explicitly connected to DRB and therefore don't appear in the table. However, these types of objects cannot generally be displayed if they have already been archived.

4.7.1.1 Accounting Document

Source document   The principle of the source document applies in Accounting. This means that each business transaction that you can display in Accounting has a document that activates the transaction—the *source document*—however, the document itself does not necessarily have to be in Accounting. If you post a billing document in Sales and Distribution, for example, an accounting document and cost accounting document are usually created (as well as other accounting documents, if necessary). The source document for this business transaction is a billing document, although this billing document is not in Accounting. For the purpose of DRB, all accounting documents are considered linked to their source document and vice versa. In the above example, the cost accounting document is therefore not directly linked to the accounting document; rather, both are linked to the billing document. Through this billing document, a two-tier relationship can then be established between the cost accounting document and the accounting document.

We have already described above how you can branch from the document display to the Document Relationship Browser. No additional prerequisites are required here, expect that you must be able to view the document to be displayed in the document display (transaction FB03). For archived documents, this means that either the application-specific archive index has been created for the FI_DOCUMNT archiving object (table ARIX_BKPF), or that an active and established infostructure exists for one of the SAP_FI_DOC_001 or SAP_FI_DOC_002 field catalogs. In transaction FB00, you can then set the document display in such a way that archived documents are also found and displayed in DRB.

Prerequisites for displaying data in DRB

In addition, the **Document Relationship Browser role** (SAP_DRB) contains a program that is also suitable for accessing DRB from an accounting document. You can branch to DRB by double-clicking on the required document in the output list of this program. Similar to the line item reports for cost accounting mentioned earlier, you can select whether you want the program to read from the archive or the database. The method already described previously, which is controlled from table ASACCESS01, also works with this program. You only need to make the corresponding entry for the RDRBFI00 program.

You can connect archived accounting documents fully to the Document Relationship Browser as follows:

Connecting archived accounting documents

▶ If you want to use the RDRBFI00 program contained in the **Document Relationship Browser** role and you also want to make selections using the **Posting Period** (BKPF-MONAT) and **Reference** (BKPF-XBLNR) fields, you should use an infostructure for either of the field catalogs SAP_FI_DOC_001 or SAP_FI_DOC_002 , which also contain fields for **Posting period**, **Posting date**, **Document type**, **Reference (document number)**, **Reference transaction**, **Reference key** and **Logical system**.

▶ If you don't want to use this program, you don't require automatic archive access contained in this program. If you don't want to make a selection using the fields mentioned above, you can use the application-specific archive index (ARIX_BKPF), which is normally built anyway.

▶ Set the document display in transaction FB00 in such a way that data is read from the archive using the archive index.

4.7.1.2 Cost Accounting Document

Distribution to archives

Dealing with archived cost accounting documents in DRB is more complicated than dealing with accounting documents, for example. This is due to the way in which the line items are distributed in the archives. You can archive cost accounting documents with different archiving objects, such as CO_ITEM, PP_ORDER, or SD_VBAK, for example. Another problem is that the cost accounting documents are not archived document by document. With a posting that involves a production order and a cost center, part of the document is in a PP_ORDER archive, while the other part of this document is still in the database. Therefore, you cannot clearly determine in which archive file a cost accounting document is located, or whether it was already archived. This can only be determined for individual line items (single line items).

Multiple field catalogs and infostructures

Since a field catalog of the Archive Information System depends on the archiving object, you may require multiple field catalogs and therefore multiple infostructures. To access cost accounting documents, field catalogs are provided for the different archiving objects. These field catalogs begin with the prefix "SAP_COBK_." Therefore, to connect archived cost accounting documents to DRB, you need an infostructure for the corresponding SAP_COBK field catalog for each archiving object that you want to use to archive cost accounting line items. To be able to determine the links, these infostructures must contain the REFBN field. SAP provides these types of infostructures by default. Their names also start with "SAP_COBK_." Activating and building these infostructures is usually sufficient. You can improve the runtime of the program by adding the REFBT, AWTYP, and AWORG fields into your infostructures; however, this means that the infostructures also need more storage space in the database, which you may have to compare with faster processing speeds.

Based on the way in which cost accounting documents are archived, the number of entries in the required infostructures corresponds approximately to the number of line items. The important items here, however, are the line items from archive files, for which the corresponding infostructure was built. Since such an infostructure can be very large, you should carefully consider whether you need to display archived cost accounting documents.

Only the corresponding source documents are linked to the cost accounting documents (as is also the case with other accounting documents). The objects in which the costs are collected (e.g., orders and cost centers) are not considered to be linked to the cost accounting document. Otherwise, you could have a situation where several million documents would be connected to an object, which would exceed the capabilities of DRB.

4.7.1.3 Sales Order

In Sales and Distribution, a link between two documents corresponds to the relationship referred to in the document flow as the predecessor or successor. However, because the semantics of the relationship is omitted in DRB, you can no longer discern which document is the predecessor and which is the successor. To connect archived sales orders and other sales documents archived with the SD_VBAK archiving object to DRB, you simply need an active and filled infostructure for one of the SAP_SD_VBAK_001 or SAP_SD_VBAK_002 field catalogs.

The **Document Relationship Browser** role contains a special program for sales documents that enables access to DRB (see Figure 4.9).

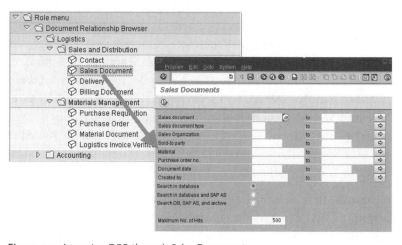

Figure 4.9 Accessing DRB through Sales Documents

In addition to the document number in the **Sales Documents** field, you can also use other fields as selection criteria. We recommend adding these fields to the infostructure.

Search options

Also note the three selection buttons on the selection screen. You can use these buttons to control where the search for the sales documents is run.

- ▶ **Search in the database**
  If you select this option, the program only searches the database for sales documents. Archived sales documents are completely ignored.

- ▶ **Search in the database and SAP AS**
  If you select this option, the program searches for sales documents in the database and the infostructures of the Archive Information System listed above. However, no archives are accessed. Consequently, not all the fields in the output list may be filled and not all the required records may be found, since the program views fields that are not contained in the infostructure as empty and therefore does not continue searching for sales documents.

- ▶ **Search DB, SAP AS, and archive**
  If you select this option, the program searches for sales documents in the database and in the Archive Information System. For documents already found in the Archive Information System, any missing data is read from the archive. Therefore, only documents located in a suitable infostructure are read in this case.

Known pitfalls

This selection only controls what is displayed in the output list of the program, and not the linked documents that DRB will subsequently find. Archived documents may therefore be displayed as linked objects in DRB, despite the fact that you selected the **Search in DB** option. In many cases, you should only use the two options: **Search in database** and **Search in DB, SAP AS, and archive**. Although the **Search in database and SAP AS** option is often faster than the latter option mentioned, it often presents the end user with confusing results because the end user doesn't always know which fields are contained in the infostructures and what effect this has on the selection.

Displaying archived logistics documents

In contrast to accounting, archived logistics documents are not displayed in DRB in the same way as documents that are still in the database. However, the display for archived documents is based on the relevant display transaction for documents from the database. This also ensures that the important fields are displayed. If the documents are still in the database, the usual document display transactions, such as VA03, for example, are used.

All other object types for logistics are connected to DRB in the same way as the sales orders. The only differences are with the field catalogs used and the fields through which data can be selected, and which should be integrated into the infostructures. For more information, refer to the documentation for application-specific components of the Document Relationship Browser.

4.7.2 Configuring the Document Relationship Browser

The previous DRB discussion focused mainly on using the Archive Information System and other data archiving functions to access archived data. In terms of configuration, we concentrated primarily on how infostructures are defined. In addition to this main option for making selections, however, there are also other options available for optimizing access to archived data and for adapting functions to suit the needs of the end user.

In this context, we will address the following configuration options:

▸ Presetting the entry programs
▸ Selecting entry list fields
▸ Selecting object types to be displayed
▸ Selecting fields in DRB

In principle, all settings can be user-specific. All settings, except the one for selecting object types to be displayed, are not actually specific for the Document Relationship Browser, but originate from the tools used there. But, since these settings are extremely useful for adapting DRB better to data archiving, we would like to discuss them in more detail below, and to demonstrate how you can make access to archived data even more convenient for the end user.

4.7.2.1 Presetting the Entry Programs

Although the **Document Relationship Browser** role in the standard delivery contains some suitable programs for accessing DRB, these programs are set up in such a way that they cannot access archives. For logistics programs, the **Search in database** search option is preset. For accounting programs, the automatic archive access is not activated by default in the ASACCESS01 table. Below we describe how you can assign these programs to a role to activate an automatic archive access.

Creating selection variants

First you must create a selection variant for each program that you want to use. In the field properties of the selection variant, you can preset and hide the **Search in...** fields. If the program is now started with this variant, the user no longer sees these fields on the selection screen and the required value is used automatically.

You can proceed in the same way for the entry lists for accounting documents and for the line item reports in cost accounting. However, you cannot hide the fields for selecting the data source here since these fields don't appear on the selection screen in any case. Nevertheless, they are saved with the variant. You can, of course, also control the entry lists for accounting and cost accounting documents in table ASACCESS01, as described above. In this case, the performance changes for all users. If you really want to set up the system in such a way that the line item reports in cost center accounting are automatically read from the archive for all users, you should implement the setting in table ASACCESS01.

Assigning a selection variant to a role

After you have created corresponding variants for all programs to be used, you can enter these programs into a role in transaction PFCG. If you call this type of program from the role to which it was assigned, this program starts automatically with the default settings from the variant. In this way, you can compile a role that contains all programs that call DRB and that are configured to access the archive automatically. You can, of course, also use this method to preset selection criteria other than those mentioned here.

4.7.2.2 Selecting Entry List Fields

All programs contained in the **Document Relationship Browser** role were implemented using the SAP List Viewer. Therefore, whenever you display a list, you can change its layout, save this changed layout, and set it as the default setting. These settings can be made for specific users or for all users.

4.7.2.3 Selecting Object Types to Be Displayed

Complex business transactions and processes are also usually displayed in a relatively complicated format in the Document Relationship Browser. Furthermore, due to the large number of object types that support DRB in SAP ERP, runtime problems can occur when links are being determined, because the program tries to resolve all links, even though the user does not generally require all object types.

Let us assume, for example, that a user is interested in the supply chain of a business process, but not in the accounting details. In this case, it would make sense to simply hide the unwanted object types in the display. The method you use to achieve a selective display is called *personalization*. Depending on whether you want the settings to apply for individual users or for a role, you can implement the personalization in user maintenance (transaction SU01) or in role maintenance (transaction PFCG). Settings made for a role can automatically be made for all users assigned to this role. The selection of object types in the Document Relationship Browser role is set in such a way that all objects are displayed.

Personalized display

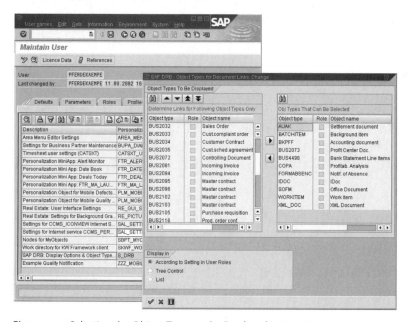

Figure 4.10 Selecting the Object Types to Be Displayed in User Maintenance

When you hide object types, note that the documents in question are not only removed from the display, they can also no longer be used to determine additional relationships. This means that not only are the explicitly hidden objects removed from the display, but they are also the objects that depend on the hidden objects.

4.7.2.4 Selecting Fields in DRB

Only the type and description of an object are displayed by default in the navigation tree of DRB. You can enhance this display by adding additional relevant fields. Apart from the technical equivalence of the object key and object type, there are two fields of particular importance here:

The Logical system and Origin fields

▶ **The Logical system**: This field indicates from which system the data originates. This is relevant if cross-system processes or business transactions are involved.

▶ **The Origin field**: In terms of data archiving, this field in particular is worth mentioning. This field indicates whether a displayed business object is located in the database or in the archive. In the same way as entry lists, you can also control the field selection here using layouts. You can also save and preset user-specific layouts.

This chapter is made up of two parts. First, it deals with the technical basis that is integral to understand the existing archiving solutions and those solutions yet to be developed. Secondly, it helps the administrator, who is already familiar with data archiving, to ensure a smooth fine-tuned production process.

5 Technology and Administration

by Gerd Buchmüller, Dr. Axel Herbst,
Dr. Jan Nolte-Bömelburg

Understanding the technology and administration of data archiving is essential for its optimal use. This chapter will therefore focus primarily on this critical requirement.

5.1 Basic Technology of SAP Archiving Solutions

Because the *Archive Development Kit* (ADK) provides the technological basis for data archiving, we will examine the ADK more closely.

5.1.1 The Archive Development Kit: Classification and Components

SAP data archiving can be used for any database system supported by the applications of the SAP Business Suite. The independence from the database system is achieved by archiving software, which handles a data flow "above" the database interface. This approach is called "database-based"—in contrast to (still existing) database-integrated solutions. Database-based archiving enables the use of different database systems, while simultaneously taking into account the business relationships.

Database-based archiving

Despite the different characteristics of archiving programs with regards to data selection and application-specific check logic, all programs use the same basic services with respect to the archive. These

Application-independent basic services

include services for the compact storage of data objects in archive files, or for the release-independent reading of archived data. The software layer of SAP NetWeaver, which provides these basic services at the development and runtime of archiving programs, is the ADK, which we have already mentioned.

ADK components In a real sense, the ADK includes not just the ADK runtime system, but administration environment as well (the transactions SARA and DB15), along with an environment for the definition of archiving objects and classes (transactions AOBJ and ACLA). Administrative data and metadata (e.g., technical properties of archiving sessions and structure definitions of archiving objects) are administered in internal ADK tables in the same database as the SAP system, the so-called *ADK Repository*.

5.1.2 ADK as Runtime Environment

Figure 5.1 clarifies the interplay among the database, archiving programs, ADK components, and file storage based on the data and control flows during the write phase.

The archiving program is scheduled as a job through Archive Administration. Within the archiving program, an ADK call generates a new archiving session, which is entered into the ADK Repository. Application data, read in an archiving object-specific manner and checked for archiving suitability, is passed record by record to the ADK and bundled into data objects using ADK functions.

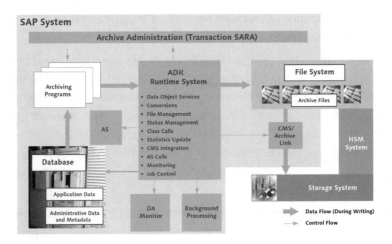

Figure 5.1 ADK as Runtime Environment of Archiving Programs

Other ADK-internal data object services transform and compress a completely assembled data object in a platform-neutral and release-independently readable format. Depending on the composition of the data, compression rates of up to 1:10 can be achieved on the one hand, and even better with records with many initial values. On the other hand, data originating from cluster tables cannot be compressed further. In all, compression factors between 2 and 5 can often be achieved.

Data object services

Before the first data object is written to a file, the ADK takes care of the transfer of the metadata required for the technical interpretation of the archive files from the ADK Repository and the ABAP Dictionary. In particular, the so-called *nametabs* of all tables and structures belonging to the archiving object are transferred by the ADK.

During archive access, the ADK runtime system checks whether the following conversions are needed due to changed system environments, and executes them if necessary:

Conversions

► **Platform adjustment**
This is necessary if the codepage or the numeric format has changed. When reading archive files of non-Unicode origin into a Unicode system, there is always a codepage conversion of the character data (for more Unicode details, see Section 5.1.4).

► **Schema adjustment**
This is necessary if the archived tables and structures have changed with respect to their current definitions in the ABAP Dictionary. Structural changes, however, must be assignment-compatible. The same semantics apply here as for the ABAP command MOVE-CORRESPONDING. At the time of archiving, any structure components not yet existing are returned with initial values, and components removed during upgrade are not output. For like-named components, the usual ABAP conversion rules between different data types apply.

These conversions are performed only temporarily at the runtime of the read, delete, or reload program, that is, the archive files are never changed. If the system environment has changed in ways more significant than described above, however, special conversion programs can be implemented using the ADK for permanent archive conversion.

ADK file manage-
ment

Along with the other runtime system services listed in Figure 5.1, the ADK also handles other technical and application-independent tasks for archiving programs. ADK file management handles the automatic creation and naming of new archive files during the write phase, once the limits established in the archiving object-specific Customization have been reached. The selection of the path that is valid for each syntax group for file access is also not a part of the logic of an archiving program.

Additional ADK
services

Moreover, the ADK also encapsulates and handles:

▸ The assignment and checking of archiving session and archive file status (see Section 5.2.2)

▸ Data exchange with archiving classes (see Section 5.1.3)

▸ The calculation and storage of statistical data (see Section 5.2.4)

In order to complete the following tasks, the ADK also includes and supplies interfaces to other components and services of SAP NetWeaver:

▸ File storage via CMS/ArchiveLink (see Section 3)

▸ Scheduling of sequential jobs, like the automatic start of the delete job once an archive file has been written (see Section 5.4.2)

▸ Provides the Data Archiving Monitor (see Section 5.2.2.2)

▸ Updating of archive information structures for the Archive Information System (AS) (see Section 4.4)

5.1.3   ADK as Development Environment

ADK API

Besides of its function as a runtime environment for all archiving programs, the ADK also assumes the function of a development environment. This primarily includes an application programming interface (API), which consists of a series of released function modules in the ARCH function module group, and is provided by the ADK for all archiving objects. The ADK API enables the development of new, as well as the extension of existing, SAP archiving objects. The archiving solutions delivered by SAP are also based on the use of the ADK API. A detailed description of the functional scope of the ADK can be found in the SAP Library, as well as in the documentation of the function modules. Information and examples of the development of custom archiving solutions can also be obtained through SAP seminar BIT670, see Appendix C.

SAP develops archiving solutions for SAP standard business objects. If you want to archive data from custom tables, you can use the ADK to develop a corresponding archiving solution.

5.1.3.1 Developing New Archiving Objects

The development of an archiving solution for custom tables in the customer namespace largely consists of the definition of an archiving object and the creation of suitable archiving programs using the function modules of the ADK API.

Archiving objects are complex objects of mutually dependent tables. When defining an archiving object, the so-called *structure definition*, you can determine the database tables which make up the archiving object. The structure definition is created using transaction AOBJ.

Archiving object

Figure 5.2 Structure Definition of FI_DOCUMNT

An archiving object includes, among other things, the following programs entered into transaction AOBJ:

▶ **Write program** (required)
The write program is used to read the archived data from the database, bundle it into data objects, and write it sequentially into archive files in the file system. During the write phase, there is no deletion from the database.

▶ **Delete program** (required)
The delete program is used to delete the data in the data objects in the archive file from the database. The basis for this is always the archive files already generated.

▶ **Read program** (optional)
The read program can be used to evaluate the archived data.

Alternatively or in addition to a read program, you can connect the archiving object involved to the Archive Information System (see Section 4.5) by providing the necessary field catalog and information structures.

The function modules of the ADK API enable the archiving of data and access to and processing of archive data; however, they cannot be used for the actual deletion of data from the database or for the reloading of data into the database. These tasks are handled by the delete or restore programs, for instance, in the form of OPEN SQL statements.

Archiving classes   Archiving classes are used for the archiving of data, which does not represent standalone objects from a business point of view, but belongs together from a technical or logical perspective. This data is generally used by multiple business objects and archiving objects. But, it generally doesn't have the status of a business object. Typical examples for the use of archiving glasses are SAPscript text and change documents. Access to archived data is also implemented using archiving classes.

Archiving classes are exclusively developed by SAP, but can also be used in customer programs. Their use, however, is only possible in combination with an archiving object.

5.1.3.2   Extending SAP Archiving Objects

An extension of SAP archiving objects may be necessary if, for instance, custom append structures have been added to a standard table, or there exist custom tables which logically belong to SAP standard tables. Depending on the type of change to the data structure, an extension to the standard archiving solution may require essentially broad modifications to the delivered standard.

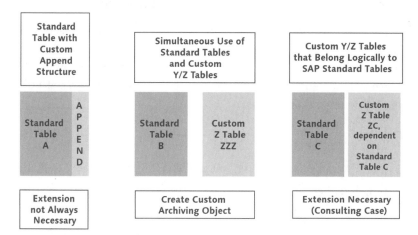

Figure 5.3 Extension Options of Archiving Objects for Standard Tables and Custom Tables

If an SAP standard table has been extended with a custom append structure, changes and extensions of the SAP standard archiving functionality is not necessary in every case. An analysis of the standard archiving program is the essential first step. If the original table entries are archived in the write and delete programs of the archiving object, no change is necessary, since the fields added by the append structure are automatically archived. If the original entries are first passed into a structure in the archiving program, then you need to adjust both the structure and the archiving program itself. The reason for this is that this type of structure has a fixed design, and does not contain the added table fields.

Append structures in standard tables

For custom tables in the customer namespace, you should first check whether they could be archived through a custom archiving object. In that case, you don't need to make any modification to the standard. For archiving, you can then develop a new archiving object with the appropriate archiving programs. This is also the case if the custom tables are logically related to SAP standard tables and therefore to an SAP standard archiving object. In that situation, archiving of the data in the standard object and in the custom object should be performed independently of one another as close together in time as

Custom tables in the customer namespace

possible. To take into account the special relationship of the data in the standard object with that of the custom object, you can also write a reporting program, which reads the archive files of both archiving objects and relates the application logic correspondingly.

If the procedure described is impossible, you should contact your consultant or SAP Consulting. This may be the case, for instance, if the custom table is very closely related to the standard archiving object. The extension of a standard archiving object requires at least the following modifications:

▶ Extension of the structure of the archiving object with the tables to be archived

▶ Copying of the standard write and delete programs into the customer namespace, as well as adaptation of the programs to the new requirements

▶ Copying of the standard report into the customer namespace and adaptation of the program

Before you undertake an extension to a standard object, you must carefully analyze whether there might be any dependencies on other standard archiving objects. Moreover, you must examine whether additional checks for archivability of the objects involved may be necessary for business reasons.

5.1.4 Data Archiving and Unicode

The system support of different user languages belongs to the most important requirements resulting from the increasing internationalization of business scenarios. Data exchange with newly integrated systems, in particular—in which text appears in languages other than the languages offered in the existing system network—can run up against technological limitations. For instance, if a European company founds a subsidiary in Asia, or a supply chain must be built between partners speaking English and Vietnamese, database, processing, and presentation software must be designed for the expanded set of characters.

Typically, only subsets of characters have been supported previously, in the form of character sets. For each character set, there are different manufacturer- and hardware-specific encodings—so-called *code-*

pages—which assign each character a hexadecimal value—the *code point*. An example for a codepage often used in Japanese installations is Shift-JIS. Even if a Japanese user speaks French or German, he cannot read these languages correctly under Shift-JIS if characters are included that fall outside 7-bit US ASCII. The core problems can be summarized as follows:

▸ A codepage includes only certain languages.

▸ A character may have different code points in different codepages, but the underlying codepage is not always known in multi-code-page environments.

▸ Codepages cannot be arbitrarily combined.

Unicode not only defines a universal set of characters, but for the first time, unique, mappable encodings—so-called *Unicode transformations*—have been globally standardized. Unicode has also become established as the character representation of the Internet, and is used in Java, HTML, and XML, for instance. For the ABAP-internal encoding, SAP has decided on the UTF-16 Unicode transformation. On the one hand, this means that texts in all worldwide languages can be processed in a program and exchanged with other Unicode systems with no loss of information; but, on the other hand, every character now requires two bytes (and sometimes four) in main memory. Unicode-capable databases sometimes use 8-bit transformations, so there is only a small increase in the storage required for Roman characters, but require three bytes per character for Asian languages. You should note that the conversion of different UTF formats is lossless (i.e., without loss of information) due to the identical character format.

Unicode
(ISO/IEC 10646)

In the following, we will look at the consequences for data archiving of the Unicode conversion of an SAP system. For more information on language combinations, multi-code-page environments, and Unicode in SAP, we recommend the article "Looking Forward to the Unicode Advantage: Internationalization and Integration" [RED02], the book *Unicode in SAP Systems* [BÜR06], and SAP Notes 73606 and 379940. For more useful information about Unicode in general, go to the website *http://www.unicode.org*.

Requirements for Unicode-based archiving

To archive arbitrary character data and later be able to report and display it independently of the login language, you must meet two prerequisites:

▶ You must use a Unicode system or convert an existing system to Unicode.

▶ You must ensure that all programs involved in the archiving or the archive retrieval are Unicode-capable.

The first requirement means that your database system must support Unicode and that the SAP system has been installed as a Unicode system. The Unicode conversion of an existing SAP system including the database can be accelerated by previous data archiving. For the second requirement, both ADK and the archiving objects and archiving classes used must comply with the stricter ABAP syntax within a Unicode-capable application. While this is satisfied for ADK, as a component of SAP NetWeaver Application Server, and also applies to the SAP archiving solutions described in this book, you must check modified or custom archiving programs for Unicode capability, as you may have to adapt them. Besides the article mentioned [RED02], the chapter *ABAP and Unicode* in the SAP Library is also helpful, as is the ADK documentation (see the last chapter, particularly the documentation of the function modules using the new parameter RECORD_REF for the reading of records) and the sample programs included for the archiving object BC_SFLIGHT.

Consequences for the data archiving administrator

For the data archiving administrator, Unicode conversion will have no significant effect. First, the disk space required for the archive files will change by approximately the amount required for the UTF-16 transformation of the data to be archived. The ADK internal compression and a more compact ADK format can counteract this increase only to a limited extent. However, depending on the Unicode support in the database, more space may be freed up during the deletion phase, resulting in more space than anticipated by the character-based estimate of the space requirements in the context of statistics (see Section 5.2.4).

No archive file conversion

As mentioned in Section 5.1.2, the ADK handles the reading of archive files, which may have been created before the switching over to Unicode as a special case of automatic platform adaptation. This is even the case if you performed the archiving in a multi-code-page environment (an MDMP system was converted to Unicode). However, please see SAP Note 449918. Under no circumstances do you need to convert archive files due to Unicode conversion.

For more information on Unicode in SAP systems, please refer to the Quick Link *UNICODE* in the SAP Service Marketplace.

5.1.5   XML-Based Archiving

Insofar as this book examines concrete archiving objects, these objects are all based on the technological basis described in the previous chapters, that is, on ADK. With SAP R/3 Enterprise Extensions 2.0, however, the first archiving object that uses an alternative technology was delivered. The impetus for introducing the so-called *XML-based archiving*, or *XML archiving*, had the following reasons:

▶ Better support of "end-of-life" scenarios in which the archived data has a longer lifetime than the application system—due to a looser coupling of the archive with the originating application system

▶ Increasing the long-term and independent capability to interpret archived data using open standard formats and interfaces (XML, XML Schema, HTTP(S), WebDAV, Java EE)

▶ Provision of an archiving technology for the Java applications in the SAP Business Suite as well

Why XML-based archiving?

These requirements led to the development of the XML Data Archiving Service (XML DAS) and the two XML DAS connectors—one each for the ABAP and Java stacks of SAP Web AS 6.30. Therefore, ABAP applications can now choose between two development and runtime environments. Because SAP determines individually, for each new archiving object, which runtime environment is better suited, you cannot simply convert an existing ADK archiving object to XML.

5.1.5.1   Positioning of XML Archiving

Even though XML DAS is the newer technology, that doesn't mean that ADK isn't being further developed. As already mentioned, both development and runtime environments run next to one another and are used depending on the archiving scenarios expected. For customer development, the XML Archive API is currently not released for either ABAP or for Java. Analogous to the introduction

Complement of "classical" archiving

of ADK, best practices for the development of XML-based archiving programs should be established before the corresponding development guides and training content can be determined. It is also not the intent of SAP to physically migrate existing ADK archives, since the associated data transport is generally unacceptable and a generic conversion without application knowledge could not bring the desired maximum usefulness. However, since multiple XML archiving objects already exist (see Section 5.1.5.3), we want to outline the important common features and differences below.

5.1.5.2 Common Features and Differences from ADK from an Administrative Viewpoint

Common features between the two technologies

The data archiving administrator still uses transaction SARA for the scheduling and monitoring of all ABAP archiving objects. The concepts of interruption and continuation discussed above (based on transaction RZ20), as well as DA monitoring and DA statistics, are also largely unchanged. The marking of Archive Administration data for archiving (and deletion), and the following usage of the archiving object BC_ARCHIVE take place in the familiar ADK manner.

Differences

On the other hand, XML archiving has the following differences from ADK archiving:

▶ **File format**
Instead of ADK files, an archiving session generates XML documents and generally an XML schema with a structural description of the individual objects. These files are written by XML DAS without compression and on an object (instance) by object basis. If you want to reduce the number of resulting files and the overall size of the data, the so-called *PACK* function is available in XML DAS administration. The PACK format is very simple compared with the ADK format; it uses standard compression and is described in the SAP Library. You may want to leave the compression to your own storage system anyway (which ideally should have no problem with the large number of files, either), so that you can eliminate the packing entirely as a separate administration step. On a technical level, you can then—provided you have the corresponding permissions—display the XML documents for testing using the browser of your choice.

▶ **XML DAS as a part of the SAP NetWeaver Application Server Java (AS Java)**
Since XML DAS is a part of AS Java, AS Java must be installed and supported. With an add-in installation, this can be the same SAP system as the application system, or it can also be a dedicated stand-alone (Java) system. In the latter case, you should consider using the same system denoted as the "XML DAS server" for multiple application systems, so that, for instance, the configuration overhead (such as the connection of external storage systems to the "XML DAS server") can be reduced in a distributed system environment.

▶ **Separation of data via hierarchical levels**
Because XML DAS can potentially manage archived data from multiple application systems, there is already a need for separation according to point of origin. With ABAP, the separation by client is also possible. The next level of the resulting XML DAS-wide archive hierarchy is formed by the archiving object. Additional hierarchical levels can be added on an application-specific basis, but are terminated at the (leaf) level for the individual archiving sessions. Despite this hierarchical arrangement of archived data, new in comparison to ADK, searches in the archive are not limited to navigation along existing paths. Similar to ADK, applications offer search forms for value-based queries, without, for example, your needing to know the session. One drawback that you should note is that these search forms are predefined by SAP, because the Archive Information System cannot be used for the indexing of XML archives.

▶ **Connection via WebDAV**
The connection to storage systems takes place using the SAP-independent WebDAV[1] protocol, not ArchiveLink/CMS. Alternatively, you can—just as with ADK—also archive in the file system.[2] In contrast to ADK, however, the file system is not used as intermediate storage; instead, you decide for each archiving object[3] whether you want to write the archived data into a directory of a file system or directy into a so-called *collection* of a WebDAV-capable archiving system. There are already archive providers that sup-

---

1 WebDAV = Web-based Distributed Authoring and Versioning [WEBDAV].
2 Or in a storage system with a file interface, such as an HSM system.
3 Or via path extension with Archive Routing; see Section 5.3.

port both ArchiveLink and also WebDAV as access protocols. You can obtain an overview of WebDAV archive providers currently certified by SAP from the Partner Information Center at *http://www.sap.com/partners/directories/searchpartner.epx* if you select the SAP-defined integration scenario **BC-DAR—WebDAV for Data Archiving 6.40** in the **Search for Solutions** section.

In any case, it is the administrator's responsibility to model the logical archive hierarchy on one or more physical file or storage systems, by performing a mapping of the archiving object levels to storage (sub)systems. Figure 5.4 shows a fictional example of the archiving of European sales documents ("SalesInEurope") in the physical storage AS2. AS2 could, for instance, represent a directory on a Network Attached Storage (NAS) server.

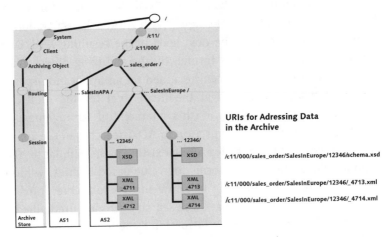

Figure 5.4 Example of an Archive Hierarchy for XML Archiving

▶ **Number of parallel delete jobs arbitrary**
In the deletion phase, there is an invisible difference, but a useful one. The number of delete jobs for an archiving session is not dependent on the files written. The administrator is free to choose how many delete jobs should be scheduled in parallel in order to distribute the work of deleting the corresponding data in the database.

5.1.5.3 Availability and Documentation

XML DAS and its connectors for ABAP and Java are components of SAP WebAS 6.30 and, naturally, also in SAP NetWeaver 2004 and SAP NetWeaver 7.0 (2004s), they are a part of the standard installation (usage types AS ABAP and AS Java). The following applications currently rely on them; others are in development:

Component of SAP NetWeaver

Environment	Archiving Object
ABAP	Demo archiving object BC_SBOOK_X
	Execution Steps—SAP R/3 Enterprise SCM Extensions 2.00
	iPPE—Integrated Product & Process Engineering ▶ Three archiving objects in SAP ERP 6.0 ▶ One archiving object Interchangeability Master Data
Java	XI 3.0 Adapter Engine and Partner Connectivity Kit (PCK) ▶ Message Archiving: Messages in the Adapter Framework ▶ Security Archiving: Messages with S/MIME settings
	Adaptive Computing Controller 1.0 ▶ Archiving in the Controller Log
	Guided Procedures (based on SAP NetWeaver 7.0)

Table 5.1 Overview of XML Archiving Objects

The documentation on XML archiving in the SAP Library (see the Introduction, Table 1) is structured in such a way that an experienced (ADK) data archiving administrator can easily recognize the different concepts and steps. SAP Note 826000 names a few additional documentation sources.

Documentation

5.2 Tasks of the Data Archiving Administrator

In many larger enterprises, the role of a data archiving administrator has been established, which primarily involves the implementation and execution of data archiving. Below, we introduce a few of the typical tasks of such an administrator, which are also reflected in the SAP user role of that name.

5.2.1   The Data Archiving Administrator Role

Portals   The core notion of role-based portals is to provide the user with simple, personalized access to all the significant information, tools, and systems required for daily work. In an SAP environment, this is performed by the SAP NetWeaver Portal, which contains roles (*portal content*) as its core component for the modeling of activity profiles.

Content of the role   As will be shown in this chapter, the administration of data archiving includes far more tasks than simply the operation of the central transaction SARA (see also the article "Data archiving essentials—What every administrator needs to know" [GS01]). The role of **Data Archiving Administrator** includes transactions relevant to the following tasks, as well as links to the corresponding help pages in the SAP Library:

▸ Selection of suitable archiving objects according to analysis of database and table growth (DB15, DB02, SE16, TAANA)

▸ Scheduling, controlling, monitoring, and reporting on archiving sessions (SARA, SAR_SHOW_MONITOR, SARI)

▸ System settings, particularly the customization of the storage of archive files (SAR_OJB_IND_CUS, FILE, SF01)

▸ Useful tools in the area (SA38, AL11)

Figure 5.5 shows the menu of roles, which appears in the role maintenance transaction PFCG and should be adapted. The technical role name is SAP_BC_CCM_DATA_ARCHIVING.

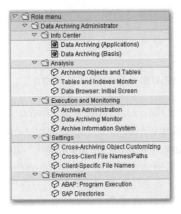

Figure 5.5 Menu of the "Data Archiving Administrator" Role

Chapter 7 describes the analysis phase, particularly the assignment of archiving objects to growing tables. Details on the monitoring of data archiving are provided in the next chapter; system settings, which determine the relationship between security and performance, are explained in Section 5.2.3. At this point, we would only like to recommend the customization of the platform-independent file names.

The archiving programs are generally executed on different servers, but at the latest, when the archived data is read, the same files are accessed. Also, Archive Administration should be able to perform an access check from a (dialog) server. Consequently, the directory in which the archive files are written must be accessible from all the servers, which might need it. Providing this access based on "mounts" or suitable software is the network administrator's responsibility.

Directory for archive files

Now you must also ensure that ADK and Archive Administration can form the syntactically correct path expression for file access according to the operating system group. In the archiving object-specific customizing, you first have a logical file name available for that purpose. To define the logical file name, you need a name and a path part. The path part is itself of a logical nature, that is, there is a naming convention, which appropriately regulates the physical expression of the path at runtime (platform-dependent) according to your specification.

Logical file names and paths

As an example, we'll use the following naming conventions for the logical path ARCHIVE_GLOBAL_PATH:

Customizing example

▶ Syntax group UNIX:

```
<P=DIR_GLOBAL>/data_archiving/<FILENAME>
```

▶ Syntax group WINDOWS NT:

```
<P=DIR_GLOBAL>\data_archiving\<FILENAME>
```

Here, the placeholder <P=DIR_GLOBAL> is replaced at runtime with the global directory of the SAP system according to profile parameter DIR_GLOBAL. The required placeholder <FILENAME> takes its name part from the definition of the "calling" logical file name assigned to the archiving object, which is MY_ARCHIVE_FILE in our example. An example of its definition is shown in Figure 5.6.

Figure 5.6 Definition of a Logical File Name

For the placeholder <PARAM_2>, the ADK uses a counter to ensure a unique name assignment for each archive file. This placeholder must always be included in the definition of the logical file name.

> **Note**
>
> If possible, don't just use the placeholder <PARAM_2>, but also the placeholders <DATE> and <TIME> in the definition of the logical file name in order to guarantee the unique, time-dependent assignment of a name.
>
> Moreover, you can arrange your archive files within a directory according to the archiving object, or write them into dedicated directories if you use the <PARAM_3> in the logical file name or in the logical file path. The ADK automatically replaces <PARAM_3> with the name of the current archiving object.
>
> If you want to store your archive files, the placeholder <F=ARCHIVELINK> can be placed into the logical path. Then the files will be generated directly in the basis path of the content repository assigned to the archiving object, and after archiving, there is no internal copying process.

We use MY_ARCHIVE_FILE in the archiving object MYOBJECT and thereby generate, on a Unix server for instance, the directory

/usr/sap/BCE/SYS/global/data_archiving/

on January 21, 2006, the archive file having the physical name

MYOBJECT_20060121_152226_0.ARC.

For more details and recommendations, for example, for the subsequent storage of archive files, besides the application help there is also SAP Note 35992.

5.2.2 Monitoring Archiving Sessions

In the administration of data archiving, the monitoring of archiving sessions plays an important role. Here, archive management is available and, from SAP R/3 4.6 on, the Data Archiving Monitor as well. You can call the archive management function from Archive Administration (transaction SARA) using the **Management** pushbutton.

5.2.2.1 Archive Management

Archive management provides an overview of all archiving sessions and archive files for a selected archiving object. From archive management, current information on archiving sessions and archive files, as well as for archiving jobs, can be displayed. Moreover, archive management also provides direct options to go to the display of logs, to the spool list of the write job, to Customizing for data archiving, the archiving objects and tables (transaction DB15), the Archive Information System, and the data archiving statistics.

In the overview, the archiving sessions for an archiving object are displayed depending on their status. Besides the status of archiving sessions described in more detail below, there are other possible statuses whose descriptions can be found in the SAP Library or in archive management via **Legend**.

Overview of archiving sessions

▶ **Archiving sessions with errors**
The write phase was canceled before the first archive file was completed.

▶ **Incomplete archiving sessions**
The write phase has not yet ended, or the delete program has not yet run for all archive files.

▶ **Complete archiving sessions**
Both the write and the delete phase have been concluded successfully.

▶ **Archiving sessions marked for deletion**
The management data of the archiving session can be archived and deleted with the archiving object BC_ARCHIVE.

▶ **Replaced archiving sessions**
The archiving session has been reloaded or converted.

▶ **Invalid archiving sessions**
The archiving session has been declared invalid.

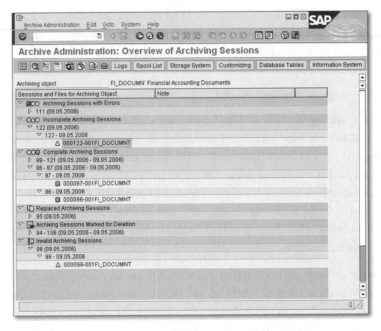

Figure 5.7 Overview of the Archiving Sessions for FI_DOCUMNT

The archiving sessions are initially arranged into status areas. Within a status area, the sessions are grouped into blocks of 20. By expanding an archiving session, another level is shown in which the archive files belonging to the archiving session are listed.

Details on the archiving session

For each archiving session and each archive file, you can double-click on the archiving session or the archive file to get detailed information. For the archiving session, among other things, the date, time, and user are displayed. In change mode, you can enter a remark for the archiving session into the detail form, and set the archive flag or the invalid flag. Management data for the archiving sessions for which an archiving flag has been set is archived on the next session of the BC_ARCHIVE archiving object. There is no further read access possible to the archiving sessions whose management data has been archived.

> **Note**
>
> To declare several archiving sessions invalid according to certain criteria or to flag archives, you don't need to edit each session individually. Instead, start the program RSARCH_FLAG_SESSIONS (e.g., through transaction SA38) and make your selection there.

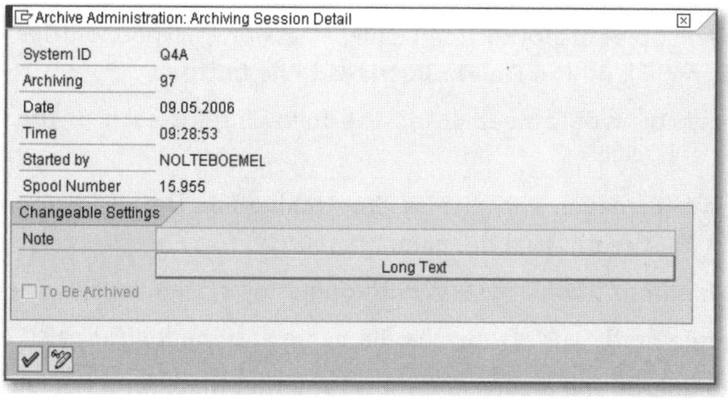

Figure 5.8 Detail Screen for Archiving Session 97

The detail screen for the archive file includes information on the size of the archive file and the number of objects in the archive file. If the archive file is stored in a storage system, the **Storage** field shows status **Stored**. In change mode, you can change the name of the archive file and the logical path, or enter a remark and a long text for the archive file.

Details on the archive file

If a name is entered for an archive file, the system assumes that the archive file is located in the file system. In this case, when the detail screen is called, a check of accessibility of the archive file in the file system takes place. The result of this access test is shown in the last line of the detail form. If the test is positive, the status **Archive file is accessible** is displayed (symbolized by a green traffic light.) Otherwise, the archive will have the status **Archive file not accessible** (red traffic light). If the archive file is stored in a storage system and no file name is entered for the archive file, it is determined whether access to the file can be obtained in the archive system. Depending on the status of this check, the file has the status **Archive file is accessible in storage system** (yellow traffic light) or **Archive file not accessible** (red traffic light).

Access verification

Note

To speed up reports accessing already stored archive files (or for the reloading of data from archiving sessions with stored files), use the action **Retrieve Files** to create a copy of stored files in the file system. After the report is complete, you generally want to remove the files from the file system again. **Goto • Retrieved Files** provides you with a list of retrieved archive files from archive management. You can limit the selection by selecting, for instance, stored archive files for all archiving objects or only for a certain archiving object or session.

To delete retrieved copies of stored archive files, mark one or more entries in the list and then click on the **Delete Retrieved File** button.

In earlier releases, you would need to do the following for each of the retrieved files:

▶ From the archive management, display the **Archive File Detail** (dialog box) to determine the physical file name.

▶ Remove that file from the file system with operating system tools.

▶ Switch to change mode and delete the file name and the logical path.

Another call to details on the archive file shows you that there is no longer a physical file name for the archive file, and the status changes back to **Archive file accessible in storage system**. Repeated storage is neither needed nor possible, since the preparation and deletion of the copy hasn't changed anything in the state of the stored archive file.

Archiving sessions or archive files, for which there are canceled archiving jobs, are symbolized by a lightning bolt in the archive management. Incomplete archiving jobs are symbolized by a clock in the overview. In the detail screen for the archiving session or for the archive file, the name of the job belonging to each session or file is shown. If you double-click on the archiving job, you jump directly to the overview for the selected job, where you can monitor the status of the job. There you can also display the job log, the spool list, and the details for jobs.

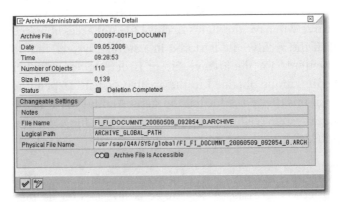

Figure 5.9 Detail Screen for Archive File 000097—001FI_DOCUMNT

Displaying selection criteria

The **User Input** function in archive management allows you to show the selection criteria that was selected when the write program for the archiving session was scheduled. This selection criteria continues to be shown when the corresponding variant of the program no longer exists.

Go to · Stored Files shows you an overview of the archive files stored in the archiving system. You can limit the selection by selecting, for instance, stored archive files for all archiving objects or only for a certain archiving object or session. In the result list, besides the content repository where the file is located, the technical key of the archive file in the storage system is also displayed. Moreover, the overview also contains information about the status of the archive file in the storage system.

Stored archive files

5.2.2.2 Data Archiving Monitor

A central monitoring tool for the entire IT environment (particularly the SAP systems) is the CCMS Alert Monitor. It consists primarily of collections of dedicated monitors for individual system components [CCMS01]. A system administrator who, for instance, is already observing *availability and performance* with the monitor, or is using the monitors *Background Processing*, *Filesystems*, and *Knowledge Provider*, will know how valuable the integration of data archiving into the monitoring infrastructure can be. The usefulness is surely even greater when so-called *auto-reaction methods* are implemented, which ensure active notification (e.g., by sending an email or an SMS message) in case of problems.

CCMS Alert Monitor

The Data Archiving Monitor offers the following archiving-specific functions for process tracking, problem recognition, and problem analysis:

Functional scope of the Data Archiving Monitor

- Complete overview of all archiving sessions executed (in contrast to archive management, without previous selection of an archiving object)
- Progress indicator regarding the processing of archive files
- Compact information about technical details on write and delete jobs like starting time, runtime, size of the archive files, and number of data objects archived
- Detection of potential need for action via so-called *alerts* (e.g., yellow alerts for remaining or incomplete delete jobs and red alerts in certain failure situations)

▶ Support of the analysis of alerts in the form of a jump to the job which triggered it and its logs

Sample scenario   The following scenario gives you an idea of the use of the Data Archiving Monitor.

In Figure 5.9, the root node **Data Archiving** is highlighted (in the SAP system, it would appear in red), indicating a problem with the monitored archiving sessions. In the example, the error message that occurred in the write phase of BC_ARCHIVE in system AL0 has triggered a red alert. The most critical node evaluation is always passed towards the root.

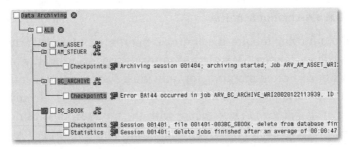

Figure 5.10 Example of Current State of the Data Archiving Monitor

The alert report automatically takes the DA administrator to the canceled job (see Figure 5.10).

Figure 5.11 Job Display for Analysis of the Alert

Finally, a look at the job log, shown in Figure 5.11, shows the actual cause of the error. In this case, it is the missing definition for the logical file path used. Another typical cause for errors here is lack of storage space.

However, the Data Archiving Monitor cannot indicate all the potential runtime exceptions (e.g., job termination due to an ADK-independent system error). So it is recommended that you use this monitor in combination with the other monitors listed above, or configure a custom monitor specifically tailored to your needs.

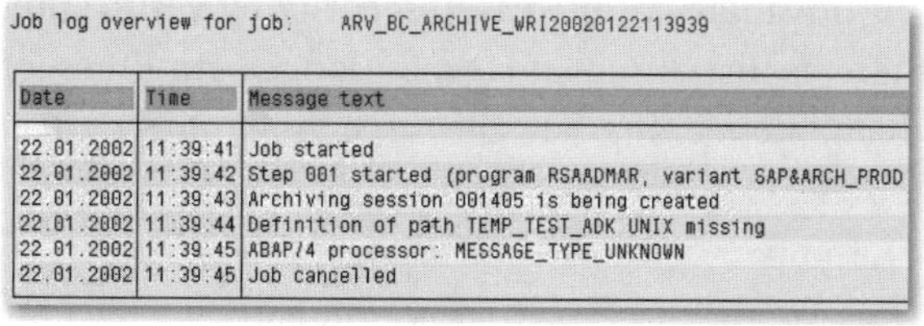

```
Job log overview for job:    ARV_BC_ARCHIVE_WRI20020122113939

┌──────────┬─────────┬─────────────────────────────────────────────────────────┐
│Date      │Time     │Message text                                             │
├──────────┼─────────┼─────────────────────────────────────────────────────────┤
│22.01.2002│11:39:41 │Job started                                              │
│22.01.2002│11:39:42 │Step 001 started (program RSAADMAR, variant SAP&ARCH_PROD│
│22.01.2002│11:39:43 │Archiving session 001405 is being created                │
│22.01.2002│11:39:44 │Definition of path TEMP_TEST_ADK UNIX missing            │
│22.01.2002│11:39:45 │ABAP/4 processor: MESSAGE_TYPE_UNKNOWN                    │
│22.01.2002│11:39:45 │Job cancelled                                            │
└──────────┴─────────┴─────────────────────────────────────────────────────────┘
```

Figure 5.12 Log of the Canceled Job

The Data Archiving Monitor can be called from the CCMS monitor sets (transaction RZ20) through **SAP CCMS Monitor Templates • Data Archiving**, directly as transaction SAR_SHOW_MONITOR, or from the role described above. Besides the application help, the long texts in the node descriptions document the published information and function of the monitor.

5.2.3 Security versus Performance

Given that data archiving is the processing of mass data and that access to the archive data must be secure and effective for years, it is the data archiving administrator's job to ensure a relationship between security and performance in archiving, which is optimally tuned to the business requirements.

5.2.3.1 Verification of Archive Files

One important decision involves the runtime cost for the verification of the integrity of archive files. During the write phase, verification information based on a CRC-32 checksum (*Cyclic Redundancy Check*) is stored in the archive file for every data object. Based on this information, an archive file can be "check read" for technical integrity during subsequent activities, like deletion, reading, or reloading, before the actual processing through all the data objects. Defective archive files are detected and indicated immediately, and subsequent activities like the deletion of archived data from the database will not even be started. In case of defective archive files, it's best to contact SAP Consulting or an experienced data archiving consultant.

CRC-32

You can set the intervals at which verification should be performed in cross-archiving-object Customizing (see Figure 5.12).

Verification
extends runtime

Corresponding to the advantage of increased security by verification of archive files, there is the disadvantage of longer runtimes of archiving jobs, which, depending on the archiving object, may increase by 10% to 30%.

Figure 5.13 Cross-Archiving-Object Customizing—Verification of Archive Files

5.2.3.2 File Access Check for Archive Selection

When selecting archive files for deletion, reading, or reloading, the existing archive file can be checked, that is, it is checked whether the archive file is accessible by Archive Administration and whether the metadata of the archive file is readable. Archive files for which this access check returns a negative result are displayed in the selection screen with a lightning bolt symbol.

As shown in Figure 5.14, the access check can be selected in cross-archiving-object Customizing both for archive files still located in the file system and for archive files that have been stored in a storage system.

Figure 5.14 Cross-Archiving-Object Customizing—Access Check for Archive Selection

Access check
takes time

The access check in the context of archive file selection can be very time-intensive for stored archive files, particularly when many archive files are in the storage system. It should therefore only be used after some careful consideration. The same applies for archive files located in a file system that is coupled with an HSM system.

> **Note**
>
> If you can forego the access check when selecting files, you should deactivate these settings in Customizing.

5.2.3.3 Reverse Order: Storage before Deletion

After the creation of the archive files in the write phase, there are two options for the order of the deletion and storage phases in cross-archiving-object Customizing:

▶ **Delete phase before storage phase**
After the write phase comes the delete phase, in which the data in the database is deleted based on the data in the archive files. In the subsequent storage phase, the archive files are stored in a storage system.

With this option, it is important for the archive files to be written on mirrored disks or into a RAID file system (see Section 3.1.1.2), or saved before the delete phase.

▶ **Storage phase before delete phase**
After the write phase comes the storage phase, in which the archive files are stored into a storage system. In the subsequent delete phase, the data is deleted from the database *only* after a successful storage.

As you can see in Figure 5.15, in addition to the order of the delete and storage phases, the storage system (**Content Repository**) and the automatic start of the storage of archive files (**Start Automatically**) can be configured in archiving-object-specific customizing.

Figure 5.15 Archiving-Object-Specific Customizing—File Storage into the Storage System

Furthermore, in the case of storage before the delete phase, the read behavior of the delete program in the delete phase can be controlled with the checkbox **Delete Program Reads from Storage System**:

Read behavior of the delete program

▶ If this checkbox is checked, the archive file is deleted from the file system after it is stored successfully. During the delete phase, the delete program reads the data from the archive file in the storage system. This guarantees that the delete program retrieves the data in the same state in which it was transferred to the storage system.

▶ If this checkbox is not checked, the archive file is not immediately deleted after successful storage in the file system. During the delete phase, the delete program reads the data from the archive file in the file system. This improves the performance of the delete program without eliminating the early storage.

To start the delete program automatically after generation of the files or after storage, in the **Settings for Delete Program** the checkbox **Start Automatically** must be checked, as shown in Figure 5.16. Only for the sequence **Store Before Deleting** is it immaterial whether the delete program is started in test or production mode. For the sequence **Delete Before Storing**, no files are stored when using the **Test Mode Variant**.

Figure 5.16 Archiving-Object-Specific Customizing—Settings for the Delete Program

Enhanced security or performance

The order of the delete and storage phases must be determined on a case-by-case basis by the data archiving administrator. If security is in the foreground, the delete phase should only take place after the storage phase. This ensures that the data is only removed from the database when the archive files have been properly stored. The option that the delete program should read the archive files in the storage system and not in the file system serves to strengthen this security aspect. If, on the other hand, performance is a higher priority, the delete phase should take place before the storage phase.

5.2.4 Data Archiving Statistics

Collecting statistical data

During the write, delete, and reload phases, ADK collects statistical data, compresses it, and stores it in the database for later reporting. Using this information, the data archiving administrator can:

▶ Detect resource bottlenecks on a timely basis

▶ Better plan for future archiving goals

▶ Document the usefulness of data archiving for the reduction of data volume in the database

Besides the runtimes of the archiving jobs and the number of data objects processed, the statistical data collected includes information about the physical disk space, which is consumed by the archive and the storage space and potentially freed in the database by data archiving.

Storage space information

While the disk space needed for the archive files can be determined rather precisely, the storage space in the database is calculated based on the data in the ABAP Dictionary and can therefore only be used as an estimate of the storage space in the database, which will actually be freed. In order to reuse the storage space in the database immediately, which has been freed by data archiving, a reorganization of the database is generally necessary. For more information, see Section 5.2.6.

For the display and evaluation of the statistical data collected, the data archiving administrator has a reporting transaction available.

Displaying statistics

Figure 5.17 shows the reporting transaction that is used to display statistical data (for all archiving sessions) that is stored persistently during data archiving. The reporting transaction can be called either directly from the initial Archive Administration screen or from archive management, via **Statistics**. You can also use transaction SAR_DA_STAT_ANALYSIS.

To select the desired archiving sessions for display, the **Client**, **Archiving Object**, **Archiving Date** (i.e., **Archived On**), and the **Status of the Archiving Session** can be used. To process the statistical data further, the data archiving administrator has the comprehensive functions of the ALV Grid Control (SAP List Viewer), like printing and exporting.

A detail screen for the statistical data as shown in Figure 5.17 is possible on the level of each archiving session. The incomplete FI_DOCUMNT archiving session 856 needs 58.6 MB disk space and still requires an estimated 156.9 MB storage space in the database. The write job needs 42 minutes to write the 56,762 data objects of the archiving session into the archive.

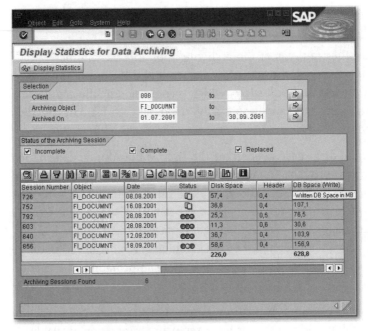

Figure 5.17 Reporting Transaction for Statistical Data

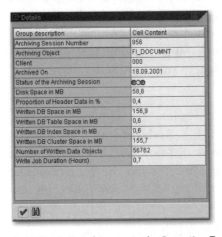

Figure 5.18 Detail Screen in the Reporting Transaction

5.2.5 Data Archiving Logs

Using the log function, you have central access to the logs generated during data archiving. You can get to this function either from Archive Administration or from archive management, either using **Logs** or **Goto • Logs**.

The following logs are written during the execution of an archiving program, such as the preprocessing, write, or delete program, and can be displayed using the log function:

Available logs

▶ **Job Overview**
Information on the background job of the archiving program.

▶ **Job Log**
Log of the individual steps performed for the background job.

▶ **Spool List**
List generated by the archiving program and stored in the spool. In general, this list contains the so-called *standard log*, which will be described below.

▶ **Application Log**
Log of all objects processed (summary and details). Not all archiving objects support this type of log.

Job overview, job log, and spool list are only created for programs run in the background; the application log, on the other hand, can be generated for programs, which run either in dialog mode or in the background. Whether the log of objects processed is written to the list (spool) or the application log can be determined in the variant maintenance for the program involved.

After the log is called, in the left screen portion of the log window, you see the logs available, sorted by archiving object, action (e.g., preprocessing, writing, deletion, etc.), date, and time. The latest log is marked; see Figure 5.19.

Displaying logs

Note
You can limit the display of logs to a certain archiving object by entering its name into the initial screen of Archive Administration. To have access to the logs of all archiving objects, you must leave this field empty.

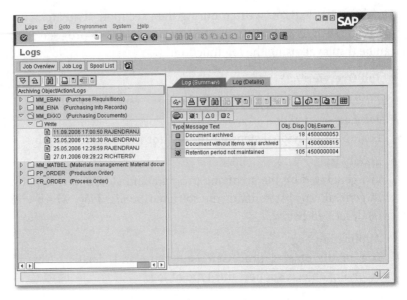

Figure 5.19 Logs in Data Archiving

5.2.5.1 The Application Log

The *application log* is displayed in the right part of the screen in the log window (see Figure 5.19). It informs the user of the results of processing all the business objects selected for processing. In the case of the write program, for instance, the user can see which business objects were archived and which business objects could not be archived for whatever reasons.

Summary or detailed log — The two tabs can be used to switch between the display of a summarized and a detailed application log (if available). If detailed information is available for an object, you can display it using the magnifier icon in the **Detail** column. Clicking on the question mark in the **Long text** column shows you the long text of the message. If no application log was created, a corresponding message appears. Possible reasons, for instance, are that the archiving program involved doesn't support this function, or that the user wanted the log output in the list (spool) and not in the application log.

5.2.5.2   The Standard Log

During writing, deleting, reading, or reloading, the executing program always writes a log. This is either a so-called *standard log*, or an application log, as described above.

The standard log consists of an archiving-session-specific or archive-file-specific section and a business-object-specific section.

Depending on the archiving action performed, you can find information here about the archiving session or the archive file, as well as information about the business objects processed (see Figure 5.20):

Archiving-session-specific/archive-file-specific information

▸ Number of the archiving session

▸ Number of data objects processed

▸ Size of the archiving session in MB

▸ Number of header data items in percent

▸ Table space required in MB for

　▸ Tables

　▸ Indexes

▸ Number of structures processed

This information is exclusively written to the list (spool) and can be displayed with **Spool List**.

The archiving-session-/archive-file-specific information in the standard log is stored in a database table and can be archived from there together with the ADK management data using the BC_ARCHIVE archiving object.

This section of the standard log informs the user of the results for all the business objects selected for processing.

Business-object-specific information

First the results are summarized; then, if requested by the user on the selection screen of the archiving program involved, the detailed log is displayed. If detailed information is available for an object, it can be displayed by double-clicking on the object desired. If detailed information is available for a message, it can also be displayed by double-clicking on it.

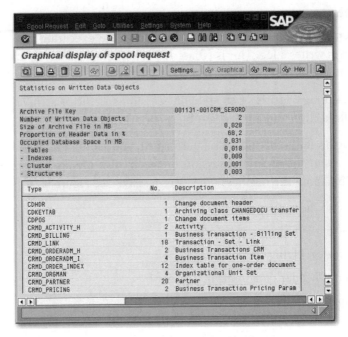

Figure 5.20 Standard Log—Archive-File-Specific Information

If no application log was created, a corresponding message appears. Possible reasons for the lack of an application log are, for example, that the archiving program involved doesn't support this function, or that the user wanted the log output in the list (spool) and not in the application log.

How you can access the information
In the variant maintenance of the archiving program, if it is determined that the log output for the business-object-specific information

▶ should be written to the application log, you can display this information directly using the log function (see Figure 5.19)

▶ should be written to the list (spool), you can display this information from the log function or from archive management using **Spool List** (see Figure 5.21)

Figure 5.21 Standard Log—Business-Object-Specific Information

5.2.6 Reorganizing the Database after a Data Archiving Session

Data archiving is primarily used for two reasons:

▶ On the one hand, the performance of the database system should be improved, for instance the access speed, the I/O behavior, and the quality of the database buffer.

▶ On the other hand, the storage space required in the database should be reduced.

The storage space that is freed up during the delete phase by deletion of the data from the database can generally not be used immediately for new data. Only data blocks whose contents have been deleted beyond a minimum limit are available for new data. To be able to use the space in only partially freed data blocks, after data archiving a reorganization of the database is necessary.

Below we will show you the effects of data archiving on the database system and what measures must be taken to achieve the goals formulated above. Due to the different architectures and terminologies of the existing database systems, we need to decide on just one architecture at this point. Here, we use the example of the Oracle database system to examine the details. The measures shown, however, can theoretically be used for any other database system.

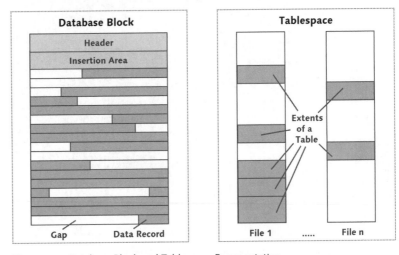

Figure 5.22 Database Block and Tablespace Fragmentation

Fragmentation of the database

As already explained above, during the delete phase, large numbers of records are deleted from the database tables, so that both the data blocks and the tablespaces become extremely fragmented. This is shown in Figure 5.22.

To correct the negative consequences of fragmentation on the database system, the reorganization types of index, table, and tablespace reorganization are all available.

Index reorganization

Of these types of reorganization, index reorganization is the most important measure for improving the performance of the database system. To achieve short database access times, a high hit rate is essential for the data to be read in the data buffer. Precisely for indexes, the probability that the data needed will already be in the buffer should be close to 100%. This assumes that the indexes consume as little working memory as possible.

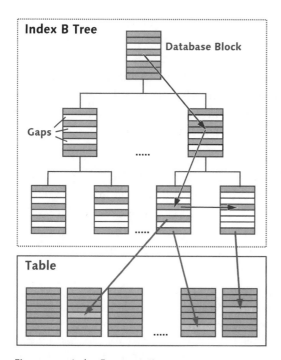

Figure 5.23 Index Fragmentation

If data is archived or simply deleted, gaps are formed in the indexes of the tables involved (see Figure 5.23). These gaps can, under some circumstances, no longer be filled by the database system, because the prescribed order of index entries may predetermine the data blocks that can be used for new entries. If there is no more space available, new data blocks must be used. Despite data archiving, the space requirements for indexes therefore continues to grow, which can result in degradation of the hit rate in the database buffer, and therefore perceptible degradation of performance in the database. This effect can be corrected using an index reorganization (ALTER INDEX ... REBUILD ...). It is significantly faster to reorganize an index than to delete it and rebuild it from scratch. An index reorganization should hypothetically be run after every large data archiving.

If the database system uses a *Cost Based Optimizer* (CBO), the statistics are obsolete after the delete phase; however, we do not recommend rebuilding the statistics for optimization of access paths using UPDATE STATISTICS. It has been shown that such a fresh rebuild, par-

Cost-based optimizer—database statistics

ticularly for large database tables, is often unnecessary or can even be counterproductive. Generally, for smaller sets of data optimizers decide on a *Full Table Scan* even though a faster index access would have been possible. The risk of an incorrect decision by the optimizer decreases as the data volume increases. For that reason, it is not always advisable to rebuild the statistics directly after data archiving, when the data volume is at its lowest.

Table reorganization

In contrast to the gaps in indexes, poor space utilization in data blocks has only a small effect on performance, since the probability that the poorly utilized data block must be loaded into the database buffer is much smaller than for indexes. Since the costs of a table reorganization are significantly higher than for an index reorganization, a table reorganization should only be performed in well-founded exceptional cases.

> **Note**
>
> Under no circumstances should an attempt be made to change the database parameters, for example, pctused, to make partially filled data blocks available for new inserts. That would only lead to fragmentation and performance losses in the newly inserted data. The value of pctused=40 % selected by SAP is actually at the upper limit of what makes sense from a performance standpoint.

Tablespace reorganization

In principle, the greater fragmentation of tablespaces after data archiving has no effect on the performance of the database system. So a tablespace reorganization is not absolutely necessary. However, it can be quite useful to do the following:

- *Reclaim storage space from the database system* if data no longer needed has been archived and the tables are subject to only slight additional change. On the other hand, if the archived tables can be expected to be subjected to the same data growth again, you shouldn't perform a tablespace reorganization.

- *Create storage space for other tables.* The alternative to this would be to consider that after repeated archiving sessions the gaps will be consolidated by the free space management of the database in such a way that they will be large enough, even without tablespace reorganization, and therefore, will be reusable for new data.

Online reorganization

To ensure high availability of the database system even during a reorganization, database manufacturers, third-party providers, and SAP now provide programs for online reorganization, such as BRSPACE [BRTOOLS].

In summary, we can say with assurance that an index reorganization should always be performed after every large data archiving operation for performance reasons. You can roughly determine when a table or tablespace reorganization should be performed by using the history of the average allocation of database blocks.

Index reorganization after every large data archiving

Even without these additional reorganization measures, data archiving leads to a stabilization of database size. If multiple archiving sessions are required, every data block should still sooner or later be completely free of its old data, and then, at the latest, would be available for new data again. When compared with data archiving with subsequent reorganization measures, this stabilization of the database size does not occur immediately and is not at a high level.

Under certain circumstances, data archiving can be used specifically for the improvement of system performance, after other options have already been tried. You can find more information on performance-oriented archiving in Section 1.4, in SAP Note 572060, and in the publications *Performance Aspects of Data Archiving—Factors for Optimal Results in Archiving Projects, Data Archiving Improves Performance—Myth or Reality?* and *Data Archiving—The Fastest Access to Your Business Data?* [DAPERF01, DAPERF02, DAPERF03], in which the use of performance-oriented archiving is examined in more detail.

Performance-oriented archiving

5.2.7 Archive File Browser

You can use the Archive File Browser (AFB) to display the contents of archive files. It offers a technical view of the archived tables similar to that shown by the Data Browser (transaction SE16) for data from the database. You can start the AFB using transaction AS_AFB.

Displaying the contents of archive files

The Archive File Browser is intended primarily for administrators (of data archiving) and people looking to detect problems with data archiving and problems inherent in the archived data. This is not a tool for end users. The data is presented only in technical form throughout. No business formatting is performed, and the AFB will not use any knowledge from the corresponding applications.

A tool for experts

Besides the display of the archived data itself, AFB also supports a search on field contents. This search is also more of a technical nature, that is, it is based only on the field contents of a table (analogous to transaction SE16) and is designed for the location of missing data. Improving performance is not the main impetus, but rather safeguarding the completeness of the data. There is no index built on the archived data; you have the Archive Information System for that purpose.

Figure 5.24 shows a view of a data object in the archive file with key 000096—001CHANGEDOCU for archiving object CHANGEDOCU.

The user interface consists primarily of an overview of the archived data, a display area, and a message area where messages are displayed. Besides the view of a data object, the display area contains the view of the content of individual tables in the archiving object, as well as a view of the header information from the archive file. You can find detailed information on the functionality of the Archive File Browser and its operation in the SAP Library.

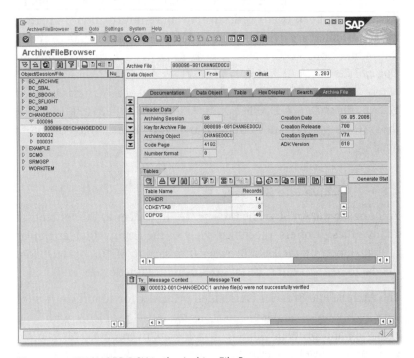

Figure 5.24 CHANGEDOCU in the Archive File Browser

5.3   Archive Routing

New legal specifications for the retention of data pertaining to storage location and retention period have led recently to an increasing need to better control archiving in these respects. The specification of a storage location, for instance, may be necessary because data with a particular business origin, or data that pertains to a certain geographical region, may need to be stored in that region (e.g., the archiving of tax-relevant invoices to US suppliers stored on a server in the USA).

Enables compliance with legal requirements

Of course, you have always had the option of archiving data for each archiving object into a dedicated directory or content repository, and therefore segregate "physical archives" (in the sense of the set of all archive files) by application. But you couldn't determine the storage location for subsets of the data to be archived for an archiving object, that is, for financial accounting documents of a particular company code, for example. It is precisely that type of fine-grained definition of the storage location, which is enabled by *Archive Routing*. By routing, we mean:

1. The rule-based determination of a storage location,[4] and

2. The storage of data from an archiving session into that storage location.

You should note that the unit of Archive Routing is the archiving session, and not an archive file, whose scope always represents a technical segment of the session itself, which is not influenced by business considerations. Assuming you assign specific values to suitable selection criteria for an archiving object (or more precisely, selection parameters/variant attributes for the write program), you can set up your archiving session in such a way that exactly that data is archived together in a session which should reach the same storage location. A reason for this might be that this data all has the same retention period.

Archiving session as the smallest unit

To introduce Archive Routing, you need to formulate so-called *routing rules* in the context of archiving-object-specific Customizing. A

Routing rules serve as the basis

---

4   Here, we mean a storage location in the broadest sense, that is, not simply a content repository, but also a directory in the file system—particularly if you aren't using a storage system connected via ArchiveLink/CMS.

routing rule consists of a condition ("What data?") and a storage location ("Where to store it?"). Naturally, the content repositories and/or directories given must exist, or be created in advance by the system/storage administrator. For each rule, multiple conditions are possible, and they are then combined together. Every condition compares a business selection parameter (or an expression derived from different selection parameters using a Business Add-In[BAdI]) with a specified value.

Routing rules in the example of SD_VBAK

For instance, you could make the following assignment for the archiving object SD_VBAK:

Rule no.	Sales Organization	Created on	Content Repository	Logical File Name
1	0002			ARCHIVE_DATA_FILE_0002
2	0001	01/01/2002 to 12/31/2004	RPR02	
3	0001	01/01/2005 to 12/31/9999	RPR03	

Table 5.2 Routing Rules in the Example of SD_VBAK

The storage location must be unique

During the subsequent archiving, you should note that the selection of the data to be archived must take place in such a way that the "right" rules determine the storage location uniquely. If this is not the case, the system will fail to archive with these values.

For instance, if you only archive sales documents for sales organization 0002 with the routing rules given above, they will be written into the directory derived from the logical file name ARCHIVE_DATA_FILE_0002—according to rule number 1. If you select a variant in which only sales organization 0001 is given, you will get an error message. If you then limit the variants only to the sales documents, which were created, for example, in 2006, the archive files are first written to the exchange directory determined in the classical way using the logical file name specified in the archiving-object-specific Customizing. In a subsequent (manual or automatic) storage process, the intermediate files are passed to content repository RPR03. In the following figure (Figure 5.25), you can see the display view for the "right" rule number 3. You can find more information on routing rules in the archiving documentation in the SAP Library.

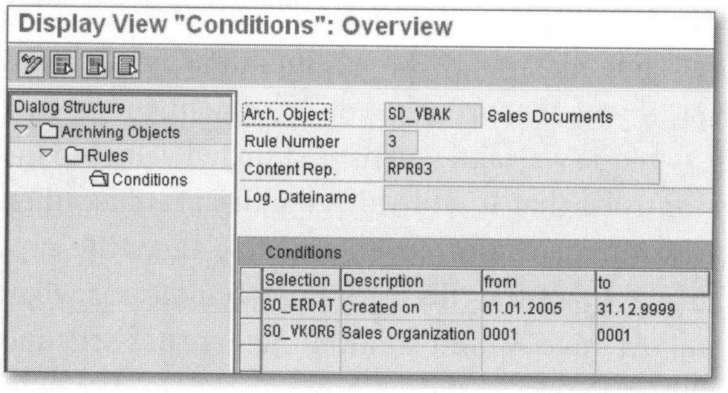

Figure 5.25 Routing Rule Number 3 from the Example

Archive Routing can be used for any application based on SAP NetWeaver 7.0. Furthermore, we should also mention that this also applies for XML archiving (see Section 5.1.5). In contrast to ADK archiving objects, however, not all XML archiving objects are a priori routing-capable, but instead are prepared for Archive Routing step by step, depending on the actual requirements for SAP development. From a technological perspective, the difference with XML archiving objects is that you can assign arbitrary path extensions for the XML DAS hierarchy, and in this way separate your data not just logically, but—by the assignment of dedicated storages to the routing rules as path extensions determined as "where?"—you can also select the desired physical storage or storage system.

Available as of SAP NetWeaver 7.0

5.4   Automated Production Operation

There are usually two phases in a data archiving project. The first is an introductory phase, in which a relatively large amount of effort is expended to archive an initial volume of archivable data for analysis, customizing, and testing. The second phase is continuous operation. In this second phase, the manual administrative expense drops. It becomes more important to optimally coordinate system resources and other IT processes, as well as to automate the overall process as much as possible.

Two phases of an archiving project

5.4.1   Periodic Archiving

When scheduling a data archiving session, Archive Administration (transaction SARA) determines whether the selected variant is being

Data is archived only once

used by another write job. If it is in use, then this could be a possible indication that the same data may be unintentionally archived repeatedly. However, if you are sure that you have defined the data selection criteria in a unique way and you have supplied values to the new archiving session such that it will store the desired data, then you can ignore this warning. You can even schedule the write program to run periodically by setting the **Periodic job** indicator when you set the start date. Archive Administration then creates scheduling jobs periodically; the specific write program starts these jobs with the same procedure, and without a further check. The period should be selected in such a way that the delete jobs belonging to each archiving session end before the next write job starts.

Prerequisites for periodic archiving

The archiving object and the variant alone determine if periodic archiving is possible. Data selection using absolute (document) numbers, items, or times would initially suggest that periodic archiving is not possible. However, if certain status indications, plus application-specific Customizing other than the variant, residence times, or other relative times, can signal an object's archivability, then the archiving object is potentially suitable for periodic scheduling.

Excluding absolute selection values

In some cases, you can exclude absolute selection values to enable periodic archiving. Material documents are archived in this way. In the write program (RM07MARCS for archiving object MM_MATBEL) variant, the material document number does not have to be entered. Archivability is determined in the application-specific Customizing of the document life for each transaction type and plant. To accelerate data selection, however, the material document year should be entered in the variant. You then have to modify the variant only once a year.

5.4.2 Scheduling Data Archiving Jobs

5.4.2.1 Job Types

A characteristic of data archiving is the background execution of programs (*batch*). Only for evaluation programs does Archive Administration offer the option to read data in dialog mode without scheduling a read job. The following table presents a list of data archiving job types (an archiving object may be assigned a subset of these):

Job identifier	Job type
PRE	Preprocessing
WRI	Write
DEL	Delete
REA	Read
IDX	Index
STO	Store
RET	Retrieve
REL	Reload
FIN (END)	Postprocessing (jobs starts automatically)
SUB	Scheduling

Table 5.3 Data Archiving Job Types

Figure 5.26 shows the dependencies between the archiving job types, and also the sequence in which ADK automatically schedules the various job types if you use the automatic start function. The sequence shown refers to the **Store Before Deleting** Customizing setting. Of course, it is also possible for the write job to first (or only) start the delete jobs automatically. The figure also shows the Archive Administration scheduling options. The usual modes are available when you choose the start date: immediate start, timed start, start after a certain job or event, start when entering a certain operation mode, and start according to a factory calendar.

Job scheduling by Archive Administration or ADK

The scheduling job ensures that the job it starts—usually the write job—becomes job class A. In this way, the privileged write job can run on the most restrictively-configured database server. ADK tries to schedule a write job on the database server, especially when the archive directory is located in a file system that is connected locally to the database server. Avoiding network traffic not only accelerates the write phase (which is not normally processed in parallel), but also reduces the risk of I/O errors during the creation of archive files.

Job class A

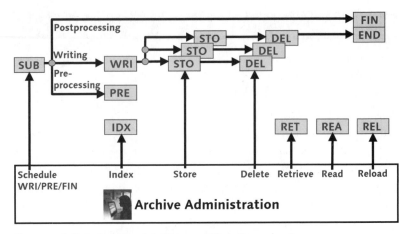

Figure 5.26 Data Archiving Job Types and Their Dependencies

5.4.2.2 Using Server Groups

CCMS job server groups

As is the case with RFC server groups, the centrally-administered server groups of the SAP NetWeaver Application Server are also available in CCMS for background processing. In this way, you can limit the distribution of jobs to selected servers using background processes. For ADK in SAP NW AS 6.10, the introduction of job server groups in CCMS was the reason that uniform, expanded functionality replaced the archiving-specific server group concept of SAP R/3 4.5. Also, job server groups are no longer allocated to individual archiving objects. Instead, they affect the data archiving jobs of all archiving objects. Nevertheless, the following still applies: If a group has a server that runs on the database server, then the write job will be scheduled there.

Example procedure

To execute the aforementioned job types only on servers *S1* to *Sn*, you have to create a group for *S1* to *Sn* using transaction SM61 and enter the group name in cross-archiving-object Customizing. Figure 5.27 shows a group that is called "ADK_GROUP."

Interrupt the Write Phase Automatically After	
Max. Duration Hrs	1.0
Max. MB per Session	

Server Group for Background Processing	
Server Group Name	ADK_GROUP

Figure 5.27 Server Group and Interruption Criteria Customizing

5.4.3   Interrupting and Continuing Archiving Jobs

Even if data archiving is usually performed in the background, low system resources or unplanned contingencies may cause the write phase to end prematurely. The data objects transferred to ADK up to this point should be stored in archive files, and the files should be closed properly. The ADK provides an interruption concept for this purpose. The data archiving administrator can explicitly (manually) or implicitly (automatically) continue interrupted archiving sessions at a suitable later time, and end them in compliance with the selection criteria. However, archived data must first be deleted from the database, i.e., the delete jobs must be finished before continuing. If an archiving session is continued, the same session number will be used; archive files will continue to be added.

ADK interruption concept

You can implicitly interrupt an archiving session if you want to ensure that reserved storage space is not exceeded. You might also want to use this feature if, for example, the write phase will exceed the narrowly-defined time windows during which the write phase was to take place. In the example shown in Figure 5.28, the write jobs should be interrupted after an hour. You can explicitly interrupt archiving sessions from Archive Administration. Interrupted archiving sessions are listed under the STOP symbol (see Session 14479 in Figure 5.28).

Reasons for interrupting an archiving session

Figure 5.28 Interrupted Archiving Session in Archive Management

Not all archiving objects support the interruption function, which means that Archive Administration offers it only for certain archiving objects. You can use transaction AOBJ to find out in advance whether the write jobs of a certain archiving object can be interrupted. In the detail screen of the archiving object, the **Interruption Possible** indicator must be marked, and **Do Not Start before End of Write Phase** is not marked.

5.4.4 Options for Automating Dependent Processes

Event-driven delet- Data archiving and SAP event control are connected in two ways. On
ing one hand, external processes can control data archiving—by making
delete jobs depend on certain system statuses or other processes, for
instance. For example, a departmental user may need to check a
detail log created in the write phase. The data may not leave the database until the user confirms that the data has been selected properly.
With this example, a release process that triggers an SAP event (system or user event) needs to be implemented. The delete jobs will not
start until this event occurs. You can configure event-driven deletion
in archiving-object-specific Customizing (see also Figure 5.16). Then
you need to enter the event name and, if applicable, an event parameter in the delete program settings. Figure 5.29 shows that although
ADK has scheduled the necessary delete jobs, they are not started
until event *E* occurs.

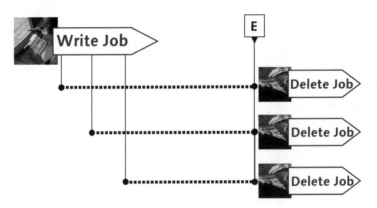

Figure 5.29 Event-Driven Deletion

ADK-triggered In contrast to the connection described above, data archiving can
events also control related processes. File backups can be automated.
Backup copies should be created using suitable software after all
archive files have been written, if not before. To achieve this, you
need a program that supplies your data backup software with the
names of the archive files that are created during the write phase.
You should schedule this program periodically by selecting the SAP_
ARCHIVING_WRITE_FINISHED system event that is always triggered by
ADK at the end of the write phase. Figure 5.30 shows this event as
E1. If you want to react to the end of the delete phase, use the SAP_
ARCHIVING_DELETE_FINISHED system event (*E2*). In both cases, ADK

transfers the number of the archiving session as the event parameter. With the ARCHIVE_GET_FILES_OF_SESSION function module, an ABAP program can easily determine the physical file names from this parameter.

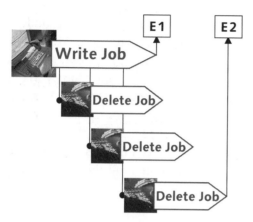

Figure 5.30 System Events for Process Control, Triggered by ADK

5.4.5 Controlling Data Archiving Jobs Using External Job Schedulers

To increase the reliability of data archiving in production mode, manual interactions should be kept to a minimum. Archiving jobs in particular should be able to be scheduled *outside* Archive Administration. If you already use a job scheduler for your IT processes, you will also want to control, optimize, and monitor data archiving using this scheduler. For all "external scheduling" scenarios (without transaction SARA, or without the automatic, immediate starting of dependent jobs by ADK), it is important to consider the special features of the job concept in data archiving which are described below.

Scheduling jobs outside Archive Administration

5.4.5.1 Scheduling Write Jobs

For every archiving object, the name of the write program is entered in transaction AOBJ. If you schedule the write program outside Archive Administration, the following archiving-object-related checks are not performed:

Checking before the write phase

1. Existence of incomplete archiving sessions

2. Use of the same variant in another, executing write job

3. Conflict with any future local currency conversions (euro conversion)

In addition, you alone are responsible for selecting a suitable server, job class, spool parameters, etc.

Checks 1 and 2 above help to prevent the multiple archiving of identical data. If you cannot guarantee that data will not be archived multiple times, then you should use the scheduler to make sure that this does not occur. For Check 1, this could entail calling the ARCHIVE_ADMIN_CHECK_STATUS function module. In contrast, Check 3 is not critical because an additional, ADK-internal check occurs when the write program is run. Even externally-scheduled jobs that use a different naming convention are visible in the Archive Administration job overview, although they are not visible until they are actually running. (For up to and including SAP R/3 4.6C, please refer to SAP Note 133707.)

5.4.5.2 Scheduling Delete Jobs

Direct scheduling
What is special about the delete phase is that neither the number nor the names of the archive files created during the write phase are known in advance. ADK usually transfers the file information to each delete job that is automatically created during writing. If you determine the name of the delete program using transaction AOBJ and schedule the program directly, you will implicitly select the file. ADK finds the archive file (for an archiving object) with status "Writing complete" that has the smallest key value. In other words, this file is the oldest archive file that still contains data for deletion. This direct delete program scheduling provides the scheduler with the most flexibility and complete control over the job. The single basic condition is that the variants stored in the delete program settings must be the only ones used for the test and production modes.

Indirect scheduling
Figure 5.31 compares direct and indirect scheduling. Indirect scheduling is already available in earlier SAP releases, and is described in SAP Note 205585. With indirect scheduling, the scheduler starts only the RSARCHD program, which in turn schedules the delete jobs. For the most part, you determine the archive files to be processed yourself.

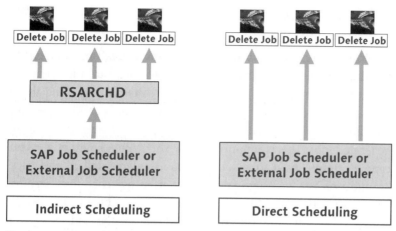

Figure 5.31 External Scheduling of Delete Jobs

In the RSARCHD variant, you need to enter parameters such as the archiving object, the maximum number of files to be selected, and the maximum number of delete jobs running in parallel in the system. After taking the sequence and statuses into consideration, RSARCHD determines the final number of delete jobs to be started for each execution of RSARCHD.

You can use the variant to control different operating modes of RSARCHD:

Monitoring the delete phase

▸ The program is ended immediately after the delete job is scheduled to start

▸ The program ends as soon as all scheduled jobs have the status **Finished** (or one of the delete jobs has the status **Canceled**). This mode simplifies the delete phase monitoring, since only the RSARCHD job needs to be monitored. If the RSARCHD job is ended properly, then the same applies for the entire delete phase. If the job is cancelled, though, the RSARCHD job status will ensure that the cancellation is immediately recognized. To achieve this behavior, you need to set the checkbox **Wait for job end or termination.**

▸ RSARCHD schedules delete jobs until the number of archive files determined by Max. number of sessions and Max. number of files have been processed. There are always at most as many delete jobs active in parallel as specified by the Max. number of jobs parameter. If all the specified archive files have been processed or one of the delete jobs is canceled, RSARCHD terminates as well. To achieve this behavior, you must check the **Process all files** checkbox (see also SAP Note 820023).

Assuming that all the jobs involved are known in advance and can be scheduled externally, it is relatively easy to construct a job network and control it centrally from a scheduler. Alternatively — and this is necessary, for instance, for the write jobs in data archiving — a job scheduler must be capable of assuming control over dynamically generated jobs. This is supported since SAP Web AS 6.40 by the concept of "intercepted jobs," which was implemented in the background processing system and is supported by schedulers certified compliant with BAPI XBP 2.0. This makes it possible to suppress the release of certain jobs (in archiving, these are the DEL, STO, and END jobs) so that the external scheduler has the opportunity to accept the control of these "intercepted" jobs. This kind of automatic job detection and assumption of control means that additional functionality will be added to an external scheduler, which is the responsibility of the scheduler manufacturer.

You can find more information on the use of this functionality in SAP Notes 458670 and 604496.

For SAP R/3 4.6 C, SAP Note 458670 provides a solution via modification, which ensures that the archiving jobs named will continue to be generated by ADK, but not released.

5.5 Application-Independent Errors and Their Resolution

5.5.1 Abnormal Program Termination Behavior

The procedure for restarting the archiving process after abnormal program termination during an archiving session depends on the following factors:

▶ The archiving object used

▶ The time of the termination (in the write or delete program)

▶ The cause of the error

To determine the cause of the error, it is usually helpful to read the system log (*syslog*) or the archiving job log. The following sections will describe the role of the termination point in more detail.

5.5.1.1 Abnormal Program Termination During the Write Phase

If the program terminates abnormally during the write phase, basically three error scenarios can arise. Each is discussed separately below.

Scenario 1

A correctly-closed archive file has not yet been created for the archiving session because the archiving session was canceled before the first archive file could be written.

No correctly-closed files have been created

When creating a new archive file, the system generates the corresponding management entry for access and internally sets the status to **Created**. Archive management does not change the status to **Writing complete** until the archive file has been closed correctly. ADK is then able to provide this archive file to a read or delete program or to the Archive Information System for selection. The incorrect file is not displayed in archive management.

Procedure

1. Perform a new archiving session with the same selection criteria as for the cancelled write run.

2. Set the **To be archived** indicator in archive management for the archiving session affected by the termination listed under **Incorrect Archiving Sessions**. You can then archive the management data for this session using the BC_ARCHIVE archiving object.

Scenario 2

The delete program was not started for any of the correctly-closed archive files that were already created when the archiving session was canceled. This could have occurred if the automatic start of the delete programs was not set in Customizing, or if the **Do Not Start Before End of Write Phase** indicator was already set in the archiving object definition (transaction AOBJ).

No data has been deleted

In this case, we recommend that you completely restart the archiving session using the same selection criteria as for the canceled write run.

Procedure

1. For the affected archiving session, set the **To be archived** indicator in archive management so that the archive files of the archiving session will no longer be selectable for evaluation.

2. Perform a new archiving session with the same selection criteria as for the canceled write run.

3. Check the newly-generated archiving session for errors. If this session was performed completely and without errors, you can delete the archive files for the canceled session from the file system.

4. You can then archive the management data for the canceled archiving session using the BC_ARCHIVE archiving object.

If the method described above is not possible due to time constraints, the procedure described in Scenario 3 can usually be performed. However, there are some archiving objects that archive a "snapshot" of the database, such as the evaluation of the fixed assets of a company at a certain point in time. If the write job terminates during this type of session, this snapshot is incomplete, since not all data could be written into the archive files. In this case, you cannot schedule the delete programs individually. Instead, you have to repeat the entire archiving session. Before you restart archiving, you should first read the documentation for the archiving object being used.

Scenario 3

Data has already been deleted

The delete program has already been started for one or more of the created archive files (e. g., the automatic starting of the delete program was permitted).

In the write phase, archive files are created sequentially, i.e., several archive files cannot be written simultaneously. Therefore, you can use all archive files that were created up until the process was terminated, with the exception of files that were being created as the termination occurred. For the last processed archive file that was not correctly closed, ADK sets the internal counter for the number of previously-written data objects to zero. These files are not sent to the delete program, thus ensuring that delete programs can be scheduled only for correctly-created archive files.

Procedure

1. Schedule the delete jobs for the correctly-closed archive files. Wait until the scheduled delete jobs have been completed successfully.

2. Delete the defective archive file in the file system.

3. Perform another archiving procedure using the same selection criteria.

For the new session, only the data remaining from the first session is selected, since the rest of the data was already selected and deleted in the first session.

5.5.1.2 Abnormal Program Termination During the Delete Phase

A delete program may terminate abnormally for a number of reasons. The delete program may not be able to open the archive files, especially in heterogeneous system environments, because it cannot access the directory in the file system. You need to analyze the problem and try to resolve the error. The system log or the delete job log usually contains information about the cause of the error; SAP Notes may also give you some hints. If the session terminates during the delete phase, you should also consult the documentation for the affected archiving object, since special application-specific problems may occur when you restart deletion.

Three scenarios can arise when this abnormal termination occurs. Each is discussed separately below.

Scenario 1

The archive files for the affected archiving session can be read without error.

Archive files can be read without error

Procedure

1. Try to determine the cause of the error.

2. Resolve the error that led to the termination of the delete program.

3. Restart the delete program for the affected archive files.

Scenario 2

At least one of the archive files is corrupted. The program terminates while the archive file is being verified.

Archive files are corrupted; termination occurs during verification

If the delete program terminates at this point, you can be sure that no data from this archive file has been deleted from the database. This means you do not have to reconstruct data from the corrupted archive file. The corrupted archive file should be removed from the archive management display, either by your customer service representative or by SAP Consulting. After the corrupted file is removed, you can perform a new archiving session using the same selection criteria in order to archive and delete the data that still remains in the database.

Scenario 3

Archive files are corrupted; termination occurs during the delete procedure

At least one of the archive files is corrupted, and termination occurs during the delete procedure.

Since the delete program may have already deleted data from the database, an attempt must be made to reconstruct the corrupted archive files using a "repair program." This program tries to read as much of the archive file as possible and to write the read data to a new archive file. The new archive file must then be entered in archive management as a replacement for the corrupted archive file, after which the delete program starts for this archive file. The data that could not be read is still located in the database. You can delete it in a separate archiving session, although SAP Consulting usually performs this task.

5.5.2 Typical Pitfalls

The following section describes some typical errors that may cause archiving programs to terminate, and closely examines their causes.

5.5.2.1 The File System Cannot be Accessed

The archiving sessions and archive files cannot be selected, even though they are listed in archive management and are marked with the correct status. The affected archiving program terminates with the message that the archive file is not accessible, even though the archive file exists at the operating system level and the access authorizations have been assigned correctly.

In reality, the directory (file system) in which the archive files are located on the operating system level is sometimes not accessible to all application servers in the system. You should first check to see if you can make the directory accessible to all application servers. If this is not possible or not desired, you can enter a server group for background processing in cross-archiving-object Customizing. All application servers of this server group must be able to access the corresponding directory. In order to be able to select archiving sessions from archive management or the Archive Information System (e. g., for evaluation purposes), you should be logged onto the server that can access the directory.

5.5.2.2 Insufficient Storage Space in the File System

This error usually occurs when the storage space in the file system has been exhausted, so no additional archive files can be created. In this case, the procedure may terminate abnormally during the write phase.

We recommend that you estimate the required storage space before archiving starts, and then provide sufficient space. To estimate the required space, you can determine the size of the archive file being created in test mode, either using operating system resources, or from Archive Administration using the **Archive Directory** function (see Section 2.2.1).

5.5.2.3 Log File Overflow for Database Changes

This error occurs if the database storage area in which the data record changes are temporarily stored is too small, or if the data volume being processed is too large.

To resolve this error, you can try the following measures in sequence:

1. Decrease the value of the commit counter for the delete program. You can change this setting using transaction AOBJ in the **Customizing Settings** view.

2. Decrease the maximum archive file size in archiving-object-specific Customizing.

3. Increase the storage space reserved by the database system for data record changes. In this case, the procedure depends on the database system being used.

5.5.2.4 Database Error ORA-1555—Snapshot too Old (Only in Oracle Database System)

This error occurs if very large data volumes have been transferred to the database for processing, as is the case when the user performs an extensive data selection. The database is no longer able to process this data volume correctly. The archiving program terminates processing with the "ORA-1555" SQL error. A program often terminates with this error when delete programs run parallel to a write program, which usually occurs when the automatic start of the delete job is set in Customizing and large data volumes are processed.

This problem may be prevented by reducing the data selection during archiving, or by increasing the corresponding database parameters (see SAP Note 60233). You may also be able to restart the archiving session with identical selection criteria at a time when the system load is lower. If this does not help, you should ensure that the delete programs do not start in parallel with the write program by resetting the indicator for the automatic start of the delete job in Customizing. You can then manually schedule the delete job when the write job has been completed.

5.5.2.5 Database Lock Problems

The number of database locks that can be maintained simultaneously within a database system is limited. If a lock request made by a delete program exceeds this limit, the program may terminate. The maximum number of simultaneously-maintained database locks and the behavior of the database after this value has been exceeded both depend on the database system used. Therefore, we can describe the possible solution only in very general terms.

▸ Reduce the value of the commit counter for the delete program and schedule fewer parallel delete programs. Lock releases will occur earlier, and the delete program will request fewer locks in total.

▸ Check and, if required, increase the parameter for the maximum number of database locks. This procedure depends on the database system used, and is described in the respective documentation.

This chapter describes concrete data archiving solutions in critical SAP components. It discusses established solutions as they are used in SAP ERP Financials, for example, and uses financial accounting documents and controlling data as an example. Moreover, it describes the data archiving solutions provided in SAP ERP HCM and in new developments such as SAP CRM and SAP NetWeaver BI.

6 Data Archiving in Various SAP Applications and Components

by Dr. Veit Bolik, Dr. Bernhard Brinkmöller, Dr. Martin Fischer, Dr. Gernot Kuhr, Iwona Luther, Thorsten Pferdekämper, Rainer Uhle, Dr. Michael Wulf, Dr. Peter Zimmerer

There are numerous SAP applications and components available that provide solutions for archiving application data. Depending on the application, these solutions can differ considerably with regard to the archiving functionality and process. This chapter describes the archiving solutions of the most important applications.

6.1 SAP ERP

Being the central application within the SAP Business Suite, SAP ERP contains the largest number of archiving solutions, some of which differ from each other to a large extent. Since we cannot describe all these solutions in detail, we will focus on archiving data from financial accounting and cost accounting as well as from HR.

6.1.1 Data Archiving in Financial Accounting

The following archiving objects are used in SAP ERP Financials to archive application data from financial accounting:

Archiving Object	Archived Data
FI_ACCOUNT	G/L account master data
FI_ACCPAYB	Vendor master data
FI_ACCRECV	Customer master data
FI_BANKS	Bank master data
FI_DOCUMNT	Financial accounting documents
FI_ELBANK	Electronic account statements
FI_TF_CRE	Vendor transaction figures
FI_TF_DEB	Customer transaction figures
TI_TF_GLC	G/L account transaction figures
FI_PAYRQ	Payment requests
FI_SCHECK	Prenumbered checks
FI_TCJ_DOC	Cash journal documents

Table 6.1 Archiving Objects in Financial Accounting

FI_DOCUMNT— the most important archiving object

FI_DOCUMNT is by far the most important archiving object in financial accounting. It assumes a special role with regard to the aspects of data growth, data security, and compliance with legal requirements, and it therefore has the biggest functional scope of all archiving objects in financial accounting. The document archives that are created using FI_DOCUMNT are most widely integrated in the standard applications.

For this reason, we will focus exclusively on the archiving object FI_DOCUMNT and financial accounting documents in this chapter, while also discussing some important aspects such as data management, Customizing, and archive access techniques.

6.1.1.1 Data Management

If possible, it is much more efficient to avoid creating large data quantities from the start instead of first creating such data and then archiving it. In financial accounting, you can reduce the number of document line items (Table BSEG) via document summarization. In addition, you can suppress the creation of FI secondary indexes for G/L accounts.

Document Summarization

Usually, when an item is posted in financial accounting via the accounting interface, for each line item in the original document, a corresponding line item in the financial accounting document is created (see Section 4.7.1.1). For example, a material withdrawal in materials management causes as many line items to be created in financial accounting as in the material document. This can be avoided with the help of document summarization. The fields that are selected for summarization are no longer filled with data in the financial accounting document, so that fewer document line items are created overall; however, the field content is subsequently no longer available for selection, for clearing, and for reconciliation with other applications. Still, in the original document, all information continues to be contained.

Limiting the number of document line items

A newly established summarization will not have an immediate effect on the amount of data in your system, since it only affects future postings. Old documents are not adapted.

No retroactive summarization

To check whether the document summarization will be successful, you should first carry out a summarization simulation. To do that, you can use the program RSUMSIFI. For information regarding the use of this program, see the SAP Note 310837. You can select the fields you want to summarize in the initial screen of the simulation. The program also determines the maximum possible summarization effect, which would be the result of selecting all fields for summarization. This information can be helpful in determining whether further simulations would be useful.

Summarization simulation

If the document summarization simulation reveals that summarization would be useful for certain fields, you should check which of the fields in question are really required. You should do this with the assistance of the departments responsible for these fields, and look at only those reference activities, which, according to the simulation, would generate the greatest effect if summarized. You can then perform the summarization for each individual reference activity.

The document summarization can be configured using transaction OBCY.

Line Item Management for G/L Accounts

With G/L accounts in financial accounting, you can define—in the master record of the company code—whether an account should display line items. If the line item display has been activated, then an entry will be saved for each document position in an FI secondary index table (Table BSIS). Often line item display is activated for accounts that don't require or use this kind of display. If the FI secondary indexes for certain G/L accounts are not required, then the line item display for these accounts should be deactivated, because Table BSIS is one of the database tables that tend to grow considerably. The question regarding whether to deactivate the line item display for a certain account should be discussed with the relevant department.

When you deactivate the line item display, you should note that you must start the program RFSEPA04 after you have changed the master record, as described in the corresponding documentation. This program adapts the line items to the new account control.

6.1.1.2 Customizing

Technical Customizing

In technical Customizing, you can set the standard parameters, such as file size, program control, and so on, for archiving object FI_DOCUMNT. You can make the corresponding settings in archiving-object-specific Customizing under **Settings for Delete Program**. As of SAP ERP 2005, archive files are indexed exclusively using the Archive Information System (AS). The application-specific archive index in Table ARIX_BKPF that was previously used is no longer updated, but you can continue to analyze it for old archives, should they exist.

Application-Specific Customizing

Tradeoff between business and technical requirements

In *Application-Specific Customizing*, you define the minimum amount of time that the financial (FI) accounting documents, including the corresponding FI secondary indexes, must be stored within the system (document type life). The document type life is analyzed during the execution of the write program. When electing the settings, you must find a compromise between the requirements of the involved departments and the technical requirements. While the database administration department would like to remove the data of the financial accounting documents from the database as early as possible, the financial accounting department usually has an interest in keeping the data in the system as long as possible.

Another aspect that you should consider when setting the document type life is that certain application functions will no longer be able to access the archived data to the same extent as they did before the settings were made. For the archived documents themselves, almost all display functions continue to be available via the standard transactions. To ensure fast display, it is merely necessary to create an archive index using the Archive Information System. All operational or editing functions for the financial accounting documents, such as a cancellation or clearing reversal, are no longer possible. Evaluations using the archived documents are still possible to a limited extent. If the data is required for further processing, such as the preparation of annual financial statements, then the document type life setting should be selected in such a way that this data is archived only after the conclusion of such tasks.

Considering possible access restrictions

The FI secondary indexes are primarily needed for displaying line items in an account. The consequence of deleting the FI secondary indexes is that the line items will no longer appear in the display, and therefore the complete overview of the accounts for previous years will be lost. In the case of pure line item controlled G/L accounts, the total balance will no longer correspond to the balance of the transaction figures that is shown in the balance display.

FI secondary indexes

SAP Note 596865 describes how you can carry out line item reports without FI secondary indexes.

The length of time that financial accounting and FI secondary indexes are available can be controlled using the company code, the account type, and the account. For financial accounting documents, you can also define the document type life using the company code and the document type. All lives are indicated in terms of days. The setting of account type life and document type life is carried out in Archive Administration (transaction SARA) in application-specific Customizing, or using transactions OBR7 and OBR8.

Controlling the document type life

Account type life

CoCd	Account Type	From Account	To Account	Life	Secondary Index Runtime
*	*	0	9999999999	365	1096
*	*	A	ZZZZZZZZZZ	365	1096
*	A	0	9999999999	365	1096
*	D	0	9999999999	548	1096
*	K	0	9999999999	548	1096
*	M	0	9999999999	365	1096
*	S	0	9999999999	365	1096
0001	*	0	9999999999	730	1460
0001	S	8000000000	8999999999	1096	1460
3000	*	0	9999999999	548	1096
3000	S	4711	4711	1826	1826

Table 6.2 Examples of Account Type Lives

Account type lives: definition rules

The following rules apply for the definition of account type lives:

- The company code and the account type can be wildcarded by using an asterisk (*). Entries of this type are then valid for all company codes or account types. If, however, there is a specific entry in which the company code or the account type is explicitly documented, then the wildcarded entry is disregarded. If several entries are equally specific, then the maximum life is selected.

- In the **From Account** and **To Account** fields, account type lives can be specified in greater detail at the level of the account number. This is of particular interest if you wish to keep the documents and secondary indexes of certain accounts available in the system for a longer period of time. The account fields always refer to G/L accounts. Therefore, if you enter an account number interval for the D or K account types, the numbers of the reconciliation accounts must be used.

- In the **Life** column, you can enter the minimum number of days during which the documents should be stored in the system. In the **Secondary Index Runtime** column, you can enter a corresponding value for the secondary indexes.

Document Type Life		
Company Code	Document Type	Document Life
*	*	730
0001	*	365
0001	SA	1096
3000	*	548
*	SA	730

Table 6.3 Examples of Document Type Lives

The following rules apply for the definition of document type lives:

Document type lives: definition rules

▶ As with the account type lives, you can wildcard the company code and the document type using an asterisk so that these entries are valid for all company codes and document types. The logic with which wildcarded entries are treated, in contrast to specific entries, also corresponds to the logic that applies to account type lives.

▶ In the **Document Life** column, you must enter the minimum number of days during which the documents should be stored in the system.

6.1.1.3 Data Archiving

A complete archiving session of accounting documents with the archiving object FI_DOCUMNT includes writing the document data into the archive, deleting the archived documents from the database, and deleting the FI secondary indexes using a postprocessing program. The archiving of financial accounting documents can be carried out independently of the archiving of other data.

Complete archiving

Writing Data to the Archive

During the write phase of the archiving session, all the data that belongs to specific financial accounting documents is selected in the corresponding database table, after which archivability checks are carried out and the documents are copied into one or more archive files. A financial accounting document, together with all corresponding table entries, represents a business object that is stored in an archive file under a certain offset. The following procedure is recommended for selecting documents in an archiving session.

It is useful to archive financial accounting documents according to individual company codes, fiscal years, and, depending on the quantity of data, perhaps also by certain periods, in order to make the selection of archive files for a later evaluation easier. Usually, though, not all documents of such an archiving session can be archived, since in some cases individual documents may have been balanced only at a later time, or have not yet been balanced at all. You can collect such documents in a separate archiving session, which may then contain a few documents from different fiscal years.

> **Note**
>
> Make sure to enter a meaningful description of the archiving session at the beginning of the write phase. This will make the selection of archive files for later evaluation easier. It also makes the management of archive files clearer.

The write program carries out a number of archivability checks so that only those documents that are no longer required in the database are selected. In the first instance, these checks are carried out at the document header level (Table BKPF) and subsequently at the level of the line items (Table BSEG). You can implement additional checks using the Business Add-In (BAdI) FI_DOCUMNT_CHECK. To be suitable for archiving, a document must meet all the requirements of these checks. The check results for each individual document, at the level of both the document header and the items, can be reviewed using transaction FB99. All life checks refer to the key date that you have entered in the selection screen. A key date can also be defined separately for each session; however, the key date cannot be later than the date of the execution.

The checks that are carried out are described in more detail below:

▶ **General checks**

The document header must conform to the following archivability criteria:

▶ The document type lives, previously defined in Customizing, cannot be exceeded. This check verifies the posting date of the document.

▸ The document must have been stored in the system for more than the minimum number of days. This criterion is defined in the selection screen of the write program, and is checked against the creation date and the change date of the document.

▸ Permanent documents, parked documents, and sample documents are not archived.

The line items must conform to the following archivability criteria:

Line items

▸ All items of documents in open items managed accounts must be balanced.

▸ The account type life defined during Customizing must be exceeded. During this check, items in open items managed accounts are verified against the clearing date and other items are verified against the posting date of the document.

▸ Documents that include a withholding tax are archivable after 455 days. During this check, items in open items managed accounts are verified against the clearing date and the clearing entry date, and other items are verified against the posting date of the document.

▸ **Other checks**

▸ If an external tax audit is in progress, the system checks whether the audit has been completed for a particular document.

▸ If a subsequent settlement of conditions is planned, the program determines whether an agreement linked to the document has been carried out and whether the residence time defined for the document in the Customizing of the subsequent settlement has expired.

▸ **Additional checks via user exits**

If you require additional checks and would like to implement these via a user exit, you can use Business Add-In FI_DOCUMNT_CHECK, which is very versatile and can be used for several purposes.

Deleting Data from the Database
The delete program reads the archived documents in the archived file, including all corresponding table entries, and deletes the corre-

sponding records from the database. FI secondary indexes are an exception to this procedure. They are deleted by the postprocessing program. Tables for a subsequent adjustment to the balance sheet are another exception. They are not written to the archive; instead, the delete program simply removes them from the database.

In addition to the actual deletion of data, two other tasks are carried out during the execution of the delete program.

Building the archive indexes

One task consists of automatically updating the relevant data for each deleted document into the active infostructures of the Archive Information System.

Setting the deletion indicator

The other task consists of setting a deletion indicator in the FI secondary indexes of the deleted documents. This indicator must be set in order for secondary indexes to be deleted. The deletion indicator guarantees that only indexes of archived and deleted documents can be removed from the database.

Deleting Secondary Indexes

The postprocessing program enables you to schedule automated index deletion in archiving-object-specific Customizing. The account type life and document type life that are defined during Customizing are checked against the key date, which can be entered in the selection screen of the program. When the program is executed, this key date may not be in the future.

Preconditions for deleting an index

A precondition for the deletion of an FI secondary index is that the corresponding financial accounting documents must have been archived beforehand. A check will also be made to determine whether the life of the secondary index has expired on the key date. The posting date will be used for G/L accounts that are managed on a line item basis, while the clearing date is used for accounts that have open posting management. When deleting the secondary indexes, you should pay special attention to the option that instructs the program to take into account the display balance. If this option is selected, only completed clearing procedures will be deleted from the secondary index. If this option is not selected, the item display of the account may show a display balance that does not equal zero; however, selecting the option during index deletion requires a longer program runtime and means a less effective reduction of the database load.

You can use correction program SAPF048S to reintroduce the FI secondary indexes into the database at a later point in time.

Reloading Archived Data

In theory, you should be able to reload all archived financial accounting documents into the database. The only archive files that are excluded from this are archive files that were created before the changeover from a local currency to the euro, and which contain data from adapted company codes.

6.1.1.4   Accessing Archived Data

Single Document Display

Standard single document display (transaction FB03) is linked entirely to Archive Administration. In general, for the end user, there is no perceptible difference between this access to archived data and an access to data in the database.

From the single document display, you can go directly to the Document Relationship Browser by selecting **Environment • Document Environment • Relationship Browser** from the menu.

Carrying out an Evaluation

The programs described below are standard reports, which permit a simultaneous evaluation of financial accounting documents in the database and in the archive. Documents from archive files that were created before a changeover to a local currency are automatically recalculated to the current local currency.

Report	Description
FAGL_ACCOUNT_ITEMS_GL	G/L account line item list
RFBELJ00	Compact document journal
RFEPOJ00	Line item journal
RFITEMAP	Vendor line item display
RFITEMAR	Customer line item display
RFITEMGL	G/L account line item list
RFKLET01	Accumulated balance audit trail

Table 6.4 Evaluation Reports That Can Read Archived Data in Financial Accounting

Field catalogs and infostructures for FI_DOCUMNT

Archive Information System

By default, the Archive Information System provides the document header-based field catalog, SAP_FI_DOC_001, the account-based field catalog, SAP_FI_DOC_002, and the field catalog for the G/L view, SAP_FI_DOC_003. Furthermore, the infostructure SAP_FI_DOC_DRB1 is provided for use in the Document Relationship Browser, and infostructure SAP_FI_DOC_002 is provided for both account searches and the Document Relationship Browser. Since these infostructures already contain a suitable database index, they are particularly well suited for a quick access from the applications described.

To access archived data from the G/L view, you need an infostructure based on field catalog SAP_FI_DOC_003. This type of infostructure is not included in the standard package, but you can create it by yourself as per your requirements.

6.1.2 Data Archiving in Cost Accounting

The following archiving objects are used for archiving cost accounting (Controlling, CO) application data in SAP ERP Financials:

COPA1_xxxx	COPA2_xxxx	CO_ALLO_ST
CO_BASEOBJ	CO_CCMAST	CO_CEL_RCL
CO_COPC	CO_ITEM	CO_KABR
CO_KSTRG	CO_ML_BEL	CO_ML_DAT
CO_ML_IDX	CO_ML_ML1	CO_ML_SPL
CO_ORDER	CO_PROCESS	CO_TOTAL

Table 6.5 Archiving Objects in Cost Accounting

In addition to these CO-specific archiving objects, there are also archiving objects from other components, which not only archive the data of their own component, but also data from cost accounting tables:

PM_ORDER	PP_ORDER	PR_ORDER
PS_PROJECT	RE_BUILDNG	RE_BUSN_EN

Table 6.6 Other Archiving Objects That Archive CO Data

| RE_MGT_CNT | RE_PROPRTY | RE_RNTL_AG |
| RE_RNTL_UN | RE_STLM_UN | SD_VBAK |

Table 6.6 Other Archiving Objects That Archive CO Data (cont.)

Data archiving in cost accounting can become rather complex. Often the size or growth rate of Table COEP is what triggers the archiving of cost accounting data. Therefore, in this section we would like to describe the importance of this table for CO archiving and the best way to keep this table under control. By doing so, many similar problems in this application will resolve themselves.

Table COEP—the linchpin of CO archiving

We will not cover the entire subject of cost accounting, but only a part of it: namely, overhead cost controlling. There are other areas in cost accounting in which large quantities of data, such as costing-based profitability, are sometimes created. However, we will concentrate on overhead cost controlling below, since this area usually shows the highest data growth.

We will also touch on other useful aspects of CO archiving in our discussion of Table COEP, even though this table is not the reason for our having to perform data archiving in the cost accounting area.

6.1.2.1 Table COEP in Context

The term *CO objects* is frequently used in connection with cost accounting data. A CO object can be any business object that contains cost accounting data (*CO data*). Examples include cost centers, internal orders, line items of sales-related documents (items in sales orders), cost objects, and production orders. Figure 6.1 shows the structure of a CO object, using the example of an internal order.

CO objects

Depending on the application, the master record is stored in different tables. For example, the master record for internal orders is contained in Table AUFK, and for sales-related document items in Tables VBAP and VBAK. The master record contains a short text as well as organizational data, such as the controlling area, company code, or plant. The object currency is often stored in the master record, or derived from information in the master record. In contrast to the master data, the totals records and single line items of cost accounting are contained in the same tables for all applications. The totals of the primary costs are, for instance, always stored in Table COSP, regardless of whether they belong to a cost center or a sales order.

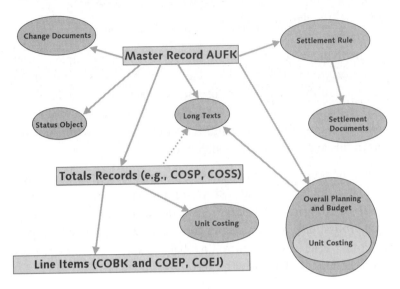

Figure 6.1 Structure of a CO Object

6.1.2.2 Object Number and Object Type

For all applications that use cost accounting, cost accounting data is stored in the same tables, so a concept is required for the uniform identification of CO objects in different applications. This concept is the *general object number*. The key of the CO object is stored in this number; for example, for an order or sales-related documents item, or for a cost center. The object number contains both the object type and a key, from which the corresponding object can be unambiguously identified. The object type represents the property of an object, that is, it describes whether the object is an order, a sales-related documents item, a cost center, and so on. The object number to which the corresponding record belongs is found in cost accounting tables, usually in the OBJNR field, such as COEP-OBJNR for example.

6.1.2.3 Analyzing Overhead Cost Controlling Tables

Analysis programs
RARCCOA1 and
RARCCOA2

An exact analysis of Table COEP and other relevant tables of this application should be the basis for every archiving concept in the area of overhead cost controlling. In particular, you can use programs RARCCOA1 and RARCCOA2. Program RARCCOA1 creates an extract of the data that can be evaluated using program RARCCOA2. You will obtain a list, which compares the archiving objects that can, theoretically, archive data from the CO tables to the number of entries in these tables.

The list shown in Figure 6.2 comes from a development system and does not display a realistic result. Examples of analyses from real production systems will be provided later.

RANK	Object	OTy	COAr	F.Yr	ALL	COEP	COEJ	COSP	COSS	COST
* Total	CO_COSTCTR				425.969	218.153	131.877	14.807	56.180	4.952
* Total	RE_RNTL_AG				65.965	49.387	0	16.578	0	0
* Total	PP_ORDER				65.957	13.156	0	24.634	28.167	0
* Total					63.277	32	10	37.673	25.562	0
* Total	CO_ORDER				29.736	18.543	3.199	5.065	2.929	0
* Total	SD_VBAK				16.614	2.703	0	13.276	635	0
* Total	PM_ORDER				15.927	2.681	0	5.591	7.655	0
* Total	PS_PROJECT				15.039	2.607	336	5.914	6.182	0
* Total	CO_PROCESS				11.487	2.051	7.866	0	1.464	106
* Total	PR_ORDER				8.898	809	0	4.468	3.621	0
* Total	CO_KSTRG				5.335	1.452	2.985	25	873	0
* Total	CO_ITEM				2.667	2.594	73	0	0	0
** Total					726.871	314.168	146.346	128.031	133.268	5.058

Figure 6.2 Analyzing Overhead Cost Controlling Tables

The programs try to assign each entry in a table to an archiving object. For table entries that can be archived by several archiving objects, the archiving object that is typically selected is the one that enables you to archive and delete the largest number of tables of the corresponding object type. This, however, does not mean that this archiving object is the most appropriate one in any specific case. This applies in particular to CO_COSTCTR.[1] You can use this archiving object to archive entries from all tables that belong to a cost center; however, line items listed under CO_COSTCTR should be archived using archiving object CO_ITEM instead.

How the programs work

You can find additional information on the analysis programs RARCCOA1 and RARCCOA2 in the program documentation and in SAP Note 138688.

---

1 Please note: Archiving object CO_COSTCTR has become obsolete in SAP ERP 6.0; see SAP Note 623870. Instead, you can use archiving objects CO_CCMAST, CO_ITEM, and CO_TOTAL. Although the RARCCOA* analysis reports still show CO_COSTCTR, you can use the alternative archiving objects instead.

6.1.2.4 Data Management—Line Item Summarization

Summarization simulation

Usually it is far more efficient to avoid creating large data quantities right from the start, instead of first creating the data and then archiving it. In overhead cost controlling, you can use line item summarization for this purpose. To check whether line item summarization would be successful, you can simulate the summarization using program RARCCOA5.

Documentation on this program and further information on line item summarization can be found in SAP Note 195480. You can configure the document summarization in Customizing (IMG) by selecting **Controlling · General Controlling · Document Summarization for External Accounting Documents**.

6.1.2.5 Selecting Archiving Objects

After you have detected that Table COEP is growing rapidly, or that it has already grown to a substantial size, you should identify the archiving objects that would be most useful in decreasing the table size. The programs RARCCOA1 and RARCCOA2 described above provide a good basis for this decision. Usually, two or three archiving objects cover 90 % of the data that must be archived; however, this doesn't mean that you can actually archive 90 % of the data because usually some of this data is still needed in the database. You can, however, assume that the archiving objects found are most likely the most useful ones.

Archiving line items

You should also note that the line items listed under CO_COSTCTR in the analysis result can also be archived using archiving object CO_ITEM; in fact, they should generally be archived with this archiving object. You can use CO_ITEM to archive all line items. For this reason, it wouldn't make sense if the analysis result were to include the assignment between CO_ITEM and the cost center line items, since this would not represent any new information. In most cases, it makes more sense to use CO_ITEM for the cost center line items and, if required, to archive the totals and master data subsequently using CO_TOTAL and CO_MAST respectively.

Examples of how to select the right archiving objects

The following two examples illustrate how to select the right archiving objects. We will use extracts from analyses of actual production systems and, on the basis of these analyses, we will indicate which archiving objects are recommended. In this regard, you must bear in mind that the requirements of the corresponding departments have not yet been taken into account. It is therefore entirely possible that the archivability of the data may still change because of further requirements.

For the sake of simplification, a number of lines and columns have been omitted from the analysis. The totals therefore do not correspond exactly to the individual values. However, only lines and columns containing small values were omitted. Since the analyses do not involve current values, only the approximate date of the analysis run has been documented. The recommendations for archiving must therefore be taken with regard to this date.

Example 1

Archiving Object	Year	Total	COEP	COSP	COSS
CO_COSTCTR	2003	15,533,291	15,472,547	41,778	6,352
CO_COSTCTR	2003	14,642,565	14,629,032	1,802	6,801
CO_COSTCTR	2004	13,435,134	13,371,090	51,072	8,831
CO_COSTCTR	2004	12,127,723	12,114,878	1,839	9,323
CO_COSTCTR	2005	7,448,672	7,398,534	41,976	8,162
CO_COSTCTR	2005	6,476,771	6,467,164	508	8,591
CO_COSTCTR		**70,159,499**	**69,927,862**	**159,311**	**48,255**
CO_ORDER	2004	7,462,580	6,881,785	204,274	376,279
CO_ORDER	2004	3,601,633	3,267,759	115,514	218,360
CO_ORDER		**11,225,161**	**10,292,126**	**335,874**	**596,919**
CO_ITEM	2004	554,655	554,655	0	0
CO_ITEM	2003	421,285	421,285	0	0
CO_ITEM	2005	338,175	338,175	0	0
CO_ITEM	2002	85,777	85,777	0	0
CO_ITEM		**1,399,900**	**1,399,900**	**0**	**0**
Total amount		**82,787,347**	**81,619,888**	**497,972**	**645,174**

Table 6.7 Analyses 1

In this analysis from August 2005 it is striking that by far the largest part of the data is allocated to archiving object CO_COSTCTR. Nevertheless—and especially in view of the remarks above regarding archiving object CO_ITEM—we recommend that you archive line items, that is, the entries from Tables COEP and COEJ using CO_ITEM. For example, all line items up to and including 2004 can be archived with CO_ITEM.

Furthermore, we suggest that you perform regular, perhaps annual archiving using archiving object CO_ORDER. While you could also archive the line items using CO_ITEM, internal orders are more like measures that are completed at some point in time and can be completely archived after a certain residence time.

On closer examination of the records listed under CO_ITEM, it emerges that the records are exclusively of the object type ABS (reconciliation objects), which can be archived up to and including 2004 using archiving object CO_ITEM.

Example 2

Archiving Object	Year	COEP	COEJ	COSP	COSS
CO_COSTCTR	2005	162,027,929	659,877	265,051	13,708
CO_COSTCTR	2006	36,839,252	341,476	103,929	341,702
CO_COSTCTR	2004	7,980,104	0	54,072	10,056
CO_COSTCTR	2003	6,286,166	0	50,325	4,024
CO_COSTCTR	2005	5,087,469	0	2,891	0
CO_COSTCTR	2006	1,162,064	0	1,499	0
CO_COSTCTR	2002	816,463	0	54,523	746
CO_COSTCTR	2002	337,696	0	5,875	284
CO_COSTCTR	2004	327,080	0	2,671	0
CO_COSTCTR	2003	217,258	0	2,868	0
CO_COSTCTR		**221,187,950**	**1,001,353**	**585,295**	**376,822**
Total amount		**221,187,950**	**1,001,353**	**585,295**	**376,822**

Table 6.8 Analyses 2

In this February 2006 analysis, only data for cost centers was found. Here line item summarization was successfully implemented.

In this case, too, we recommend using archiving object CO_ITEM, although only CO_COSTCTR is listed in the above table. Archiving with the archiving object CO_COSTCTR is not recommended for relatively recent data since totals and master records are also archived. Moreover, problems with available storage space can arise when using CO_COSTCTR, since all of the line items corresponding to a cost center in a business object are stored. Data up to the middle of 2005 can probably be archived using CO_ITEM. CO_COSTCTR is recommended for archiving the remaining data up to fiscal year 2003.

6.1.2.6 CO_ITEM: Central Archiving Object

From the considerations above, it becomes clear that archiving object CO_ITEM is one of the central archiving objects in cost accounting. CO_ITEM enables the archiving of all line items of overhead cost controlling. In some cases, however, it may be more appropriate to archive line items with a different archiving object.

> **Note**
>
> When using CO_ITEM, please make sure that no archiving session is running in parallel and using one of the other possible archiving objects. For example, if an archiving session for orders (CO_ORDER, PM_ORDER, PP_ORDER, or PR_ORDER) runs in parallel with archiving using CO_ITEM and object type **ORD**. In any case, order archiving should be finished before a CO_ITEM run is started, and vice versa. An archiving session is finished in this context only when all of the files have been given the status **deletion completed**. If you can't verify that this has occurred, CO_ITEM should not run in parallel with any archiving that can, in principle, archive entries of Table COEP. To establish which archiving objects are involved, you can use transaction DB15.

The runtime for archiving with CO_ITEM depends largely on the entries in the selection screen. We recommend that you observe the following rules:

Recommendations regarding CO_ITEM runtime

▸ Always start the archiving session for only a single object type.

▸ Always start archiving for only a single controlling area.

▸ Archive as many periods as possible in one session. It is best not to enter a to-period or any to-fiscal year. (In this case, only the residence times have an effect). It is also not advisable to use multiple archiving sessions for different to-periods or similar characteristics. Limiting the selection to certain periods or years will usually have little effect on the runtime of the write program.

▶ If you already know that only a small number of objects are relevant for archiving in the corresponding object type, then you should create a group or record set with these objects and process only the relevant objects on the basis of the parameters Group or Set parameter.

Group or set   You can use the Group or Set parameter to limit the selection to certain objects, such as orders or cost centers. The Group or Set parameter also enables you to distribute the data quantity to be archived across several archiving sessions. This type of subdivision is more appropriate than, for instance, a subdivision by periods or fiscal years. You can find more details on the Group or Set parameter in the field help function or in the help file of the CO_ITEM application.

6.1.3   Data Archiving in SAP ERP HCM

HCM—an application for controlling central HR management processes   Data archiving in SAP ERP Human Capital Management (HCM)—SAP's HR management application that is often also referred to as HCM—was included at a later stage not only in this book, but in the entire SAP system as well. The main reason for this is that the necessity of archiving HR management data was not important in the past due to the fact that old information needed to be accessed frequently.

Right from the beginning, the design and development of an archiving solution in SAP ERP HCM focused on those areas of application in which the archiving of data would involve the biggest load reduction of the database. At the same time, we also intended to ensure that the data archiving activity would not affect the flow of most of the HR management processes or that it would even necessitate any changes.

In contrast to data archiving in other areas of SAP ERP, the archiving of data in HCM has the following characteristics:

No use of the Archive Information System   ▶ The Archive Information System is generally not used in SAP ERP HCM for several reasons. First, the HCM application already provided efficient access to archived data before the Archive Information System was developed. Secondly, the flexibility of the Archive Information System is not needed in HCM, because, in most cases, there is only one possible key that enables you to access archived data. Third, a strict authorization check is required in HCM. This authorization check is automatically implemented when you use indexing in HCM, whereas you would have to implement this feature yourself in the Archive Information System.

▸ To display archived data, SAP ERP HCM uses the same programs as used for displaying data from the database. Depending on the program, you can define whether or not you want the archive to be read automatically. In general, you should note that not every program that processes data has read access to archives. The decision as to which program is equipped with this function is made by SAP Development; however, basically, there is always one program that can display archived data.

Archives and database are displayed in the same program

SAP ERP HCM contains two types of archiving, which are described in the following sections: archiving in the area of payroll and archiving of other HCM application data.

Two types of archiving

The essential difference between these two types of archiving is that some extra preparations are necessary in the HCM application, in addition to using Archive Administration (transaction SARA) to be able to archive payroll data.

6.1.3.1 Data Archiving in Payroll

The checks to be carried out prior to archiving payroll data are very complex due to the retroactive accounting that is often necessary (for legal reasons and because of collective agreements).

Retroactive accounting must be considered

For this reason, we decided to offer a separate HCM-specific function as a complement to the options provided by the generally available archiving functionality via transaction SARA. The use of this customized function occurs prior to the general archiving process and is intended to serve as a preliminary step.

The following areas are relevant for archiving payroll data:

Which areas of HCM are involved?

▸ Time evaluation (archiving object PA_TIME)

▸ Travel expenses (archiving object PA_TRAVEL)

▸ Payroll (archiving object PA_CALC)

The archiving of the corresponding posting in financial accounting (archiving objects PA_PIDX and PA_PDOC) requires a check that is described in detail in Section 6.1.3.2.

> **Note**
>
> The archiving objects described here are used to archive data records from tables PCL1 and PCL2. These tables are cluster tables. They are subdivided into separate areas that are identified by cluster IDs and have separate meanings. For example, each country has its own cluster ID for its payroll results. You can find more information on the contents of these tables and on possible data management actions in the Data Management Guidelines [DMG]. Also refer to the notes on table analyses provided in this chapter.

Why a separate functionality?

There are strong interdependencies between the functions described above. Therefore, without any specific HCM functionality, the archiving of data would have been possible only with profound expert knowledge and would have involved the strict adherence to organizational measures.

These interdependencies result from the necessity to carry out retroactive accounting in payroll if facts change that affect the past.

Let's look at an example:

Example—data archiving and retroactive accounting

In time management, some facts have changed that affect the past, such as clock-in and clock-out entries or the posting of overtime hours. As a result, payroll must be carried out again for the period in question. The corresponding changes are then settled in the current payments to the employees.

For one of the employees, the time management data was archived after three months. After that, payroll carries out a retroactive accounting because the salary of the employee for the last four months has changed retroactively.

Regarding the period for which the time management data was archived, the system would now determine that the employee did not work and it would therefore claim the remuneration back. On the other hand, for the retroactive accounting period for which time management data is available, the system would take the salary increase into account.

Still, this is not the situation we want to end up with when archiving data.

The process of archiving data in payroll comprises the following steps:

How does an archiving process work?

▶ Creating an archiving group

▶ Using the archiving group

Creating an Archiving Group

First you must create an archiving group. The archiving group contains all the information that is required for archiving:

Archiving group as a starting basis

▶ The data to be archived (time evaluation, payroll, travel expenses)

▶ The country version (if payroll is involved)

▶ The date up until which you want to archive data

▶ Other data that may depend on the specific country

You can create archiving groups using transaction PU22, as shown in Figure 6.4. A wizard (see Figure 6.3) guides you step by step through this process and thus facilitates the entry of the relevant details. The wizard also checks the data with regard to possible interdependencies. You can define whether you want to use all archiving objects (PA_CALC, PA_TRAVEL, PA_TIME) together, separately, or in any combination. In any case, the wizard will inform you about possible interdependencies.

A wizard supports your entries

Each step involves a plausibility check of the data you have entered. These checks are country-specific with regard to payroll data; in some cases, they can even be industry-specific. For more details on these checks, please refer to the documentation that is available in the SAP Library. There you can find documentation on both general archiving and each individual step. Figure 6.3 shows the second step in the creation of an archiving group using the wizard.

The initial screen for archiving payroll data contains information on the country versions for which a country-specific support is available. For countries not included in this list, a general international version is available as of SAP R/3 4.6C; however, you should note that the users in those countries must ensure that they have complied with legal requirements.

Multiple country versions, one international version

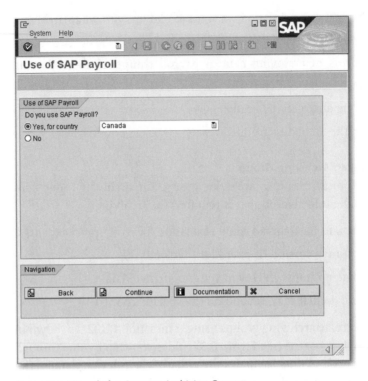

Figure 6.3 Wizards for Creating Archiving Groups

Using the Archiving Group

Once you have created the archiving group, you must use transaction PU22 to process all the necessary steps with this group (see Figure 6.4), including the navigation into the actual archiving session in Archive Administration. For this purpose, you must select the archiving group from the selection tree and then carry out the necessary steps using the available pushbuttons. The system supports you in such a way that it activates only those pushbuttons that are relevant for the respective process context and grays out those pushbuttons that are not relevant.

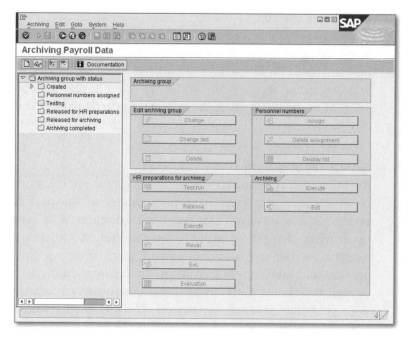

Figure 6.4 Initial Screen of Transaction PU22

The process steps are divided into four groups:

- **Edit archiving group**
  Here you can make last changes to attributes as this is no longer possible once the personnel numbers have been assigned (e.g., you can then no longer change the country version of payroll).

- **Personnel numbers (assignment to archiving group)**
  Once you have created the archiving group, you must assign the personnel numbers for which you want to carry out the archiving session. In doing so you can use the selection options available in the logical database, PNP. In addition, you can retroactively assign or remove additional personnel numbers.

- **HR preparations for archiving**
  This is the most important step in the archiving process for payroll data. During this phase, the system is set into a status similar to that which occurs when the data has been archived. However, based on our experience, the entire preparation phase requires only 10 % of the runtime of the overall process. In this phase you can do the following:

> The most important step in the archiving process

► **Carry out a test run**
You can optionally carry out a test run in order to check the archivability of all personnel numbers. The checks carried out here are based on the personnel numbers, whereas the checks (e.g., regarding legal evaluations) carried out during the creation of an archiving group are of a more general nature. You can remove personnel numbers from the archiving group after the test run has completed.

► **Release the preparations**
By doing this, you can lock the system during the preparatory time in order to protect it against updates of the payroll results. In this way, you can avoid inconsistencies that may occur when changes are made to the database tables that are needed for the preparations. Payroll takes this lock into account and allows only calculation simulations during this period. You should therefore schedule this step in accordance with your time schedule for payroll. The lock involves only personnel numbers that are contained in the archiving group.

► **Execute the preparations**
The system is set into a status that, from the HCM viewpoint, corresponds to a completed archiving session. All checks that are based on personnel numbers are carried out again. These checks are identical to those carried out during the test run. If errors occur at this stage, the preparations for the respective personnel numbers will discontinue. If necessary, you can correct errors that have occurred and then carry out the preparations for the defective personnel numbers once again. Alternatively, you can remove the respective personnel numbers from the archiving group.

► **Reset the execution**
If you find out that, after the archiving session has completed, you have inadvertently archived personnel numbers or periods that were not supposed to be archived, you can reset the archiving of this data.

► **Exit the preparations**
This completes the current step. Once you have done that, payroll can be carried out again. Note, however, that if you have previously reset the archiving, you can no longer undo this.

What happens technically?

The actual data (data records in tables PCL1 and PCL2) is not moved at all. The system merely moves the data records to be archived from the internal result directory (RGDIR in Cluster CU) into a different directory that is provided for archived results only (RGDIR in Cluster CA). In addition, an entry in Infotype 0003 (payroll status) ensures that retroactive accounting in periods, in which data has been archived, cannot occur. For this purpose, you can use the fields **Earliest personal retroactive accounting date** (PRDAT) for payroll (also for travel expenses) and Earliest personal recalculation date for time evaluation (PRTEV) for time management.

The archived data records can be managed using Infotype 0283. The system stores the data of the archiving group along with the information on archived results for each personnel number in this infotype. Each archiving object has a separate subtype. The infotype is written only by the system and you cannot change it manually.

▶ **Executing the archiving session**

If you select **Execute** in the **Archiving** section of transaction PU22, the system displays a screen in which you can select the data to be archived. Depending on the archiving objects contained in the archiving group, the list can consist of one or several items. Once you have confirmed your selection, the system takes you to the variant maintenance section of the respective archiving object in Archive Administration (transaction SARA). From this point on, you can use the functions and procedures available in general data archiving for HCM archiving as well, such as the scheduling of a write job in the background.

Although each archiving object is executed separately during the archiving session, you only need to select the archiving group in the variant maintenance, because the archiving group contains all the information that is required. The program, in turn, provides only those archiving groups for selection that are eligible for archiving. In a final step, the program checks whether all archiving processes have been completed successfully.

The left-hand side of transaction PU22 displays all available archiving groups, sorted by status.

> **Note**
>
> You can use the ARCHIVE analysis variant of the table analysis (transaction TAANA) to determine which archiving objects are most useful in the payroll environment. The analysis uses Table PCL2 as a basis, which stores the payroll results for all countries, as well as the results from time management.
>
> The table analysis provides you with a first overview of the areas in which you can obtain the largest part of storage space. After that, it is still necessary to perform a detailed check with regard to which data can actually be archived. For this purpose, a close collaboration between the user department and the IT department is inevitable.

6.1.3.2 Archiving Other HCM Application Data

Direct call from Transaction SARA

SAP ERP HCM contains other archiving objects that can directly be called from transaction SARA. The two most important archiving objects are as follows:

▸ **PA_LDOC (long-term documents)**
This archiving object enables you to archive the change documents that are written by the system during the maintenance of infotypes. The only selection criterion used here is the archiving period. This period refers to the date on which the document was written. You cannot use the personnel numbers or infotypes as selection criteria.

▸ **PA_PDOC and PA_PIDX (posting to financial accounting)**
PA_PDOC enables you to archive the documents that are created when data is posted from payroll to financial accounting. In addition, you can use PA_PIDX to archive the posting indexes.

> **Note**
>
> We recommend using both archiving objects (PA_PIDX and PA_PDOC) simultaneously in order to optimize the archiving process; however, the archiving of the index will remove the biggest portion of the database load. Note that you cannot archive the index until the associated payroll result has been archived. This check is necessary, because the index is required for retroactive accounting.
>
> For large index files, you can also extend the archiving process to a date before the retroactive accounting date. With retroactive accounting, the program reads the index files from the archive.

You can therefore reduce the database volume considerably during normal operation while having to take into account longer runtimes if retroactive accounting in archived periods is involved. The longer runtimes result from the fact that data must be read from the archive. As this function is disabled in the standard version of HCM, you must explicitly switch it on. You can find more information on this topic in SAP Note 922559. If you want to use this solution, you should ensure that the storage technology you are using offers fast access to the archives (e.g., you shouldn't use any CD-ROMs).

6.2 SAP CRM

This section describes the archiving solution for SAP CRM. This description includes details about the basic technical principles and specific features of CRM archiving, as well as a closer look at the data model of the CRM business transaction. To better illustrate the descriptions, we'll use the archiving of CRM activities via archiving object CRM_ACT_ON as an example.

6.2.1 CRM Server in the SAP CRM Application

With SAP Customer Relationship Management (SAP CRM), SAP provides a comprehensive solution for managing customer relationships. SAP CRM contains efficient front-office applications that meet the needs of all sales, marketing, and service channels, and it integrates these applications seamlessly with the back-office order processing systems, in particular, with the internal process handling and financial controlling systems of a company. The holistic concept of SAP CRM also takes into account the strong links of customer-specific processes to SAP Supply Chain Management (SAP SCM), SAP's solution for the management of supply chains.

Managing customer relationships

SAP CRM maps actual business scenarios that are derived from customer requirements. The CRM server is the logical central component within a CRM system landscape. It contains CRM Enterprise functions, CRM Middleware, and various adapters. Depending on the functional key areas to which the described scenarios belong in each case, the implementation of the solution may require additional software components. Figure 6.5 provides an overview of the possible software components that have their own data retention (indicated by a database icon) in a CRM system landscape.

CRM server as a logical central component

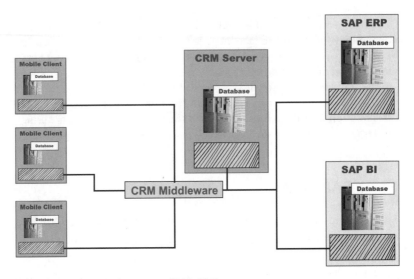

Figure 6.5 System Architecture of SAP CRM

CRM Middleware as a communication component

CRM Middleware (the corresponding parts are lightly shaded in the diagram) is responsible for the communication between the different components and is an integral part of the SAP CRM solution. The server component of CRM Middleware is always installed in conjunction with the CRM Server component [see *mySAP CRM*, BE02].

Data archiving is component-specific

As discussed in Section 1.1, data archiving is component-specific. This fundamental principle also applies to SAP CRM, where the archiving solution essentially consists of archiving data of the CRM Server component. The CRM Server is installed on the SAP NetWeaver Application Server and can therefore use the *Archive Development Kit* (ADK) function for data archiving. However, because the term *CRM Server* is only relevant at a technical level, we will use it in this book only if we need to clearly differentiate it from other SAP components. In all other instances, we will only refer to *archiving in SAP CRM or in the CRM system*.

During data archiving in the CRM system, the services of CRM Middleware are used for keeping other components informed of the data archiving process. This enables the other components to react to the archiving of data from the CRM Server. However, note that you should trigger the data archiving process in an SAP ERP system, which you may be using as a backend for your SAP CRM solution, independently of the data archiving processes in SAP CRM. Similarly, data that is stored in SAP NetWeaver BI is not affected by an archiving of CRM data. Since the result of a report in SAP NetWeaver BI must not be dependent on the archiving date of data in a different software component, an archivability check of data must be carried out independently of other software components.

Alternatively, mobile client software, for instance, ensures that data, which is archived on the CRM Server, will be deleted on the mobile clients.

6.2.2 Special Features of Data Archiving in SAP CRM

Archiving objects that are assigned to SAP NetWeaver Application Server are available in SAP CRM with the same functionality as in other SAP applications. An example of this is archiving object CHANGEDOCU, which is used for archiving change documents.

The first CRM-specific archiving objects were developed and delivered with SAP CRM 3.0. For these new developments, a number of additional features were implemented, which are usually not available in the other components. These differences are due to the fact that CRM data, based on its distinct mass character, must usually be deleted from a database faster than similar data in an SAP ERP system. The reason for this is that CRM solutions create additional data, such as the logging of customer contacts, which causes the data volume to grow rapidly. The business relevance of this data is undisputed — CRM solutions were developed expressly to store and evaluate this data. Indeed, the example of customer contacts also shows that the records that are created are not subject to change, and that after their creation they are only required for read access. After such data has been transmitted to SAP NetWeaver BI for analysis, it can therefore be archived and deleted from the database of the CRM system relatively quickly, since read access is still possible.

CRM data is usually mass data

To make these short residence times acceptable both for system users and administrators, the following aspects were also taken into consideration in the development of the data archiving solution for SAP CRM:

Short residence times required

▶ In the case of short residence times, it is necessary to carry out data archiving for different archiving objects relatively often. This process must therefore be easy to administer.

▶ Such a reduction of the residence times can also, under certain circumstances, mean that when checking archivability, a higher percentage of data may be deemed not yet archivable. An efficient way to avoid expensive multiple data archivability checks must therefore be found.

▶ The shorter the residence time, the higher the probability that the archived data must be accessed. The accessibility of archived data therefore becomes considerably more important.

Deleting without prior archiving

It can also be assumed that in many cases it is sufficient to delete part of the data that has been created in the database after a certain period without previously archiving it. The deletion of unnecessary data requires a uniform and flexible concept, which permits, but does not impose, the archiving of data prior to its deletion. To archive this, it is necessary that checks are carried out independently of the ADK write program to determine whether data should be deleted with or without prior archiving. The ability to delete data independently of the ADK delete program must also be offered for data for which deletion without prior archiving is to be offered.

Principles

In order to consider all of these points, the following principles were applied in the implementation of the new archiving objects in SAP CRM, especially with regard to checks:

▶ The archivability check for data is carried out independently of the ADK write program. The check determines whether the data can be deleted. Depending on the type of business transaction, you can either archive the data before deletion from the database, or carry out a delete run without prior archiving.

▶ The checks are carried out by either an ADK preprocessing program, or a newly-developed check program that works for all archiving objects (referred to as *cross-archiving-object delete program*). This check program should help to make the checks easier to administer, especially if they are used frequently, since it includes methods for internal parallelization and load distribution. This will be described in greater detail in Section 6.2.5.

▶ The date of the most recent archivability check is stored with the data in order to prevent repeated negative results if checks are scheduled frequently. The selection of data for checking takes into account only data that was last checked negatively some time ago.

Moreover, the residence time of the business transaction types, which can be defined in Customizing, is also taken into consideration.

▸ For the many new CRM-specific archiving objects, the access to archived data was implemented with the same function groups as access to data in the database. This means that the display of archived data is the same as, or very similar to, the original display.

6.2.3 Relationship Between Business Objects and Archiving Objects

The goal of data archiving has always been to consistently transfer all data that belongs to a business object from the database into the archive. From the very beginning, an archiving object was used as a frame around the associated data. While the relationship between an archiving object and a business object is intuitively clear in most instances, it has never been formally defined. This is hardly surprising, since the central storage of all properties of business objects used in SAP applications has been possible only since the introduction of the *Business Object Repository* (BOR). In the BOR, the properties of business objects are modeled and their relationships to one another are stored.

BOR as a central repository for business objects

While the BOR was introduced after SAP R/3—at a time when the first archiving objects already existed—it was available right from the beginning of the development of SAP CRM. This meant that the options provided by the BOR were used much more when the data was being modeled. It was therefore natural to formalize the relationships between archiving objects and business objects, and their alignment with the BOR. With the BOR it is possible to define general business object types, and also to define the specialization of these object types—the subtypes—that inherit the properties of the main type, but are differentiated by additional properties. Figure 6.6 shows the possible inheritance hierarchy between the business objects in the BOR, based on the example of the CRM business transaction.

Each new archiving object is defined for exactly one BOR object type (the logical assignment does not occur in the Business Object Repository). This assignment can be carried out on every level of the inher-

Archiving objects are created on the basis of the BOR

itance hierarchy. The archiving object is valid for those subtypes that come under the selected BOR object type in the inheritance hierarchy. If the definition is carried out on one of the upper levels, the archiving object can, under certain circumstances, cover a multitude of partially dissimilar business object types; however, you should note that the control options for data archiving are situated at the level of the archiving object. A very generally defined archiving object, therefore, limits the possibilities of controlling the data archiving process.

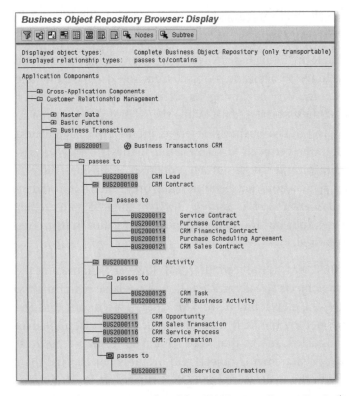

Figure 6.6 Inheritance Hierarchy of the CRM Business Transaction in the BOR

In the case of a CRM business transaction, the definition of an archiving object at the highest level of the inheritance hierarchy would mean that many different BOR object types are combined in one archiving object. For this reason, archiving objects were defined at one of the lower levels of the BOR inheritance hierarchy, as in the case of archiving object CRM_ACT_ON (CRM activities), which was created with reference to BOR object type BUS2000110 (CRM Activity). With this archiving object, therefore, data belonging to BOR object types BUS2000125 (CRM Task) and BUS2000126 (CRM Business Activity) will also be archived. This concept, of course, brings with it the need to develop further archiving for archiving the data of other BOR object types.

In CRM, the BOR is also used to display some additional functions discussed in the last section. For example, the function modules that are used in the archivability check—both for the selection of the data to be checked (preselection function module) and for the check itself (check function module)—are stored as methods in the BOR. The check program (either the ADK program or the cross-archiving-object check program described above) identifies the relevant function modules for the respective archiving object in the BOR.

Function modules are stored as methods in the BOR

6.2.4 The Three-Phase Model of Data Archiving

The creation of a uniform concept for the removal of old data from a database was one of the basic ideas for the implementation of data archiving in SAP CRM. Depending on the relevance of the data, data archiving then becomes an optional step that can be carried out between checking whether data should be deleted and the actual process of deleting it. This idea resulted in the development of a model, which includes the phases of checking, replicating, and deleting, and that is referred to as the *three-phase model of data archiving* (see Figure 6.7).

In the first phase, the data is checked to determine whether it should be archived, or whether it can be deleted without prior archiving. The second phase consists of the actual archiving process, that is, writing the data to the archive and then confirming whether the data has been safely stored in the archive. In the third phase, the data is finally deleted from the database.

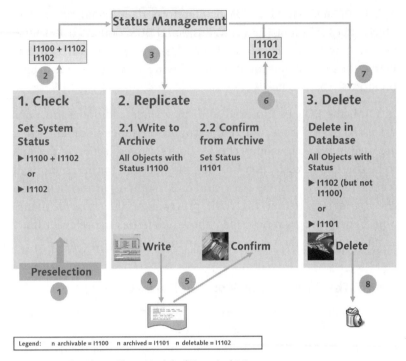

Figure 6.7 The Three-Phase Model of Data Archiving

Phase 1: Check Communication between the individual phases is effected via *status information*. This will be shown in the following example of the system status used for CRM business transactions. The data that forms part of a business object is checked in the check phase to verify whether it has reached the defined residence time. Should this check reveal that the data can be deleted, the status of the business object is set to **Deletable** (I1102). If the data is to be archived before the delete run, then the status **Archivable** (I1100) is also set. Currently, it is no longer possible to change the data. At this time, the CRM Middleware will also notify the connected systems that the data is being deleted or archived. During the synchronization of the CRM mobile clients with the CRM server, the data from the mobile client tables is already deleted, although the data is still persistent on the CRM server.

Phase 2: Replicate In the second phase—the replication phase—the data to be archived is written into the archive using an ADK write program. In this case, the status of the business object in the archive is changed to **Archived** (I1101). This status change, however, is not recorded in the database.

The deletion process was implemented in two different variants. In the "classical" variant, an ADK delete program carries out the actual deletion process. This program verifies the archive file and then deletes the corresponding data in the database. In the second variant, the deletion process is divided into a logical and a physical deletion activity. This division separates the deletion process in the database from the archiving process. The logical deletion is carried out by a check program instead of the ADK delete program. The check program checks the file and changes the status of the data in the database from **Archivable** to **Archived**. The subsequent physical deletion process deletes the data that has the status **Deletable** and, if available, the status **Archived** from the database. An archiving object can support only one of the two variants. You can check in Customizing which variant has been chosen for a specific archiving object. For archiving objects that use the variant in which the logical and physical deletion processes are separated, you can carry out the deletion of data in the database either by using an archiving-object-specific postprocessing program, or by using a cross-archiving-object delete program for multiple archiving objects.

Phase 3: Delete

There are advantages to both a direct deletion through the ADK delete program and the separation of the physical deletion. The direct deletion of data, during the check reading of archive files has the advantage that the delete program itself does not have to read the data in the database. It therefore has a slightly higher performance than a read program, which must first access the database to find the data that is to be deleted. The advantage of separating the check reading from the deletion procedure is that the programs that have to access the archive are relieved from the most difficult operation, namely, the deletion of the data, which results in a greater flexibility in job scheduling. In addition, this variant can include the deletion of data that is not to be archived.

Both methods provide advantages

6.2.5 Cross-Archiving-Object Programs for Continuous Data Archiving

Cross-archiving-object programs (these are actually so-called *framework programs* that trigger further activities) for the check phase and delete phase enable you to use new data archiving functions with relatively little administrative effort. Since the ADK preprocessing and

Cross-archiving-object programs as an enhancement of the ADK postprocessing programs can also be used for this, these newly developed programs are an optional enhancement of the ADK.

You can control the check and delete phases in Archive Administration via **Customizing • Cross-Archiving-Object Customizing • Check and Delete** (transaction DA_CONTROL).[2] In this way, you can define for which archiving objects the cross-archiving-object programs are supposed to carry out the check and delete processes. You can activate the delete program only for those archiving objects for which the physical deletion process is separated from the logical deletion process.[3] For all other archiving objects, the deletion is carried out using a classical ADK delete program. In addition, the **Check and Delete** function in archiving-object-specific Customizing enables you to define the technical parameters for executing the programs, such as the maximum number of business objects to be checked in a session.

The cross-archiving-object check program[4] is structured in such a way that it can check the relevant data in multiple simultaneous processes. You can also use the **Check and Delete** function in archiving-object-specific Customizing to define the number of processes as well as the package size. The ideal package size depends on the scope of checks to be carried out and of the business transaction.

> **Note**
>
> Please note that in applications in which the CRM Middleware informs the mobile client software about the archiving process in the CRM Server, additional work will be required within the check modules. For this reason, the package size defined should not be too large.

You can use transaction SM36 to schedule both the check and delete programs[5] for background processing. As of SAP CRM 5.0, you can also schedule the cross-archiving-object check and delete processes for CRM in Archive Administration (transaction SARA) via the

---

2 In releases higher than SAP CRM 5.0, you can use transaction DACONTROL to make this setting.

3 In releases higher than SAP CRM 5.0, the system ignores the setting of the **Deletion active** flag.

4 Prior to SAP CRM 5.0: DARGE_VERIFY_PARA, as of SAP CRM 5.0: ARCDEL_VERIFY_PARA.

5 Prior to SAP CRM 5.0: DARGE_DELETE_OBJECTS, as of SAP CRM 5.0: ARCDEL_DELETE_PARA.

Check/Delete pushbutton. The two programs evaluate the parameters entered via **Check and Delete** in archiving-object-specific Customizing and carry out the check and delete processes for the specified archiving objects.

This can be of particular interest for the check phase if you want to do a relatively prompt archiving of some archiving objects. In this case, you can ensure that the selected data receives the status **Archivable** and/or **Deletable** as quickly as possible by regularly scheduling the cross-archiving-object check program. You can avoid compromising on performance (due to frequently run checks) by using the date of the last archivability check, which is saved along with the data, and by setting the "resubmission interval" to an appropriate period of time (this can also be done through the Number of Days parameter in archiving-object-specific Customizing).

6.2.6 The CRM Business Transaction Data Model

Although in SAP R/3 the structures of individual archiving objects varied considerably, in SAP CRM, a uniform data model was chosen for several different business transactions.

Uniform data model for many business transactions

The CRM business transaction corresponds to BOR object BUS200001. A business transaction is described by a business transaction header (database table CRMD_ORDERADM_H) and one or more optional business transaction items (CRMD_ORDERADM_I). The business characteristics, that is, the *subtypes*, determine whether there are further attributes, which additionally identify the business transaction. In the BOR, the subtypes correspond to the business objects, which are subordinated to BOR object BUS20001 in the inheritance hierarchy. A special feature of the CRM business transaction data model is that one business transaction can simultaneously assume the characteristics of several subtypes. For example, a business transaction can simultaneously describe a customer contact and a sales transaction. One of the subtypes is always marked as the *leading subtype* if the corresponding BOR object is assigned an archiving object.

All components of a business transaction can be determined by the subtypes that are associated with that transaction. These subtypes exist in two possible variants: either as an extension, which contains

Extension or set

additional information on the business transaction header or one of its items, or as a set that contains information in the form of a special link table (CRMD_LINK), which can be assigned to either the header or to several items.

Reusability of code using uniform data model

The advantage of this uniform data model is the high degree of reusability of the code, which was written for dealing with sets and extensions. For the user, this means that the same functionality will always be treated in the same way in different business transactions.

The programs for data archiving are also based on this uniform model. Business-related rules are applied only during the check phase, which may be different for individual business transactions. Consequently, the check programs must be written individually for each archiving object. Conversely, the same code can be largely reused in the write, delete, and display programs of the various archiving objects.

To illustrate the above discussion of data archiving in SAP CRM, we will first look at the example of archiving object CRM_ACT_ON, which is used for archiving CRM activities. Many of the characteristics that distinguish this archiving object can be transferred to all archiving objects for CRM Business transactions.

6.2.7 The Archiving Object CRM_ACT_ON

Preprocessing program

CRM_ARC_ACT_ON_CHECK is the preprocessing program for archiving object CRM_ACT_ON. It enables the selection of the data to be checked for archivability by limiting the activity type or the object identification (ID). In archiving-object-specific Customizing, a residence time must be maintained for the data.

For selecting and checking the data, the preprocessing program uses the two function modules CRM_ARC_ACT_ON_PRESELECT and CRM_ARC_ACT_ON_CHECK, which are stored as BOR methods. Corresponding preselection and check function modules are available for all archiving objects, which can be controlled using the cross-archiving-object programs.

For performance reasons, the important check that determines whether or not the data belongs to a complete business transaction (status I1105) is carried out in the preselection function module when the criteria for data selection is applied. This minimum check is identical for all archiving objects that are used for CRM business transactions. Furthermore, the data selection in the preselection function module is designed in such a way that, apart from taking into account the defined selection criteria and residence times, the only data selected for further checks will be the data on which the last check was carried out previously. Like the maximum number of data records selected by the preprocessing program, this time limitation can be set by using the **Check and Delete** function in archiving-object-specific Customizing. In the preselection function module, the date of the check for each object selected is stored in Table CRMD_ORDERADM_H.

The majority of archiving objects for CRM business transactions use CRM_ARC_ACT_ON_PRESELECT as the preselection function module, because these archiving objects are all based on the same conditions.

In contrast to most other archiving objects, no further checks are carried out in the check module of CRM_ACT_ON. The program sets the status "deletable" and "archivable" (I1102+I1100) for all successfully checked data and informs CRM Middleware about the successful check. Status I1102 ensures that this data can no longer be changed as of this moment, while status I1100 enables the CRM_ACT_ON write program to select the data in the next archiving session.

The technical control parameters of transaction DACONTROL (which have not been mentioned so far and for which detailed information can be obtained in the F1 help or in the SAP Library), the number of parallel check processes, and the package size for the check are not considered during the archivability check executed by the preprocessing program. They serve to better control the processing load during the check phase when the check is executed by the previously mentioned cross-archiving-object check program, DARGE_VERIFY_PARA or ARCDEL_VERIFY_PARA. The same selection options are available during a check with this cross-archiving-object check program as are available during a check using the archiving-object-specific preprocessing program. The selection conditions can be stored here by indicating a variant for program CRM_ARC_ACT_ON_CHECK through the **Check and Delete** function in archiving-object-specific Customizing. In this way, the cross-archiving-object check program can take into account different selection criteria for the various archiving objects, which it will pass on to the corresponding preselection function module.

Parallelization options

The `Number of Calls/Preselection Module`[6] parameter controls how often the preselection function module is called during an archiving session of a cross-archiving-object program. The `Package Size Check Module`[7] parameter controls the size of the data package that is transmitted to the check function module during each call. The preselection function modules are called directly by the cross-archiving-object check program, while the check function modules are activated by asynchronous RFCs in other processes, several of which can work in parallel. This is very useful when the business checks are complex. However, in the case of function module `CRM_ARC_ACT_ON_CHECK`, which does not perform any further checks, you should note that the transmission of information via CRM Middleware represents an expensive operation compared to using function module `CRM_ARC_ACT_ON_PRESELECT`. Therefore, parallelization should certainly be considered here.

Since the preselection function module already stores the data of the check that has been executed, the previously selected data will be ignored during subsequent runs of the preselection function module.

> **Note**
>
> However, this does not apply if you run the check in test mode. Because the date of the last change is not stored in this instance, the preselection function module is executed only once (in this case, it is not necessary to make any adjustments in archiving-object-specific Customizing via the **Check and Delete** function). In general, no changes are made to the database if the check is run in test mode.

Write program

`CRM_ARC_ACT_ON_WRITE` is the write program for archiving object CRM_ACT_ON. From this point on it is no longer possible to influence the data selection; all activities that have the status **Archivable** will be selected. If you want to target only certain data for inclusion in an archive file, you must execute the preprocessing programs and the write programs immediately, one after the other. This is the only way in which you can ensure that the data selected in the preprocess-

---

6 Prior to SAP CRM 5.0: `Number of Calls/Packages`.

7 Prior to SAP CRM 5.0: `Package Size RFC`

ing program will be written into the archive by the write program. The status of the data does not change during the write phase. The replication phase is not considered to be successfully completed until the delete or verification program can verify that the data can be successfully called and read from the archive.

This only occurs upon the completion of the delete program CRM_ ARC_ACT_ON_DELETE. At the current stage of development, the data records that have been read from the archive by the delete program are always deleted directly, that is, a classical ADK delete program is used for this purpose. Consequently, the status indication **Archived** does not appear in the database at any point in time.

Delete program

This status appears only when the archived data is displayed again. Figure 6.8 shows an archived activity that is displayed using read program CRM_ARC_ACT_ON_READ.

Read program

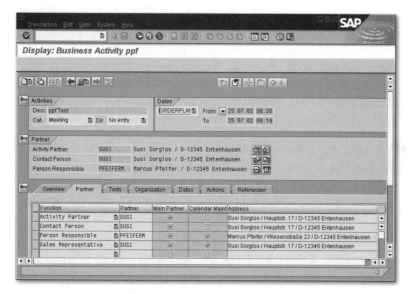

Figure 6.8 Displaying Archived Activities

With the exception of the status information, this display is identical to a display of database data. It goes without saying that it is not possible to jump from the display of archived data into the change mode. This lock is valid not only for archived data; the records are already locked once they are marked with status **Archivable**, although they are still located in the database. It is, however, possible to use archived data as a template for the creation of new documents. With this function, the archiving of CRM business transactions offers substantially improved accessibility compared to most of the corresponding SAP ERP data.

6.2.8 Summary and Outlook

The concept of data archiving has been improved in many respects in SAP CRM. Particularly noteworthy is the fact that the requirements of data archiving were already taken into account during the modeling phase of individual CRM business objects. This is evident in the improved integration of status information and the dates of archivability checks. In addition, the clear relationship between archiving objects and business objects, and the often-improved interaction between read modules for archived data and the modules for reading data in the database, represent substantial progress.

Evolutionary development

Despite these new developments, data archiving in SAP CRM is an enhanced version of the archiving concept of SAP ERP. Those who are familiar with SAP ERP data archiving won't have any problem using data archiving in SAP CRM. You can therefore expect that the innovations that have been implemented in SAP CRM will also be utilized in other components of the SAP Business Suite and that they will be considered in the development of new archiving objects.

Development still in progress

This is not to say, however, that the development of data archiving in SAP CRM is complete. As is the case with other applications, the archiving of generated data is not among the primary concerns when new CRM business processes are implemented because the development of central application functions often has a higher priority. Therefore, you should note that not all the necessary archiving objects might always be available right from the start when new functions are introduced. Instead, the archiving solution is enhanced step by step. The following table displays the most important archiving objects in SAP CRM 5.0:

Archiving Object	Data Archived
CRM_ACT_ON	Actions
CRM_OPPT	Opportunities
CRM_LEAD	Leads

Table 6.9 Archiving Objects in SAP CRM 5.0

Archiving Object	Data Archived
CRM_SALDOC	Sales transactions
CRM_SACONT	Sales contracts
CRM_COMP	Complaints
CRM_SERORD	Service processes
CRM_IBASE	Installations

Table 6.9 Archiving Objects in SAP CRM 5.0 (cont.)

On the other hand, the groundwork has been laid so that any new demands on data archiving can be met quickly (e.g., archiving other data or providing additional functions). An example of this is the option presented in Section 6.2.4 for deleting data of a CRM business transaction without prior archiving.

6.3 SAP NetWeaver Business Intelligence

SAP NetWeaver Business Intelligence (SAP NetWeaver BI) is a component of SAP NetWeaver. It represents a scalable and stable infrastructure that enables you to carry out analyses according to multiple business criteria, even with large quantities of operational and historical data, such as sales and marketing analyses, project and budget status reports, and so on. The insights gained from these analyses provide important and indispensable decision-making support for companies.

SAP NetWeaver BI provides information that helps businesses make decisions

6.3.1 Technical Basics

In SAP NetWeaver BI, mass data from operational SAP applications and any other business applications and external data sources, such as databases, online services, and the Internet, can be loaded, converted, saved, and aggregated. A broad range of users can use this data as a basis for a quick, reliable, and comfortable analysis, from both a strategic and an operational point of view. Figure 6.9 provides an overview of the complete architecture of SAP NetWeaver BI.

Data from multiple sources

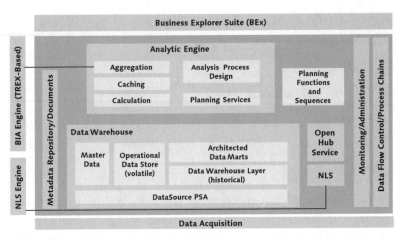

Figure 6.9 Architecture of SAP NetWeaver BI

Objects and processes in the warehouse

Data is extracted from upstream systems and subjected to a series of transformations and adjustments in the staging engine, after which it is transferred in consolidated and consistent form to the warehouse segment of SAP NetWeaver BI. The data storage areas in the staging engine are referred to as *persistent staging areas* (PSA). They are temporary, so data is held there only until it reaches the consolidated level, and until it has been sufficiently tested. In the warehouse area, however, data has a noticeably longer lifetime. Figure 6.10 shows the most important objects and processes within the warehouse segment of SAP NetWeaver BI.

Two types of data storage

For the storage of transaction data, two separate types of physical data storage media are available:

- DataStore objects
- InfoCubes

DataStore objects

DataStore objects (previously referred to as ODS objects) are designed for storing fine-grained data that is closely related to documents. DataStore objects consist of a flat database table. They are also suitable for accessing the data in edit mode. DataStore objects support evaluations only to a certain extent and, due to performance considerations, they are often used only for *drilldowns* or typical single-item reports.

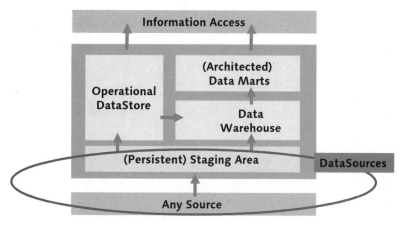

Figure 6.10 Objects and Processes in the Warehouse of SAP NetWeaver BI—Layer Concept

Thanks to their structure, InfoCubes—the second type of data storage—are particularly suitable for read access. From a logical point of view, an InfoCube is also a tabular object, with properties that represent the table key and aggregateable key figures that represent the data part. To optimize the read access, InfoCubes are mapped in the database in what is referred to as a *star schema* (see Figure 6.11). The star schema contains a series of dimension tables surrounding a central fact table, which contains fine-grained key figure values. The assignment of properties to dimension tables occurs on the basis of specific logical relationships, so that the dimensions remain largely independent of one another and the dimension tables are kept as small as possible. The link between the fact table and the dimension table is achieved via an artificial numerical identifier, the *dimension ID*. To link the dimension tables with the master data tables, which contain the actual characteristic values, an intermediary table with an additional numerical identifier, the *master data ID* (MDID), has been created.

InfoCubes

Furthermore, you can build *aggregates* for InfoCubes. Aggregates are dependent objects of an InfoCube that contain the data of the fact table in a redundant but aggregated form. Aggregates are created to improve the performance of InfoCube *queries*. However, they cause additional load during both the loading and deleting of data, the latter being also required for data archiving.

Aggregates

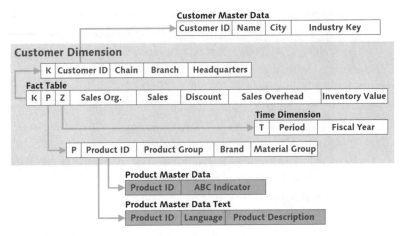

Figure 6.11 Star Schema

As of SAP NetWeaver 7.0, you can link an InfoCube with a *BI accelerator*. BI accelerators are an innovative technology that enables fast access to any data of the InfoCube with a minimal degree of administrative effort. This BI accelerator can completely replace the classical aggregates in most cases.

In the following sections, DataStore objects and InfoCubes will be summarized under the generic term *InfoProviders*.

6.3.2 Considerations for Data Archiving

Data retention in SAP NetWeaver BI differs from that of other SAP components. With its technical platform, SAP NetWeaver BI pursues a generic approach to supporting numerous different analytical solutions in the SAP Business Suite environment. Solutions that are based on SAP NetWeaver BI are provided separately from the SAP NetWeaver BI technology in the form of business content. Business content represents preconfigured role-based and task-based information models (see glossary). This means that no data storage in the form of tables is delivered with this technology. Instead, only the infrastructure for creating the tables in the customer system is provided. The tables can be created either on the basis of the metadata that is contained in the business content, or per individual customer requests. Consequently, a data archiving solution in SAP NetWeaver BI must adapt to this generic implementation.

Furthermore, in SAP NetWeaver BI, the purpose for which data is used plays an important role, which must also be taken into account in data archiving. BI data is required primarily for analysis purposes and therefore must be available for a longer time than data, which is required for purely operational purposes. Figure 6.12 shows this aspect in the form of an assumed frequency of data access, as a function of how old the data is. While the frequency at which the data is accessed in change mode often declines after a relatively short period of time, and while this phase approximately corresponds to the life-cycle of the data in the operational phase, read access can be expected over a longer period of time, especially in SAP NetWeaver BI.

Data archiving must reflect the purpose of the data

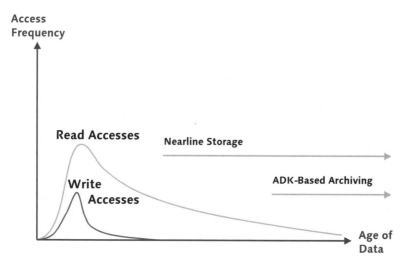

Figure 6.12 ADK-Based Archiving without Indexing versus Nearline Storage

In this context, SAP NetWeaver 7.0 provides new options for modern information lifecycle management of its BI data. A nearline storage interface (*NLS interface*) allows customers to enhance their SAP NetWeaver BI solution with third-party nearline storage solutions.

Nearline storage

The basic idea of the nearline storage (*NLS*) concept is to move partitions of less frequently needed read-only data out of the BI database and to store these partitions in alternative storage systems, without losing direct access to the archived NLS partitions of InfoProviders for analysis or loading purposes.

Integrating NLS
solutions with SAP
NetWeaver BI The NLS interface of SAP NetWeaver 7.0 provides the basic functions required to implement this concept. Selected SAP partners are thus enabled to integrate their NLS solutions into the overall SAP NetWeaver BI landscape on the basis of a set of ABAP APIs. The NLS interface provided by SAP currently supports the implementation of NLS for transaction data from InfoCubes or DataStore objects. For future releases, you will be able to store master data in the nearline storage as well.

Regarding the nearline concept, you should note that the database partitions and the NLS partitions of an InfoProvider together consistently reflect the entire data volume. This places particular demands on the process of creating an NLS partition in which the selection of the respective data partition from the database, the write process in the NLS, and the delete process in the database must be carried out in a quasi-transactional step.

This kind of InfoProvider structure, that is, the existence of database and NLS partitions for an InfoProvider, remains largely transparent for analysis and load processes that operate on those partitions. If required, a query is assigned the additional attribute **Read NLS partitions**; for load processes, you must define separate data transfer processes (DTPs) for the database and NLS partitions.

As a result, the reloading of data that is stored in the NLS does not pose any problem, which was not the case in the previous SAP BW release where the reloading of data archived in the classical manner caused some difficulties.

Classical ADK-
based data
archiving still
available Of course, if necessary, you can still use the classical ADK-based data archiving. This can become necessary if specific data sections of Info-Providers no longer play a role in currently running analysis processes, but legally stipulated retention periods require you to archive the data and to provide it for analysis purposes in emergency situations.

This way you can reduce data retention costs considerably in SAP NetWeaver 7.0. Automated archiving strategies enable the scalability of the BI database volume.

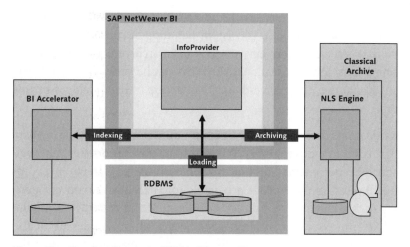

Figure 6.13 Nearline Storage in SAP NetWeaver BI

SAP NetWeaver BI thus offers solid and automated information life-cycle management capabilities in the data warehousing area, by allowing the categorization of data according to its level of importance (see also Section 1.1). In this context, the term "data archiving" is still used, but it now comprises both the NLS strategy and the classical ADK-based data archiving concept.

Data archiving processes (DAPs) enable you to model archiving objects and processes. The following sections provide more detailed information on this subject.

6.3.3   Data Archiving in SAP NetWeaver BI

For InfoCubes and DataStore objects, SAP NetWeaver BI provides an information lifecycle management functionality that contains both data archiving based on the Archive Development Kit (ADK) and an NLS partner solution service that can be addressed via the NLS interface. The data archiving process (DAP) represents the central modeling object. When defining the DAP, you must determine whether you want to use classical ADK-based data archiving, the new NLS concept, or a combination of the two.

ADK-based archiving, NLS storage, or a combination of both?

The ADK, which also serves as the technical basis for data archiving in other SAP components, contains numerous functions that were also used in the implementation of a data archiving solution in SAP NetWeaver BI. Furthermore, ADK offers many advantages that can

ADK as a basis

also be used in BI. Particularly noteworthy is the assurance of platform independence, the consistent handling of subsequent changes on data structures that have already been archived, and the Archive Administration (transaction SARA) that can be generally used. Overall, BI queries don't have direct read access to data archives of this type.

Based on its design, this type of archiving is intended for storing data that is no longer required for current analytical processes, but may still be required for building up a new InfoProvider or, in exceptional cases, must be made accessible for analysis once more. Opening ADK archive files for direct analyses in BI and perhaps—using the OLAP processor, for example—requires additional indexing of the archive files. Although ADK offers indexing capabilities through the Archive Information System (AS), they are not used for the data archiving solution in SAP NetWeaver BI.

Archiving objects in SAP NetWeaver BI

InfoCubes and DataStore objects contain an integrated set of data for a specific business area. An individual archiving object is therefore created for every InfoProvider of this type during ADK archiving—if necessary, at a later point in time. In principle, BI objects are provided and transmitted only in the form of BI proprietary metadata. The actual repository objects, such as database tables and access programs, are then generated only in the target system. This also holds true for the archiving objects in SAP NetWeaver BI. However, while reserved generic namespaces from the Change and Transport System (CTS) can be used for BI repository objects, this option is not available for archiving objects. Archiving objects are provided with a namespace with a maximum of 10 characters. The name of the Info-Provider and a name of the archiving object must therefore be mapped onto each other, but this has only local (system) validity.

> **Note**
>
> The name prefix "BW" has been designated for archiving objects generated in SAP NetWeaver BI. The following character, a "C" or an "O," identifies the archiving object as belonging to an InfoCube or a DataStore object. This is followed by the usually abbreviated name of the InfoProvider. This abbreviation is valid only within a BI system, and is generated in the same way that Microsoft operating systems abbreviate long filenames. In such instances, a name that is longer than seven characters is abbreviated by using the first five characters, a tilde (~), and the last character of the name.

Should a name abbreviated in this way have already been applied in the current system, then the suffix separated by the "~" is incremented upward until a unique name is found. For example, the name "BWOOFIAR~3" will be created for the DataStore object OFIAR_O03, which is delivered in the business content. This partially meaningful encryption of the InfoProvider name facilitates direct control of data archiving from Archive Administration.

Similar to the archiving object in an ADK-based archiving process, the *nearline object* is responsible for addressing the connected NLS solution in a nearline storage process. The nearline object is also generated out of the data archiving process for an InfoProvider. Nearline objects consist of different nearline segments that provide different views of the respective InfoProviders and can reflect different versions of the same InfoProvider. Please refer to the SAP documentation for the structural changes that you can make to an InfoProvider whose data has been partially stored in the NLS storage.

Nearline object for addressing the NLS solution

Read and delete access to data from within the archiving processes are effected using the *DataManager interface*. When reading data from InfoCubes, these are transformed in the star-shaped table schema into a flat format, which contains only the actual characteristic attributes and no navigation attributes. This means that the archive will not be affected by any possible reorganization of the IDs in the star schema. The disadvantage of this is an increase in data volume, which is, however, partially counterbalanced by a compression of the data in the archive file.

DataManager interface

6.3.4   Modeling Data Archiving Processes

A *Data Archiving Process* (DAP) is always assigned to exactly one InfoProvider and it also has the same name as that InfoProvider. You can create data archiving processes for InfoProviders that already exist and are filled with data. Vice versa, an InfoProvider can contain only one DAP.

The dialog window that allows you to define a DAP (transaction RSDAP) consists of the following five tabs: **General Settings**, **Selection Profile**, **Semantic Group**, **ADK**, and **Nearline Storage** (see Figure 6.14).

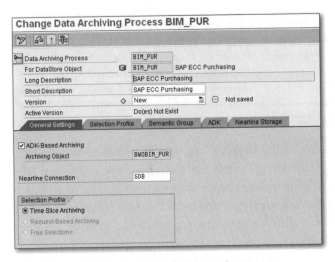

Figure 6.14 Defining a DAP for a DataStore Object

Using time slices

The **General Settings** tab enables you to define whether you want to carry out ADK-based, NLS-based, or combined data archiving. The **Selection Profile** tab allows you to define how data is selected from the InfoProvider for the archiving session. We recommend that you use *time slices for archiving*, which are intervals with a start and end time. In this case, you can select a time characteristic from the characteristics catalog of the InfoProvider. This method permits a simple automation of the archiving process.

Free choice of selection characteristics

If you don't use time slices, you can freely choose the selection criteria for the archiving session. In this case, however, the periodical scheduling of archiving sessions is possible only with additional effort.

File structure

In a next step, you must define the structure of the archive files in the **Selection Profile** tab (see Figure 6.15). This tab allows you to define the method to be used for selecting data from the InfoProvider.

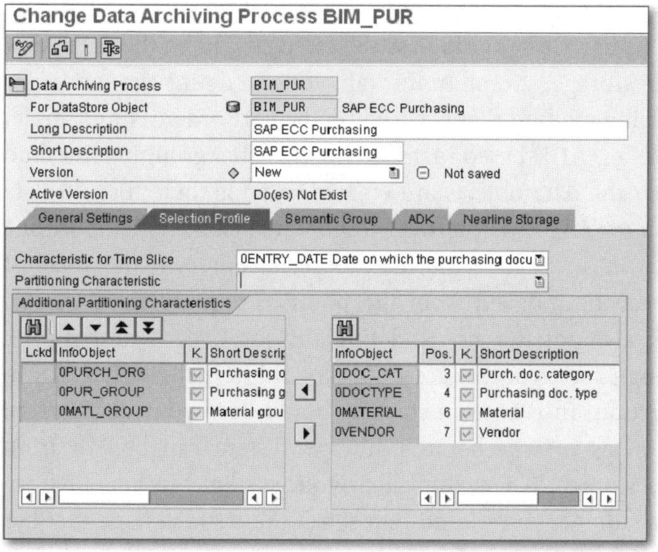

Figure 6.15 Defining the Archive File Structure—Selection Profile

If you choose a time-slice-based selection profile, an absolute time characteristic is selected from the InfoProvider structure, based on which the InfoProvider and its archive are partitioned. For a DataStore object, you should choose the time characteristic on the basis of the object key. You may also choose characteristics that are not based on the object key, but then you must combine the characteristic with another characteristic from the key, which has a monotonous time relation, such as a document number. This second characteristic is then used as the actual partitioning characteristic. You can choose any absolute time characteristic for an InfoCube.

To establish ideal conditions for the use of queries in the nearline storage system, the selected time characteristic should also have a high relevance for queries. Therefore, you should generally choose a posting date over a technical creation date. When scheduling your archiving sessions, you can then specify a relative time condition in the form of a minimum age for selecting the data records to be archived. This way you can easily schedule periodic archiving sessions without having to adapt a variant with each session. The **Selection Profile** tab provides further characteristics for selection; note, however, that these characteristics must be contained in the key if you use a DataStore object. If you select an additional characteristic, you can, for example, restrict the session to a specific organizational unit.

Time characteristic should be highly relevant for queries

Grouping the
selected data

The **Semantic Group** tab (see Figure 6.16) enables you to define the method to be used in order to pass the selected data to the archive or the nearline storage system. In this tab, you can define the sort order and a grouping method that is based on the sort order. For example, in the case of ADK-based data archiving, the grouping method defines how the data objects are created in an archive file. All data records that are selected according to the same characteristics form a data object. In an archive file, data objects represent the smallest units that can be indexed from the point of view of the ADK. Of course, it is also possible not to define any sort order—in that case, the grouping process occurs according to an internally defined technical restriction. In this context, you should base your decision on the question as to whether the storage system can benefit from sorted data storage. If you think that your system can benefit from sorted data storage, you should first select the characteristic that has the highest selection value for load processes or queries.

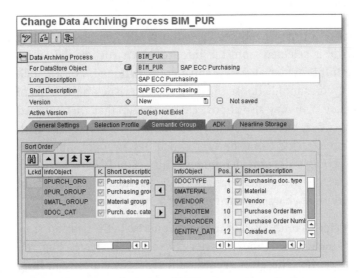

Figure 6.16 Defining the Archive File Structure—Semantic Groups

Settings for
ADK-based data
archiving

If you have selected ADK-based archiving in the first tab, the system displays another tab called **ADK** (see Figure 6.17). In this tab, you must configure the settings required for the ADK. These settings include the selection of a preconfigured logical file name. In addition, you can limit the size of the archive file by specifying a maximum size in terms of megabytes or a maximum number of data objects. This makes sense if the storage media you use requires you to limit the size of stored archive files. Moreover, you can define how and when the delete run that follows the write run should be started, and which settings you want to apply for storing the archive files in a connected content management system.

If you select a nearline connection in the first tab, another tab opens—the **Nearline Storage** tab (see Figure 6.18). In the case of simultaneous ADK-based archiving, the values in the **Nearline Storage** tab are identical to those in the **ADK** tab, and a data package in the nearline storage is identical to an ADK archive file.

Settings for NLS storage

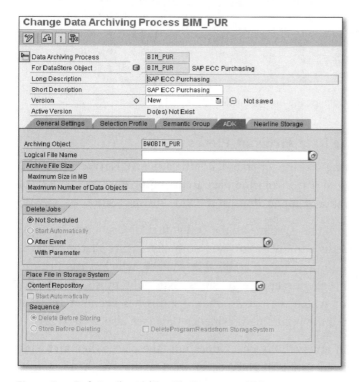

Figure 6.17 Defining the Archive File Structure—ADK

When a DAP is activated for the first time, the system creates an archiving object or a nearline object, depending on the selected archiving method. The creation of a nearline object also involves the creation of the structures required for the acceptance of data in the nearline storage system. Note that this process can differ, depending on the partner solution you have chosen.

Some settings can no longer be changed once the data is located in the archive. These settings include the selected archiving method, the selection profile, and the time characteristic.

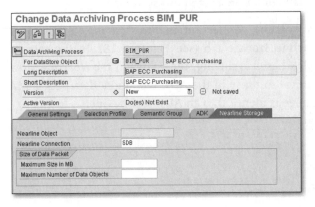

Figure 6.18 Defining the Archive File Structure—NLS

6.3.5 The Data Archiving Process

The archiving process for transaction data in SAP NetWeaver BI differs in several ways from the data archiving process in SAP ERP or other operational applications of the SAP Business Suite.

In an operational system, at the individual object level (business objects), status administration will normally ensure that the data is not archived too early. An archivability check, which is run prior to the actual write procedure, ensures that only those objects are archived for which the corresponding status has been set and that have reached the predefined residence time (see also Section 2.1).

No archivability check This type of archivability check does not take place when archiving transaction data in SAP NetWeaver BI. On the one hand, this is because, based on the implementation of SAP NetWeaver BI (see Section 6.3.2), there is no defined object in the InfoProvider to which a general status check could be linked. On the other hand, it can be assumed that for controlling data archiving in SAP NetWeaver BI, time limitations based on the age of the data are more likely to play a role. Simple selection conditions regarding time can then be linked with the partitioning of the database, and in this way allow for a high-performance deletion of data after it has been archived. It is always possible to make your selection based on a status transferred from the source system.

Another deviation from standard data archiving in an operational SAP system occurs when deleting archived data from the database. After the data has been written into the archive, an ADK delete program checks that the data has been archived successfully by reading it one archive file and one data object at a time. In SAP NetWeaver BI, the complete archiving session is first verified, and then the data is deleted in one step at the end of the verification. The details of this deletion procedure are described below.

Delete in one step

6.3.5.1 Writing Data to the Archive

SAP NetWeaver 7.0 enables you to use process chains to schedule archiving sessions for a DAP. For this purpose, the system provides the new process type, **Archive Data from an InfoProvider**, in the **Data Target Administration** section of the Process Chain Maintenance view (see Figure 6.19).

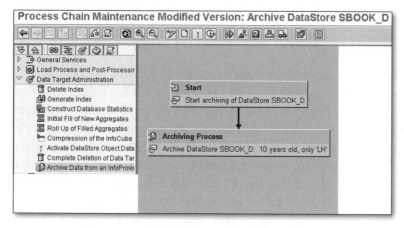

Figure 6.19 Process Chain Control for Archiving Processes

To schedule the execution of an archiving session, you must first create a variant for the process type. Based on this variant, an archiving request is then created at the runtime of the process step. This archiving request controls the entire archiving session. Depending on the archiving method you selected when defining the archiving object, the selection screen displays differently.

Creating a variant

When archiving time slices (see Figure 6.20), you can use the selection conditions for the selected time characteristic. A condition can be defined depending on the current system date as an absolute con-

Archiving time slices

dition for the time characteristic, or as a combination of both. For absolute time limitations, exclusionary conditions can also be defined. For example, you can exclude a certain time period from periodical archiving.

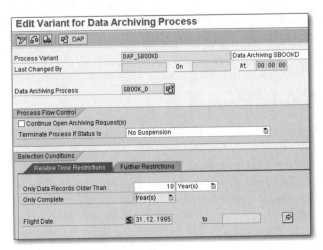

Figure 6.20 Variant Maintenance in the Time Slice Archiving Process Chain

Depending on the start time of the write process, the relative time condition is transformed into a selection condition for the time slice characteristic, and the intersection with the absolute time conditions of the time slice characteristic and the selection conditions of the other characteristics from the variant are created. Then, the section that has already been archived and the selection conditions of other archiving requests that are still open are deducted from the intersection. The resulting selection condition is saved together with the newly created archiving request, and it is used for both the subsequent selection of data in the write phase and for the delete phase later on.

If time slice archiving is not used, you can use any selection condition for each characteristic selected, with the exception of selection patterns and exclusion conditions.[8] In accordance with the characteristics selected for the definition of the data object, the data is sorted, read, and summarized into data objects in these groups.

---

8 Support for this selection profile is planned via SAP NetWeaver 7.0 support packages.

6.3.5.2 Deleting Data in the Database

In other archiving sessions, data is deleted by data objects, whereas in SAP NetWeaver BI, deletion is carried out for the entire archiving session in one step. The main reasons for this are as follows:

▶ For InfoCubes, consistency between the actual data in the fact tables and the aggregates must be guaranteed. To ensure this for queries as well, InfoCubes must also be locked for read access during the deletion of data from the fact table and the aggregates. The duration of the lock should, however, be as short as possible.

▶ If the delete conditions are summarized, then applying database-dependent delete strategies can increase performance.

Nevertheless, you must ensure that only data that has been successfully written to the archive files is removed during a delete run. In order to conform with the aforementioned ADK requirements and preconditions, the delete process is carried out in three phases:

Deleting in three phases

1. In the first phase, the verification phase, the archive file that has been assigned to the process (delete jobs are activated for each archive file individually) is opened in test mode and read in full. This ensures that the archive file is accessible and complete. In case of a successful verification, the result is stored in an individual status table for the archive file.

Archive file verification

2. In the second phase, the actual deletion of data from the InfoProvider is started. At the start of the phase, the program first checks whether the preconditions for deleting are met. This is the case, if:

Checking delete conditions

▶ The write process has been concluded successfully, in order to ensure that no new archive files or data packages are being created; and

▶ All archive files of the archiving request have been verified successfully.

If the write process has not been concluded, or if not all of the archive files have been verified, the delete process is prematurely aborted at this stage. The actual deletion is then started through the last delete process of an archiving session and with the same selection criteria that was used for the entire session, that is, the selection criteria that was used for reading data from the InfoProvider.

SAP NetWeaver 7.0 also allows you to summarize multiple archiving sessions in one delete run. For this purpose, you can execute several variants of the process type, **Archive Data from an InfoProvider**, in a process chain in order to archive disjunct sections of the InfoProvider. If necessary, you can run these variants simultaneously. The variants can then stop the process once the verification phase has completed, that is, once the **Verification completed successfully** status has been reached. After that, you can use process type **Archive Data from an InfoProvider** once again to carry out another process step to delete the data. This step summarizes the selection conditions of the open but verified archiving requests for a DAP into a delete condition. This is particularly useful if the selection conditions complement each other to form a simple condition that corresponds to one or several partitions of the InfoProvider.

The system applies different delete strategies depending on the selection criteria, the quantity of data to be deleted, and the properties of the database tables.

▶ When a complete InfoProvider is deleted on the basis of the selection criteria of the archiving session, the corresponding tables in the database are deleted and recreated using a DDL command.

▶ When the share of records to be deleted exceeds a certain threshold value (e.g., 10 %), then a copy of the table is created that includes selection conditions that complement the archiving session. The old table is then deleted and the name of the new table is changed to that of the old table.

▶ If the share of records to be deleted remains under the threshold value, a selective deletion in the database table will be carried out via *Data Manipulation Language* (DML) commands.

▶ If the fact table of an InfoCube is partitioned, a deletion will, under certain circumstances, involve the deletion of the complete partition (*drop/truncate partition*).

The same strategies used for the fact table are valid for aggregates of an InfoCube, but with one difference. When deleting aggregates, delete conditions are referenced for characteristics only if they are also used in the aggregate. This may mean, under certain circumstances, that too much is deleted from the aggregate. This is corrected by supplementing the aggregate with an aggregation of the total difference from a finer aggregate, or from the fact table, if no finer aggregate exists.

3. Once the data has been successfully deleted from the InfoProvider, the third phase follows. In this phase, all archive files of the archiving session are confirmed against the ADK. For this purpose, the archive files are opened and immediately closed in production mode.

Confirming archive files

The sequence of the entire delete process is schematically represented in Figure 6.21, in which it is assumed that the start of the delete job automatically follows the write phase. This can be set in the ADK-specific properties of a DAP.

The process of storing data in a nearline storage system is similar.

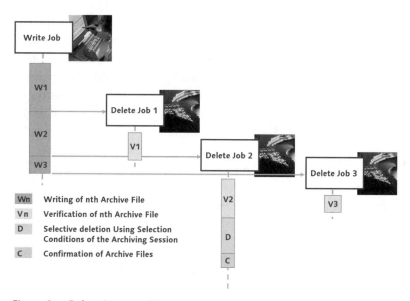

Figure 6.21 Delete Sequence Diagram

If you use a DAP for archiving data, the involved InfoProvider is not locked for the entire duration of the archiving session while it is loading new data. Instead, only those specific areas are locked where data has already been archived or where data is currently being archived.

6.3.6 Reloading Archived Data

In the case of time slice archiving, you can also use the DAP to reload completed archiving requests into the database tables of an InfoCube. Previously, this used to be possible only with time slice archiving for DataStore objects. If ADK was involved in the archiving process, you will have to trigger the reload operation via Archive Administration. If data was stored in a nearline storage without ADK being involved, you can also trigger the reload process in the **Archiving** tab of the InfoProvider administration. However, you should only reload data in exceptional cases, which is why reloading is not provided as a separate process type in the process chains.

6.3.7 Accessing Archived Data

Queries for archived data

Data of an InfoProvider that has been archived via a DAP with a near-line connection can be taken into account in queries on this specific InfoProvider. For this purpose, you must set a corresponding flag in the query definition. Note that you only need to set this flag once. The end user who runs the query usually won't realize that parts of the InfoProvider data are located in the archive. Only the runtime of a query can indicate that the nearline storage is being accessed. If the selection criteria of the query corresponds to the selection profile configured in the DAP, and if the query requests only data that has not been stored in NLS, the end user shouldn't even notice that data exists in the NLS system. If the query selects data according to characteristics that are not used in the selection profile, the response time of a query basically depends on the quality of indexing in the nearline storage system.

Direct supply of data targets from the archive

However, archived data is not available only for queries. You can, for instance, provide a connected data target directly with data from the archive via a *data transfer process* (DTP) that uses the archived Info-Provider as a source. In contrast to queries, load processes can use the archived data even if the archiving process was entirely based on ADK. The DTP allows you to switch between a selective (full) access to the non-archived and archived areas. The DTP does not require that you take into account a preselection of the archiving sessions. Prior to accessing the archive, the filter conditions of the DTP are mapped to the selection conditions of the existing archiving sessions (i.e., an intersection is created). In the event of an overlap, the corresponding archiving request is automatically opened for extraction.

6.3.8   A Look Ahead

SAP plans to provide archiving support for additional BI object types—such as master data and administrative data of DTP requests—in one of the next SAP NetWeaver releases.

Having discussed the concepts and technologies relating to data archiving, we will now show you how to apply them using real-life examples. This chapter describes a possible approach to planning and executing archiving projects and discusses the key project phases in detail.

7 Planning and Executing Archiving Projects

by Reto Gentinetta

In a live SAP system, very large volumes of data accumulate over a short period of time. Some of this data soon becomes obsolete and can overload the system. If the creation of this data cannot be avoided in accordance with the principles of data management (see Section 1.5.2), or you cannot aggregate or delete the data, you must move it out of the database via archiving. Archiving of data that is no longer required is not only important for "data hygiene;" it is also integral to proactively maintaining a high level of system performance.

Data archiving is essential to maintaining a "healthy" system

7.1 Introduction

It is only a matter of time before the mass data generated in a production system has to be removed from the database. Ultimately, all system administrators or application owners will have to face the challenges associated with archiving. To avoid potential problems, you should therefore explore the necessity of archiving as early as possible.

But, data archiving should not be used as a last resort to avoid system downtime after all hardware resources have been fully exploited. Instead, it should be part of regular system maintenance, like backups or database reorganizations. Even before an application or process is used in a production environment, the expected data volume

But: Data archiving is not a magic bullet

should be estimated and extrapolated for the future. Conversely, additional problems and costs arise if performance and administration problems make archiving essential. A successful project is very difficult to achieve under such circumstances.

We can therefore distinguish between two different scenarios in which archiving projects are implemented:

▶ Early implementation

▶ Late implementation

Proactively imple-
menting an
archiving project as
early as possible
The ideal time to start a data archiving project is determined as part of the implementation project for an SAP solution. It is advisable to implement an archiving project as early as possible. Therefore, data archiving is discussed in the *Business Blueprint* phase in the *AcceleratedSAP* (ASAP) process model (*part of the SAP Solution Manager*).

7.1.1 Early Implementation of an Archiving Project

Objective: Avoid
problems
In this scenario, the objective is to minimize the database volume from the outset and to remove data that is no longer required for production from the database.

In this scenario, the necessity of data archiving is taken into account when an application or business process is first implemented in a production environment. The application or process owner is familiar with the business process flows and the associated business objects in the SAP system. In most cases, an approximate document volume and the associated data volume is also known. These empirical values indicate the necessity of data archiving at an early stage. You can then take the necessary steps such as creating a periodic archiving plan.

Benefits
Early archiving has the following additional benefits:

▶ Early identification of incomplete business processes

▶ Low rate of database growth

▶ Shorter runtimes for jobs in data archiving

▶ Shorter runtimes for system jobs (backup, restore)

▶ No creeping deterioration of system performance

7.1.2   Late Implementation of an Archiving Project

In this scenario, the objective is to stabilize or contain the database volume. This occurs when large data volumes lead to performance or administration problems. If system bottlenecks occur, the following additional problems can occur with data archiving:

Objective: Contain problems

► Longer runtimes for archiving programs

► Additional system load due to archiving

► Time pressure on the project

If there are existing bottlenecks in the database or problems with performance, the time pressure on the archiving project increases significantly. Moreover, an additional problem is posed by the fact that the relevant business processes often have not been completed, and the documents must accordingly be completed before archiving. This correction process is time-consuming and the runtimes of the correction programs are therefore long.

7.1.3   Considerations Prior to Data Archiving

As a project manager or administrator, you should always determine whether there is any viable alternative to archiving the data before you embark on an archiving project. We don't recommend implementing a data archiving project for an archiving object if the data in the relevant tables is not required by any of the users. Therefore, before archiving, you should check whether the data is really necessary or whether it can be deleted (see Section 1.5.2). In this case, you can consult with the business department, because only the relevant users know exactly which data they require.

First, check whether the data is actually required

7.2   Procedure After ASAP Implementation Phases

Data archiving comprises more than the mere physical removal of data from the database. Since it involves revoking write access to business data by the business departments, all relevant groups must be consulted in order to carry out a comprehensive analysis and create a catalog of requirements for the data to be archived. It is impor-

Standardized procedures save time and money

tant to proceed as methodically as possible. *AcceleratedSAP* (ASAP), which is part of the SAP Solution Manager, is a proven method that is often used for the efficient execution of implementation projects. The methodology is described in *roadmaps*, which establish standardized process steps for efficient project implementation and thereby helps to save both time and money. This also enables end-to-end quality control for the project. For these reasons, we recommend that you also use roadmaps for archiving projects.

ASAP as part of the SAP Solution Manager

ASAP roadmaps are part of the SAP Solution Manager, which is the implementation and operating platform for SAP products. They can be downloaded from the SAP Service Marketplace using the quick link *ROADMAPS*. In ASAP, the implementation of data archiving is part of Phase 3: *Realization*.

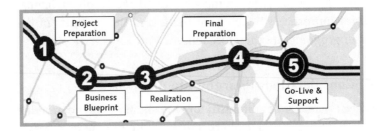

Figure 7.1 ASAP Project Phases

In this chapter, we propose a practical procedural model for planning and executing archiving projects, which is based on ASAP methodology and comprises the following main phases (see also Figure 7.1):

Basic concept

1. **Project Preparation**
   In this phase, the project is prepared and planned. The project scope and objectives are defined. In addition, the schedule for the entire project is defined. This phase is documented in a basic project concept.

Detailed or technical concept

2. **Business Blueprint**
   In this phase, the Business Blueprint defines the target concepts. The results of the workshops dealing with the requirements relating to the business processes are described in detail. Based on the general concept and the workshops, the detailed concept (also referred to as the technical concept) is created. These detailed con-

308

cepts define the sequences, dependencies, and residence times for archiving. The project team members also receive the required training during this phase.

3. **Realization**

The Business Blueprint is implemented in this phase. The business and process requirements are configured in the SAP system, and the corresponding enhancements of the programs and display functions are checked and adjusted as required. The information from the detailed concept serves as a basis for this process.

Configuring requirements

4. **Final Preparation**

In this phase, any open issues are resolved. The relevant activities are completed, which include testing, user training, and system administration. After this phase has been successfully completed, data archiving can be executed in the production system.

Resolving open issues

5. **Go-Live & Support**

Archiving goes live in this phase. After this event, archiving is then carried out on a regular basis.

Go-Live

Figure 7.2 shows an overview of the individual phases of an archiving project. Keywords indicate the potential activities or subphases that may be involved in a project phase. Each project phase produces a project milestone, which, in turn, provides a starting point for the next phase.

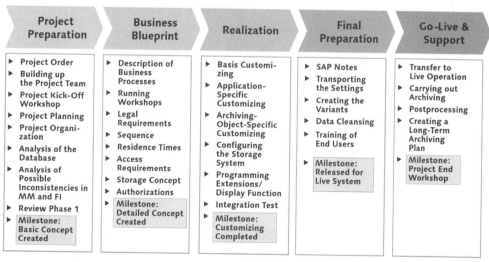

Figure 7.2 Phases in an Archiving Project (According to ASAP)

Checklist You will find an overview of all steps required to plan and execute an archiving project in the checklist in Appendix B. This allows you to determine how your archiving project is progressing and to then decide which steps to take next.

Data archiving guide for project support To support your data archiving project, SAP systems contain a data archiving guide, which you can access in transaction ARCHGUIDE. It specifies the key transactions and menu options that you can use to access the relevant functions in your system:

▶ Analysis

▶ Cross-application customizing

▶ Archive Information System

▶ Application-specific analysis and settings

▶ Execution and monitoring

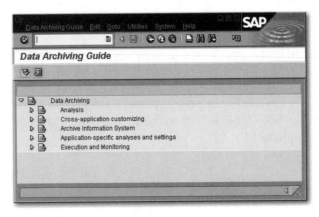

Figure 7.3 Transaction ARCHGUIDE

7.3 Project Phases

This section introduces the key components and tasks involved in the project phases specified above in accordance with ASAP methodology.

7.3.1 Project Preparation

Project kickoff workshop An archiving project generally starts with a project *kick-off* workshop for all persons involved in the project. During this workshop, the project goals should be discussed and the project team put together. In addition to these general project-planning activities, the database should also be analyzed during this phase. Furthermore, a check should be performed to detect any inconsistencies between financial accounting and purchasing data prior to archiving. The warehouse value is checked against the corresponding value in financial accounting (for more information, see the documentation about the RM07MMFI program). The results are recorded in a *general concept*.

7.3.1.1 Putting Together the Project Team

Data archiving is a cross-department activity and should be viewed and implemented as such. Data archiving involves more than simply removing the relevant business objects from the database. Rather, the business environment in which the business objects are embedded must also be considered, so that the effects on archiving can be properly assessed. Since some business objects are used in cross-application process chains, the relevant application owners should be involved in the archiving project. Where possible, the project team should include representatives from all relevant departments, depending on the size of the company.

Data archiving as a cross-departmental activity

The project team must determine whether archiving is necessary. The following indicators may be of assistance:

Indicators in favor of data archiving

▶ Significant increase in the effort involved in system administration

▶ Considerable deterioration of system performance

▶ Intensified growth in some database tables

The project team also produces a requirements catalog for archived data, helps to draft an archiving concept and, lastly, executes data archiving.

Key characteristics of successful project teams are:

Characteristics of successful teams

▶ Having a clear definition of objectives and tasks, which are shared by all team members

▶ Firm positioning of the team within the organization

▶ A cooperative environment (team spirit)

▶ Effective and competent management

> ▸ Technically and socially competent team members

> ▸ Open communication (conflict resolution)

Composition The composition of the project team is integral to the success of a project and therefore deserves careful consideration. It is essential that the team members possess extensive knowledge of company processes.

The groups listed below could potentially be involved in a data archiving project. The exact composition of the groups depends on the size and on the internal organization within the company, and may therefore differ from what is specified below:

> ▸ IT department: Database administration, SAP system administration

> ▸ Application owners of all archiving-relevant components (and related components)

> ▸ Controlling, auditing department

> ▸ External: Auditors, external service providers if required, such as consulting firms, SAP Data Volume Management (DVM), etc.

The groups involved in the archiving project are assigned different tasks based on their roles and areas of responsibility.

Project management The main tasks of *project management* are planning and control, as well as organization and management of the project. A sound knowledge of the archiving concept in the SAP system is essential. Other tasks include the integration of data archiving into broader archiving concepts, such as document storage (optical archiving), and ensuring a standardized and homogeneous archiving solution. To avoid fragmented solutions, the general IT strategy should also be addressed in larger companies.

IT department The *SAP system administrator* is usually responsible for database analysis, Customizing of ArchiveLink archives or content repositories, setting up and connecting storage systems, general archiving Customizing, and configuration of the SAP systems (batch server, etc.). The IT department also is responsible for ensuring that the archived data is stored securely for the specified period (e.g., by mirroring the relevant directories, or using an external storage system). If required, the IT department must also provide the relevant programming tools (for data cleansing, evaluation programs, etc.). In addition, the jobs and the system (e.g., the log directories of the database) must be monitored. In-depth knowledge of the SAP system and database administration is also required to complete this wide range of tasks.

Application owners must have a very sound knowledge of components and processes and be able to place the data that is to be archived in a business context. They must also be able to identify possible dependencies between business objects and the implications of these dependencies for data archiving. For example, they should know that billing documents must only be archived after rebate processing has been completed. The application owners also need to estimate the quantity structure for archiving and make the application-specific Customizing settings.

Application owners (business departments)

From the perspective of the individual business departments, the following issues, among others, must be resolved:

▸ Which data can be archived?

▸ Have the business processes been completed and do the documents have the status **complete**?

▸ When should this data be archived (e.g., once a year after the year-end closing)?

▸ Should this data be accessible?

▸ If so, how often and in what form?

▸ How should the data be formatted for display?

▸ What access time is acceptable?

▸ Will the data continue to be used by other organizational units?

▸ Are there additional requirements for retaining this data?

▸ If so, how long should it be retained?

It is the responsibility of the *Auditing or Controlling department* to specify the legal requirements for the data to be archived, taking into account country-specific regulations if necessary. In this context, a check is also required to determine whether additional requirements apply in the case of an external audit, and whether these requirements must be fulfilled prior to archiving. All activities that may be necessary, such as the creation of print lists or the use of the Data Retention Tool (DART), can then be scheduled before data archiving.

Auditing/Controlling department

If *external service providers* are to be involved in an archiving project either actively or in a consulting capacity, they require a sound knowledge of SAP data archiving. This includes:

▸ Knowledge of the relevant archiving objects and their structure

▸ An understanding of how the archiving objects fit into the system context

▸ An overview of the current market for data storage systems and how they can be connected to an SAP system

▸ An overview of the existing archiving objects

7.3.1.2 Database Analysis

Large data volumes constitute a considerable challenge in terms of the physical storage capacity of the database and the execution of data backups. In addition, the data is replicated or mirrored in many high-availability concepts. Consequently, an increased investment in the corresponding hardware equipment is required. The effects on data backup concepts are far more serious, because the duration of a backup increases in direct proportion to the data volume.

The analysis phase is the most important part of an archiving project. The analysis can be executed from two different perspectives:

▸ A technical perspective

▸ A business perspective

From a technical perspective, the size of the database and the growth of the database tables must be analyzed. This technical analysis must then be compared with the business analysis. In this step, the archiving objects to which the critical database tables are assigned must be identified. Before this step is taken, it is essential to also check whether the data volume to be archived can be reduced in the future using data management (see Section 1.5.2). The business department is also in the best position to know which data is no longer required and therefore does not need to be archived.

What should be
documented in the
analysis phase?
The results of the database analysis must be documented. The analysis should comprise the following elements:

▸ Result of the table analysis

▸ A list of tables that are not assigned to any archiving object

▶ A list proposing the possible archiving objects and the corresponding database tables

▶ Results of the analysis of inconsistencies between purchasing and financial accounting (program RM07MMFI)

Analysis of the Database from a Technical Perspective: Overview

It is difficult to make generalizations about when data should be removed from the system. It is the system administrator's responsibility to determine the actual criteria to be used as a basis for determining whether data should be removed. Routine tasks include the monitoring of the database and ensuring consistent performance during production operation. The system administrator can use a range of powerful tools for these purposes. It is essential that the system administrator is familiar with the relevant monitoring tools and knows how to interpret the values. The main tools available are listed below. The relevant transactions or programs are specified in parentheses in each case.

▶ Data Archiving Guide (ARCHGUIDE)

▶ Database Monitor (DB02)

▶ Table Analysis (TAANA)

▶ Application Analysis (ST14)

▶ Tables and Archiving Objects (DB15)

▶ Performance Monitor (ST03)

▶ Data Browser (SE16)

▶ CO Analysis Programs (RARCCOA*; can be executed in SA38)

Analysis of the Database from a Technical Perspective: Transactions and Programs

The *Data Archiving Guide* (transaction ARCHGUIDE) allows you to access all relevant reporting transactions from a central point, as shown in Figure 7.4.

Data Archiving Guide

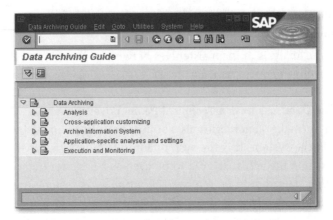

Figure 7.4 Analysis Operations in Transaction ARCHGUIDE

Database Monitor

You can use the *Database Monitor* (transaction DB02) to determine the sizes of tables and display how they have grown in the past. This transaction provides database-specific key figures. The Data Monitor display depends on the database used. With Oracle database systems (see Figure 7.5), for example, the number of free tablespaces or the size and growth rate of the individual tables and indexes are displayed.

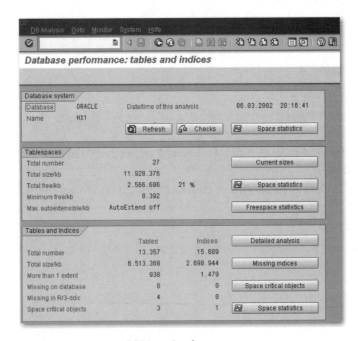

Figure 7.5 Transaction DB02 on Oracle

As shown in Figure 7.5, the Database Monitor shows three different levels on Oracle:

- ▸ **Database System** (the complete database)
- ▸ **Tablespaces**
- ▸ **Tables and Indexes**

Figure 7.6 shows the different display in the Database Monitor on a DB2 Universal Database.

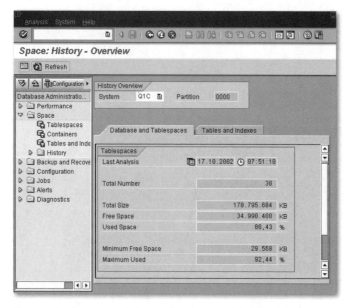

Figure 7.6 Transactions DB02 on DB2 Universal Database

You require data relating to the tables and indexes for the technical analysis. Use the **Space statistics** pushbutton for this purpose. When the hit list is displayed in Oracle, you must select the menu option **History • All Objects on/off** to display all tables. Figure 7.7 shows an example of the table sizes as determined in transaction DB02 in a live SAP installation. Here the tables are sorted by size in the display.

History for all objects

This display is similarly database-dependent. The corresponding list on DB2 Universal Database (DB2 UDB) is displayed as shown in Figure 7.8.

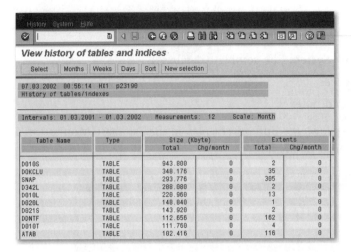

Figure 7.7 Calculating the Table Size with DB02 on Oracle

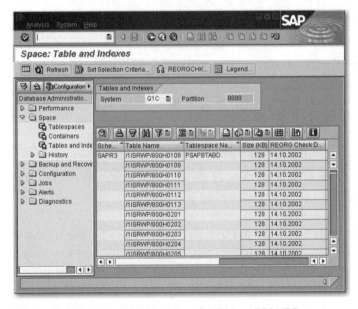

Figure 7.8 Calculating the Table Size with DB02 on DB2 UDB

In addition to transaction DB02, you can also use the BR*Tools tool [BRTOOLS] and transaction ST03 (the Performance Monitor) to determine additional indicators in relation to data archiving. Information about storage space statistics is also provided in transaction DB15 (press the **Storage Space (Statistics)** button).

Data archiving should always be recommended if the following points apply (assuming optimal configuration of the database and database server):

▶ Problems occur in relation to database administration due to a large data volume.

▶ Response time behavior is critical even if an optimal index is used to access the data.

▶ The response time of the database constitutes the greatest share of the total response time.

▶ The underlying tables are very large or have grown at a very fast rate.

More information is provided in the database administration training courses and in the documentation for the BR*Tools [BRTOOLS].

In transaction ST14, you can execute *application-specific analyses* of the table contents. You can select the relevant application on the initial screen. You can then schedule and evaluate various analyses, which provide a range of useful information about document sizes and document type runtimes. For example, Figure 7.9 shows the evaluation options available for material documents.

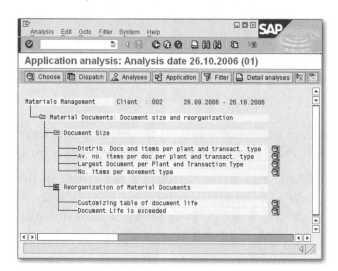

Figure 7.9 Application Analyses in Materials Management

The *Table Analysis* (transaction TAANA) allows you to analyze the distribution of the data in a table across selected fields, such as peri-

ods or organizational units. This allows you to derive selection criteria for the write program that will guarantee the greatest success
when minimizing the volume of data in the database. For example,
you don't want financial accounting data to be archived for certain
company codes in which hardly any data is posted. Therefore, you
need to know the company codes and fiscal years for which the
greatest number of documents exists. You can use the table analysis
for this purpose.

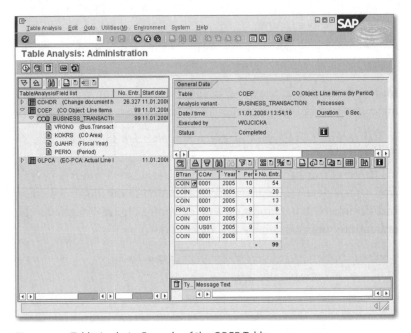

Figure 7.10 Table Analysis: Example of the COEP Table

In addition, you can use the table analysis to determine how many
records in a table could be removed with different archiving objects.

Analysis variants   Each analysis is based on an analysis variant, which you must specify
along with the table to be analyzed when you schedule an analysis.
The analysis variant determines the fields for which the distribution
of data is to be analyzed. The result of the analysis is saved to the
database.

DEFAULT variant   The DEFAULT variant exists for each table in the system; however,
this variant only assigns the table records to the client. Many applications therefore provide variants with archiving-relevant criteria for
their own tables. These variants are called ARCHIVE or STANDARD.

If necessary, you can also create customer-specific variants in transaction TAANA_AV.

> **Note**
>
> When you create your own analysis variants, bear in mind that the more selective the fields are that you select, the less meaningful the analysis will be. "Document number," for example, is a very selective field (in a customer system, millions of documents may exist; however, the total number of company codes seldom exceeds 100; therefore, the document number is far more selective than the company code. If you use such a field, every document in the database may be listed in extreme cases. Useful criteria include organizational units, company code, controlling area, fiscal year, and period or document types.

Ad-hoc variants can be used in the table analysis. The definition of these variants is not stored in the database and is therefore only available for the table analysis that you are currently scheduling. No workbench request is required for ad-hoc analysis variants. This variant type is therefore best suited for fast analyses that are only temporarily required and don't require regular scheduling.

Ad-hoc variants

Virtual fields (transaction TAANA_VF) allow you to perform the following analyses within the table analysis:

Virtual fields

▸ Analysis of part of a table field, for example, the year in a date field to investigate the distribution of data over the year. (An analysis of the entire date field is not recommended due to the high level of selectivity (see above) of this field.)

▸ Analysis using a field that is not contained in the table to be analyzed, but whose value can be determined from the available table fields or from other tables. One example of a virtual field is the field "archiving object" in the case of tables, for example, that are assigned to several archiving objects. An analysis based on this virtual field would show how the table records are distributed over the relevant archiving objects. You can thus determine the archiving object with which you can archive the most data from a certain table.

A Business Add-In (BAdI) implementation is used to calculate the field value of this second variant of the virtual fields. Knowledge of ABAP programming is required for this purpose.

When you create a virtual field, you must decide whether it is to be determined from part of another table field (subfield), or whether its value is to be calculated in a BAdI.

Value calculation by BAdI

If the value is to be determined by a BAdI, you must first specify the fields in the table whose analysis produces the value of the virtual field. Enter these in the **Fields required for the value determination** group box. Then click on the **Implementation** button to create an implementation for the TAANA_VIRTUAL_FIELDS BAdI definition.

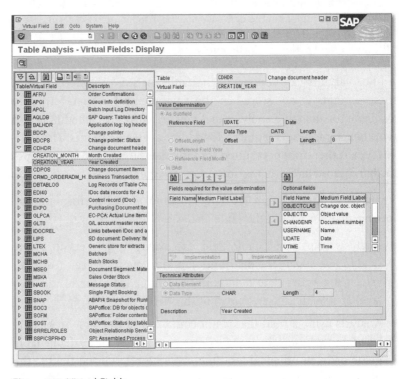

Figure 7.11 Virtual Fields

Analyzing several tables at once

With the TAAN_PROCESS_MULTIPLE program, you can analyze several tables in a single step. This is particularly useful for executing extensive analyses across a large number of tables. For performance reasons, however, you should always start these analyses in the background (transaction SA38, **Program • Background**).

If the results of an analysis are too wide-ranging (e.g., because the variant contains a field that is too selective), the system warns you that the table analysis is too large and that loading the file may take a long time when you display the results. You can press **Enter** to confirm this warning if you want to view a wide-ranging analysis.

For more information about executing and evaluating table analyses with TAANA, refer to the SAP Library.

After you have identified the critical tables, you must determine the archiving objects to which these tables are assigned. To do this, you can use the **Tables and Archiving Objects** function in transaction DB15.

Tables and archiving objects

This function allows you to find out which archiving object is assigned to which table and vice versa. You can therefore assign the tables determined in the technical analysis to a specific archiving object with which the table contents are then archived. The following functions are provided:

▸ Display the tables for an archiving object whose records are archived.

▸ Display the tables for an archiving object whose records are deleted.

▸ Display database-specific space information, such as the number of records in a table, the amount of space occupied by a table (in KB), or other table details from the SAP and database statistics.

Figures 7.12 and 7.13 show examples for the VBAK table and the SD_VBAK archiving object.

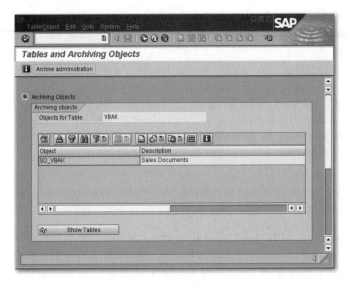

Figure 7.12 DB15, Archiving Objects for Table VBAK

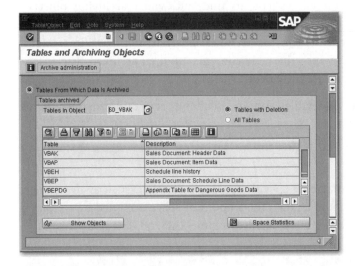

Figure 7.13 DB15, Tables for Archiving Object SD_VBAK

What to do if tables are assigned to more than one archiving object

Several archiving objects may be listed for a table in some cases. Typically, this occurs with general data such as change documents (tables CDHDR, CDCLS) and texts (tables STXH, STXL). This data is normally archived together with the actual application data using archiving classes. However, in the case of application tables (such as VBFA, COEP, etc.), you must identify the relevant archiving objects via a business analysis.

Analysis of the Database from a Business Perspective

In this analysis, the table contents are analyzed from a business perspective using standard analysis tools and are then assigned to archiving objects. Business objects can, in theory, be archived independently of each other; however, dependencies occur in some cases, which require a certain archiving sequence (see Section 2.1.1).

It may be necessary to examine the relevant business process in more detail to ascertain which processes produce a large data volume. It is important, when doing so, to view the individual objects in the overall business context, taking into account the components and corresponding processes that are actually used for production. The individual steps involved in this type of analysis are described in more detail below.

The main task of a business analysis is to clarify which data is to be archived and when this is to take place. Business objects can only be archived if the relevant business transaction has been completed. In this context, it is necessary to define when a business transaction is completed. The criteria for deciding this depends on the application. Company-specific factors must also be considered, for example, different runtimes for a business object depending on the organizational unit (company code, plant, sales organization, etc.). In addition to the analysis of business processes, the CO analysis programs (see Section 6.1.2) are also among the most important tools to help you identify data for archiving.

Identifying the data to be archived

You should also clarify whether additional data exists that is no longer required from a business perspective, for example:

Data cleansing

► Legacy data from a data transfer

► Data from spun-off business areas (e.g., after they have been sold)

► Test data

Note that this data often belongs to business processes that have not yet been completed. Therefore, you must schedule a great deal of time for data cleansing in particular.

7.3.1.3 Creating the Basic Concept

The initial results for the project are defined in the basic concept

The collective requirements for an archiving solution for the SAP system constitute the basic concept, which is based on the results of the table analysis and is created in collaboration with the project team.

The basic concept is the final step in the *Project Preparation* phase and represents the milestone for this phase. It defines the key requirements and guidelines, and provides a basis for the creation of the detailed concept (technical concept).

Scope of the Basic Concept

The basic concept should include the following points:

▶ Introduction to data archiving

▶ General requirements for data archiving

▶ Project environment (system, client, transport route, etc.)

▶ Project team members

▶ General planning issues (relating to planned upgrades of the system landscape, long periods of absence by project team members, etc.)

▶ Proposal list of archiving objects from the table analysis

▶ Additional archiving objects (e.g., master data that has already been flagged for deletion or archiving objects for data cleansing)

▶ An outline description of the archiving objects

▶ Requirements for archived data

▶ Archiving strategy

▶ Residence times

Note that a rough description is all that is required at this stage for each of the relevant points. A thorough description will then follow in the detailed concept in the *Business Blueprint* phase.

> **Note**
>
> The following points should be included in a basic concept:
> ▶ Information about the overall project environment, for example, the system in which the settings are made and the system to be used for testing, including the clients and transport routes

> ▶ The archiving project should also be synchronized with other projects to ensure that it does not overlap with a release upgrade or migration, for example.
>
> ▶ The basic concept should clarify whether other data also needs to be archived (data cleansing).

Requirements for Archived Data

The requirements for archived data provide a basis for creating the detailed concept at a later stage in the *Business Blueprint* phase. The legal, business and technical requirements for the data to be archived are specified in the basic concept. Based on these requirements, the specific business objects that can be removed are then determined for the detailed concept.

A basis for the detailed concept

First and foremost, the role of data archiving is to reduce the volume of data in the database, taking business criteria into account.

Data can only be archived if the corresponding business transaction has been completed and if write access to this data is no longer required. It does not make sense to archive data that is still required for processing in the production environment and therefore must be physically retained in the database.

Requirements for the data to be archived can be classified as follows:

▶ **Business requirements**
The business department will use business requirements to determine which data can be archived and which access or display options should be implemented.

▶ **IT/technical requirements**
Here, the focus is on implementing the requirements from the functional specification as an archiving concept and creating a technical specification, for example, for ensuring acceptable access times.

▶ **Audit-specific requirements**
Legal requirements, such as retention periods and evaluation options, must be incorporated into the concept and implemented.

The exact requirements for each archiving object are described in detail during the *Business Blueprint* phase (see Section 7.3.2).

Checking the Archiving Objects Resulting from the Analysis

Due to the high level of integration of the SAP system and the possibility of integrating business objects into cross-component process chains, the possible effects on follow-on processes must also be investigated. Specifically, this involves clarifying whether any follow-on processes access the business objects to be archived, or whether any business objects refer to the business objects to be archived. After archiving, these follow-on processes may no longer be able to access the archived data. It is therefore important that all application owners are included in the process of identifying possible interdependencies.

Archiving Strategy

An additional step in the creation of the basic concept is the definition of an archiving strategy. It has proven useful to divide the archiving objects among various phases according to certain criteria. Both technical and business aspects should be considered when doing so. Archiving objects could, for example, be divided as follows:

1. **Quick wins**
   This phase comprises the archiving objects that are likely to produce the greatest benefits (that is, the archiving objects with which a large volume of data can be archived) and can be relatively easily implemented. These quick wins are often vitally important if archiving is to be executed under time pressure. The following factors determine the ease with which an archiving object can be implemented:
   - Dependency on other objects
   - Audit-specific requirements
   - Requirements in terms of access to archived data
   - Status of the documents (the corresponding business process must be completed)

2. **Transaction data with a large document volume**
   The relevant data with a large document volume is archived in this phase. This also includes data that must be archived urgently due for business reasons.

3. **Master data**
   Because the master data cannot be archived until it is no longer referenced by any transaction data, it is archived last.

Defining Residence Times

All business departments involved in the project must jointly define how long certain business objects are to be retained in the database. Technically speaking, this is achieved by configuring a certain residence time. The *residence time* is the period of time during which a business object is retained in the database after it is created and before it can be archived. For more information, see Section 2.1.

Consensus must be reached between the business departments

The selection of residence times depends on business considerations and on the relevant business process. Any links to other business objects must be taken into account when defining residence times. In the basic concept, it is sufficient to define the residence time for each component and phase of the archiving strategy. The residence time for each archiving object is then defined in the *Business Blueprint* phase.

The *Project Preparation* phase is completed when the basic concept has been created.

Milestone

7.3.2 Business Blueprint: Design and Conception

The objective of the *Business Blueprint* phase is to determine and document all legal, business and technical requirements relating to the data that is to be archived. This information will serve as a basis for developing a specific archiving concept for removing the business objects from the database. The detailed requirements for an archiving solution for the SAP system are recorded in this phase. This detailed concept is based on the basic concept and the enhancements designed in collaboration with the project team.

Creating the detailed concept

Experience has shown that a wide range of interests may come into play, depending on whether the IT department or business department decides whether application data is to remain in the database or should be archived.

Different interests in terms of data storage

The position of the IT department is clear. It generally wants to remove as many documents as possible from the database to ensure that a high level of system performance can be maintained and to keep administration costs under control.

The business departments, in turn, want to be able to access as many documents as possible online in order to run reports, search for documents, generate lists, and so on. In the design phase, a compromise must be reached between these two positions, in other words, between the need to ensure high performance and ease of administration on the one hand, and the need for ready availability of documents on the other. The long-term goal must be to keep the data volume as consistent as possible and to be proactive about data archiving.

> **Note**
>
> It is much easier to reach a compromise in terms of residence times if the IT department can clearly demonstrate to the business departments that data does not simply "disappear" after it is archived and that it can still be displayed with standard SAP tools. It may be useful in this context to refer to the overview of archive access options [DAACCESS], which you will find on the SAP Service Marketplace.
>
> Another argument in favor of not allowing data to remain in the system for an unnecessarily long period of time are the costs that may arise as a result (e.g., the cost of purchasing and procuring additional hardware). A reference to the cost aspect often helps all sides to reach an acceptable compromise.

7.3.2.1 Creating a Detailed Concept

This subphase involves defining which business objects are to be retained for how long in the system and how data archiving can be integrated into an archiving concept that is homogeneous from both a technical and a business perspective. Regardless of which scenario applies (either proactive or reactive archiving), the requirements must be brought together in a detailed concept that takes into account business and technical perspectives. The relevant requirements are determined in the context of workshops.

Scope of the Detailed Concept

Possible content of detailed concept

The detailed concept should include the following points:

- Introduction to data archiving
- Reference to the possibilities of data management
- Requirements in terms of retention and the storage concept
- Scope of data archiving (processes, tools, handling of job terminations, etc.)

► Project details from the basic concept

► Creation of print lists prior to archiving

► A list of archiving objects

► Sequence of archiving objects

► Detailed description of the archiving objects and the relevant business processes (see the example in Appendix A)

► Dependencies between archiving objects

► Residence time for each archiving object

► Access requirements

► Required authorizations

► Notes on implementation, final preparation, and commissioning of data archiving

► Deadlines and milestones

► Checklist

Detailed Concept: The Business Perspective

Before you can begin to create a business data archiving concept, the dependencies between the archiving objects and the effects of archiving on other components and business processes must be determined and documented. A real-life example of the dependencies that must be taken into account in archiving in the sales area is discussed in detail in Section 7.5.

In order to implement the requirements from the analysis phase, you must also decide whether support from SAP Consulting is required.

The creation of the detailed concept is based on the results of the database analysis and the basic concept. You will have to consider the following aspects:

To determine the relevant business objects, you must first determine which archiving objects are to be used for archiving. The result should be a concept that defines the residence times of the individual business objects in the system. The requirements of the business departments and of the individual processes must be considered. Business objects assigned to the same business process may require different residence times in some cases, for example, because they are assigned to different organizational units. The results are defined in the detailed concept.

Determining residence times

Dependencies between archiving objects
Next, the logical dependencies between the archiving objects must be mapped, taking into account the requirements from the basic concept. The following actions will help you do this:

▶ Analyze the business processes

▶ Examine the network graphic (transaction SARA)

▶ Read the archiving object documentation

Defining the archiving sequence
The next step involves defining the archiving sequence. This is important if several archiving objects are assigned to the same business process. For example, the following sequence is recommended for the archiving of sales-related data: Shipment costs, transfer orders, shipments, billing documents, and sales documents. For more information, see Section 7.5.

Access to archived data
In many cases, an application doesn't need to access archived data, because this data belongs to business transactions that have been completed. One exception to this is archiving with very short residence times where the database grows quickly. However, a list of business objects to be archived should be used to determine whether and how often individual objects will need to be accessed before archiving takes place. Certain information about business objects may be required if a complaint is received or in regard to product liability, for example.

We therefore recommend that you produce a description of the procedure to be used in order to access archived business objects, which can be used both by the business departments and external auditors. Consider the following aspects:

▶ **Access times**
Since the data is stored on external storage media, longer access times are to be expected than are necessary for accessing the data in the database. Exact details of access times should be worked out in consultation with the relevant business departments. The IT department can then select which storage media or storage systems to use based on these specifications.

▶ **Authorization concept**
This involves defining which users may access the archived data. Should all employees who have used these business objects during production operation continue to have access to them when they are archived, or should some restrictions apply? Clarification is

also required as to which users can schedule and release background jobs. The authorization concept should define, in concrete terms, which data can be accessed by which employees.

> **Note**
>
> If you also want to archive print lists, you should bear in mind that the corresponding authorization object permits the display of all objects linked to the print list. The users that execute the jobs also require extensive authorizations (SAP NetWeaver AS plus application authorizations).

▶ **Display programs**

Appropriate read programs exist for the most important archiving objects, which allow you to search quickly and easily using specific selection parameters. The functionality of these tools should always undergo a go-live test by end users. If additional search and display programs are required, these must be programmed internally.

However, business objects are not always displayed in the same way. A technical display function always exists for all archiving objects, which displays the field names and the field contents in list form; however, a wide range of archiving objects (such as FI_DOCUMNT, MM_EKKO) also allows you to display the data in the original display transactions.

To ensure a user-friendly display for accessing and evaluating data, the requirements of the business departments and the auditing department must be defined. The following catalog of questions may prove useful in this instance:

Catalog of questions for user-friendly display

- ▶ Do different views need to be supported?
- ▶ Are the standard display functions sufficient, or do they need to be enhanced?
- ▶ What standard tools are provided by SAP (see Chapter 5)?
- ▶ Which information/attributes from the archived business objects are generally required?
- ▶ What does the information flow look like?
- ▶ Here you must determine whether the existing search options are sufficient or whether specific tools need to be developed.

The display function can be evaluated using test archiving. The following points may be relevant:

Testing the data display

▸ Which data needs to be displayed?

▸ Here you must determine whether only certain fields are relevant, or whether all fields of the business object need to be accessible.

▸ What is the form in which this data should be displayed?

> **Note**
>
> The question often arises as to the necessity of using third-party display tools. We recommend the following approach: First, check the standard display functions. If these are insufficient, check how costly it would be to develop the missing functionality. Take into account the additional costs of using third-party software. There are certain benefits to using this kind of software. For example, enhanced functionality may reduce the residence time and additional end-user training is not required.

Reloading in emergency situations only

▸ **Reloading of archived data**
SAP data archiving only provides for the reloading of archived data into the production database if data has been archived by mistake. This data should be reloaded as soon as possible after archiving to prevent a possible database inconsistency. General reloading is not supported.

Archiving is not recommended if you already know in advance that the data in question will need to be edited in change mode at a later stage. For more information about reloading, see Section 2.3.2.

Detailed Concept: The Technical Perspective
In addition to the business requirements, technical requirements also arise because archiving is integrated into the technical system environment. The technical implementation can only begin once the data archiving business concept has been defined. Since a wide range of solutions can be used, no general recommendations can be formulated.

Criteria for storage and management of archive files

However, we have listed some criteria below that may help system administrators to decide how best to store and manage archive files:

▸ **Realizing the required access times**
The selection of a storage medium depends on the required access times.

▶ **Evaluation of the storage system** (if one is planned)

The selection of a storage system depends on the purpose for which it is to be used and the requirements in terms of the archived data (e.g., access times or administration costs). Clarification is also required as to whether several SAP systems are to be used and whether the archive files are to be stored and managed centrally. Another consideration is the integration of the archive files into the system landscape. You must determine, for example, whether several SAP systems will need to access the archived data. For more information about the storage of archived data, see Chapter 3.

▶ **Storage strategy**

(if no storage system is used)

▶ **Integration of other archiving projects**

(for example, document storage)

▶ **Creation of a technical operating concept**

(that also covers the aspects of backup, restore, and administration of the archive files)

▶ **Durability of the data media**

▶ **Company-internal regulations**

Tips for Setting Up Local Storage (Without a Storage System)

It is often useful, though not essential, to use an external storage system to store archive files. If the archive files are not to be stored in a storage system, the following procedure is recommended:

▶ Create a local directory in the file system of the database host (for performance reasons), for which only the SAP system user (e.g., <SID>adm) has write authorization.

▶ Ensure that the other hosts have access to this directory.

▶ Ensure that this directory is included in the daily data backup.

▶ Save the archive files before the start of each deletion phase.

Responsibility for data security and for compliance with audit-specific requirements lies with the IT department in this case. As soon as an external storage system is up and running, the archive files can be migrated into this system.

▶ **Audit-specific requirements**

Legal requirements apply to the storage of business data, which must be taken into account when defining an archiving concept.

The concept should ensure that the archived data could still be evaluated, for example as part of an external tax audit.

In this context, it is important to comply with any existing audit-specific requirements (such as the creation of certain documents) before the relevant application data is archived.

Catalog of questions for auditing acceptability

Due to the country-specific differences in legal requirements for archived data, we will limit ourselves to a discussion of those issues that are to be taken into account when designing and executing any archiving project. To ensure the correct archiving and retrieval of data, you should consider the following questions when designing your archiving concept:

- What legally determined retention periods apply to the data to be archived?
- For how long must the business objects be accessible for an audit?
- Is it necessary to be able to display the entire business object, or only those fields that are relevant for auditing purposes?
- Are suitable tools available in the system for electronic retrieval of the archived data?
- Can readable reproductions be created if required?
- Do you need to be able to reconstruct the business process? In other words, does the financial accounting data need to be uniquely assigned?
- What access options are planned for the archived data?
- Is the archived data protected from unauthorized manipulation?

In addition, the following rule applies to the display of archived data:

- The procedure for displaying the archived data must be documented as a work instruction.
- This work instruction must describe the organizing principle for displaying the data and regulate the procedure for verifying the completeness and correctness of the data displayed.

Internal audits frequently require access to archived business objects, for example, to enable monitoring of sales goals and to provide a basis for decision-making. These audits are usually intended to assume the monitoring and control functions of management. The key objectives are to ensure the legal compliance, security and profitability of the archiving solution. Internal audits may incorporate any number of areas within the company. It therefore must be decided within the company which data is relevant for storage in addition to the data that must be stored in accordance with the legal requirements.

Taking requirements for internal audits into account in the detailed concept

---

Note

For each archiving object, you must define a retention period and then further classify this according to:

▶ Legal requirements

▶ Operational requirements (company-specific requirements, requirements based on ISO certifications, etc.)

▶ Business requirements (of the business departments and end users)

If one of the requirements changes, the other requirements do not need to be redefined. Example: The legally required retention periods for business data are shortened. This does not mean that the operational and business requirements have to be redefined. All you need to do is simply adjust the storage period of the archived data (if possible).

Completion of the detailed concept marks the end of the *Business Blueprint* phase.

Milestone

7.3.3 Realization

In the *Realization* phase, archiving is implemented and tested in the development system. All data archiving settings are made and the storage system (if one exists) is configured. An *integration test* is used to verify that all settings are correct and that all programs are running correctly and free of errors.

Make the necessary system settings

The exact procedure for data archiving where there are several archiving objects depends on the individual archiving objects used. Therefore, we can only describe here the steps that are usually relevant for data archiving. For detailed information about the individual archiving objects, refer to the SAP Library.

7.3.3.1 Configuration and Customizing

If a storage system is used, this must be configured and integrated into the system landscape. If no storage system is used, the file server must be configured accordingly. Note, in particular, that the write, delete and read programs that may run on various application servers must be able to access the archive files. For detailed information about Customizing settings for data archiving, refer to the SAP Library.

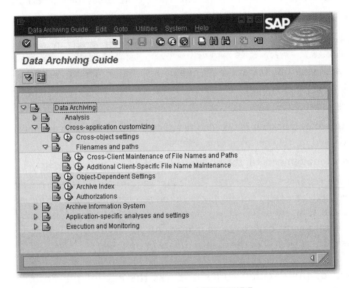

Figure 7.14 Customizing Settings with ARCHGUIDE

Customizing   The Customizing settings that are relevant for data archiving can be classified as follows (see also Figure 7.14):

▶ **General Customizing**
  Here you define the (platform-independent) logical file name (see Figure 7.15), from which the physical file path and name are generated at runtime. To ensure a clear assignment of individual archive files to an archiving object, we recommend that you use "meaningful" names (for example, include the name of the archiving object in the file name). You do this by defining a parameter in transaction FILE (see Section 5.2.1). This procedure is documented in the SAP Library.

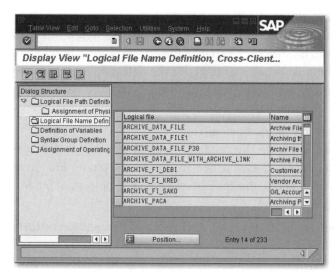

Figure 7.15 General Customizing

▶ **Cross-archiving-object Customizing**
In cross-archiving-object Customizing, you make the settings for the Data Archiving Monitor, the access check, verification of archive files, and interruption of the write phase (see Figure 7.16). You can also define the server group for background processing.

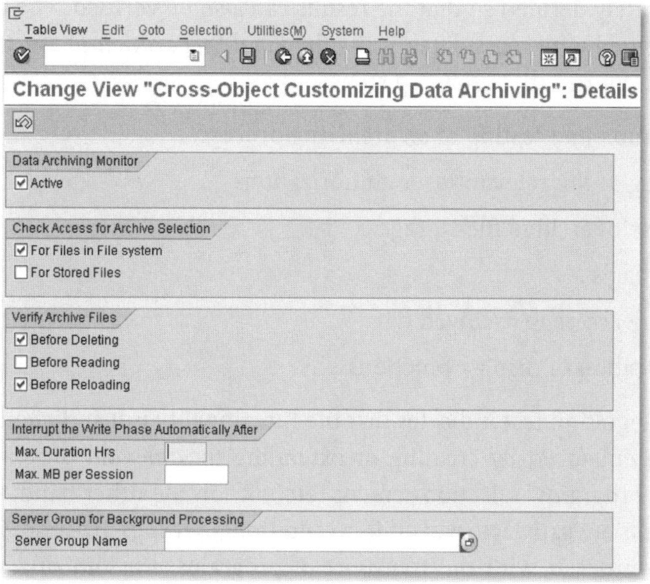

Figure 7.16 Cross-Archiving-Object Customizing

▶ **Archiving-object-specific Customizing**
In archiving-object-specific Customizing, you define the logical file name, the size of the archive file and the connection to a storage system, and make settings for the delete and postprocessing program (if applicable). In addition, you can also configure Archive Routing here (see Section 5.3).

▶ **Application-specific Customizing**
Here you configure the residence time (if possible) in accordance with the concepts established in the design phase. For detailed information about the individual archiving objects, refer to the SAP Library.

▶ **Customizing of ArchiveLink Archives and Content Repositories**
These Customizing settings are only required if a storage system is used. They should be made by an experienced system administrator. The system vendor also provides support for connecting to the storage system.

7.3.3.2 Integration Test

Verification of settings in the development system

An integration test ensures that all settings are correct, that the relevant Customizing settings have been maintained, and that the relevant programs are running without any errors. The test data should be accurately defined so that the results can also be verified. The test is performed with mass data during the *Final Preparation* phase, and should comprise the following steps:

▶ Execution and testing of all archiving processes

▶ Testing of the relevant user authorizations

▶ Testing of archive file storage

▶ Log analysis

▶ Testing access to archived data

▶ Verification of display functions

If the integration test indicates that the functionality is insufficient, it must be enhanced by creating or extending the relevant programs (display programs, selection screens, etc.). If, on the other hand, the test results are satisfactory, and if no additional settings are required, you can proceed with the transport of programs, Customizing settings, and so on into the production system.

Completion of Customizing means that the milestone of the *Realization* phase has been reached.

Milestone

7.3.4 Final Preparation

In the *Final Preparation* phase, all required settings are prepared and released for the production system.

Releasing settings for the production system

Most of the final preparations are made in the integration system. These include checking the settings and identifying new and relevant SAP Notes. In addition, tests are performed with mass data during this phase to determine whether data cleansing is required. Other activities during this phase may include end-user training and creating the required variants.

7.3.4.1 Checking Settings and Notes

All settings must be verified in the integration system as part of quality assurance. In addition, you should run a search to find any relevant new SAP Notes for each archiving object.

7.3.4.2 Test Phase

In this phase, test runs are performed for all business processes and archiving objects. The relevant test procedures and results must be documented and monitored by the project team.

Using test runs to determine whether documents can be archived

In order to test under realistic conditions, we recommend that you archive the largest possible volume of data in an integration system. This system should ideally be a replica of the production system. In certain cases, this produces the first indicators of how long archiving will take and which business objects cannot be archived. The final variants are also created at the same time.

All test results should be submitted to the business departments for final approval.

> **Procedure for incomplete documents**
>
> A document can only be archived when the relevant business transaction has been completed. Refer to the documentation about the individual archiving objects in the SAP Library for information about the differences between various document types.

In actuality, there may be many documents that cannot be archived. You should therefore schedule sufficient time to cleanse these documents before archiving. The exact procedure depends on the archiving object and therefore cannot be described in detail here.

Regardless of the procedure used, you should first search for SAP Notes relating to status cleansing so you can correct the documents that have already been generated. At the same time, the business process must be adjusted so that new documents are assigned the status **complete**.

7.3.4.3 End-User Training

Depending on the complexity of the solution, the end users may have to be trained on how to access the archived date; however, in most cases, providing end users with a description of the procedure using specific examples should suffice. Of course, experienced project team members should also be close at hand to guide the end users during the implementation phase (e.g., with a hotline).

7.3.4.4 Release for the Production System

Milestone This phase includes executing the transports into the production system, setting up the database servers for archiving, and variant maintenance. Note that variants are client-specific. The milestone for the *Final Preparation* phase is reached with the release for the production system.

7.3.5 Go-Live and Support

The *Go-Live & Support* phase includes the commissioning of the archiving solution, the setting up of a long-term archiving plan, and an end-project workshop, enabling everyone involved in the project to evaluate it.

7.3.5.1 Go-Live

The *Go-Live* phase of a new archiving solution can be broken down as follows:

1. Transfer to production operation and execution of essential preparations

2. Execution of archiving

3. Execution of any necessary postprocessing

Transfer to Production Operation and Execution of Essential Preparations

The entire archiving solution is transferred to production operation. Before archiving is executed for the first time, you should check the following parameters and correct them if necessary:

▶ General Customizing: Logical file names, size of archive file, ArchiveLink settings

▶ Application Customizing: Residence times

▶ Delete program settings

▶ Size of the database log directory (e.g., /saparch on Oracle)

▶ Check of the technical connection to a backup server (at deletion, many transactions are executed in the database, which may result in delays with high-availability backup servers)

▶ Selection subsets (save as variants if required)

▶ Execution of programs for data cleansing

The available storage space can be checked and increased if necessary in a single step. Everyone involved in the project is then informed about which business objects are to be archived.

Execution of Archiving

When archiving is executed, the archiving sequence defined in the detailed concept should be followed. The following activities should be performed:

▶ Scheduling the preprocessing programs (if relevant)

▶ Scheduling the write programs

▶ Configuring the delete program (see Section 5.2.3)

▶ Monitoring the jobs

▶ Reviewing the logs

▶ Testing read access (a one-time activity)

After archiving has been executed and the logs have been checked, the relevant business departments can be informed. Comments should be entered for the individual archiving sessions or archive files. These can be displayed later to provide important information about the stored business objects.

Postprocessing

Postprocessing includes the following activities:

- Updating the database statistics using a Cost Based Optimizer (CBO)
- Reorganization of the database, tables, indexes (if necessary) (see Section 5.3.6)
- Backup and management of the archive files
- Checking the business objects that could not be archived
- Scheduling the postprocessing programs (if relevant)

7.3.5.2 Creating a Long-Term Archiving Plan

Archiving of application data is not a one-time activity. Instead, it must be executed on a regular basis in order to maintain a controllable database status in the longer term.

A long-term archiving plan defines in detail which business objects are to be archived and when. This involves periodic scheduling of archiving jobs if the data load is high. Before such a plan can be created, you must first determine the data volume in the database. The expected data volume can then be projected based on an analysis of company-specific business processes and the growth rate of tables in the database.

A long-term archiving plan can be seen as part of a proactive archiving strategy, which aims to minimize the data volume, while taking account of archiving-object-specific residence times. When new processes or components are commissioned, the necessity of data archiving should therefore also be considered.

Other points that may be relevant for a long-term archiving plan include:

- Archiving all business objects that have exceeded a defined residence time
- Integrating data archiving into the SAP system landscape
- Managing archive files
- Removing all old archive files to tertiary storage media (only relevant if you have a large number of old archive files)

▶ Verifying table analysis on a regular basis and identifying any changes

7.3.5.3 Project-End Workshop

A project-end workshop should be held at the end of the project. This represents the milestone of the *Go-Live & Support* phase and the completion of the entire project.

Milestone

7.4 Quality Assurance for the Project

The underlying objective of an archiving project is to archive application data from the production system. Since this also involves deleting this data in the production system (a step that cannot normally be undone), quality assurance is a very important aspect of the project. There are two reasons why this is so:

▶ If an archive file can no longer be read after the delete phase is completed, this means that data is lost.

▶ Not all archiving objects support the reloading of archived data.

The objectives of quality assurance are as follows:

▶ Early identification and elimination of errors

▶ Final acceptance of interim and final results by the business departments

▶ Using the knowledge gained from errors to improve the process

Some objects of quality assurance

Tools for implementing quality assurance concepts include the following:

Implementation tools

▶ **Principle of dual control**
The correctness of an action can rarely be verified by an external party. According to this principle, correctness of form and content must always be verified by a second colleague. Customizing is also performed in the system by two people.

▶ **Review**
This is a formal method for verifying work results. In general, a check is performed to determine whether the results meet the defined requirements. The expert knowledge of the Review Team enables an expert evaluation of the work result that is checked. In

archiving projects, the milestones (basic concept, detailed concept, etc.) should be checked.

▶ **Test**
This method aims to detect any errors that may be present. In a test, actual or simulated functions are executed in a defined environment. Documentation of processes and results is required to ensure that the test is complete and can be reproduced.

▶ **Audit**
In an audit, procedures are checked and evaluated. An independent auditor checks whether the procedural model corresponds to the relevant SAP Roadmap (see Section 7.2).

7.5 Example: Executing an Archiving Project for Sales-Related Data

We will now apply the information provided above (i.e., about planning and executing archiving projects) to a sample project from the SAP ERP key functional area SAP ERP Operations, sub-area Sales and Services. This example of executing an archiving project is intended for project managers and other project team members.

7.5.1 Introduction

As with other types of documents, a compromise must be reached between the requirements of the IT department and those of the business departments when it comes to the archiving of sales-related documents.

IT department versus business departments

The IT department will want to remove as many documents as possible (in this case, shipments, sales documents, deliveries, billing documents, etc.) from the database in order to streamline the system, improve performance, and simplify maintenance (backups, monitoring, etc.). The business departments, on the other hand, will want to have online access to as many documents as possible to help them in their routine work. Since this requirement conflicts with the requirements for high performance and user-friendliness in the production environment, a compromise must be reached, whereby these two key requirements (usability and availability of documents on the one hand, and database performance on the other) can be united.

As mentioned above, possible dependencies between the business objects to be archived must be taken into account. In the sales application area , there are very clear dependencies between the individual documents, which means that an analysis of these dependencies prior to data archiving is very important.

Document dependencies

To facilitate a better understanding of the process and to provide a basis for example, Figure 7.17 shows one of the relevant parts of a typical sales business process.

Figure 7.17 A Typical Business Process Flow in the Sales Area

A sales document is used to generate delivery. Based on this delivery, a billing document is then generated, and this completes the business process from the sales point of view. The arrows in the diagram indicate the relationships between the various document types. These relationships are also referred to as the document flow, from which the following document dependencies are derived:

Process steps

▶ Preceding document (if one exists)

▶ Subsequent document (if one exists)

For more detailed information about document flow and dependencies between business objects, see Section 2.1.

7.5.2 Project Preparation

7.5.2.1 Putting Together the Project Team

You should consider the following persons when putting together the project team, which will be responsible for planning and executing the archiving of sales data:

Project team members

▶ **Representatives from the relevant business departments** across all applications. These are normally employees from sales, shipping, the billing department and accounts. Over the course of the project, additional support may be provided by colleagues from warehousing, purchasing, production, controlling, sales support, and departments that prepare statistics and reports.

▶ **Representatives from the IT department**
who are responsible for maintenance, availability and the general operation of the database and systems.

▶ **Representatives from the controlling and auditing department**
to ensure that the legal requirements are met.

7.5.2.2 Analysis

There are two different approaches to preparing this type of project, namely, a technical approach and a business approach. The following section discusses the most important aspects of both approaches and suggests possible solutions.

Technical perspective

Before you begin archiving sales data, you should ensure that the technical environment is up-to-date for the archiving objects to be used. This involves checking whether the most current archiving programs are used and whether the archiving-specific Customizing settings for the project have been made. You can use the methods described in Section 7.3.1.2 to determine how many documents exist in the database for each archiving object. The following archiving objects belong to the sales area:

Archiving Object	Archived Data
SD_VFKK	Shipment costs
SD_VTTK	Shipments
RV_LIKP	Deliveries
SD_VBRK	Billing documents
SD_VBAK	Sales documents
SD_VBKA	Sales activities
SD_COND	Condition records

Table 7.1 Archiving Objects for Sales-Related Data

Business perspective

The business perspective is concerned primarily with the question of how long the sales-related documents (sales documents, deliveries, shipments, billing documents) are to remain in the system after they are created, in other words, which residence times should be selected.

7.5.2.3 Basic Concept

The basic concept should define, among other things, the requirements for the sales-related documents, the residence times preferred by the business departments, and specific requirements for archiving objects by simply collecting and compiling this information.

7.5.3 Business Blueprint

In this project phase, you establish the legal, operational, and technical requirements for the sales archiving objects and create the detailed concept based on these results.

7.5.3.1 Detailed Concept

The general scope of the detailed concept is described in Section 7.3.2.1. Examples of the most important sales archiving objects are provided below:

Shipments (SD_VTTK)

This archiving object is used to archive shipment documents. All deliveries contained in the shipment must have the transportation planning status "C" (completely planned) (the VBUK_TRSTA field is checked). All deliveries contained in the shipment must have the goods movement status " " (not relevant) or "C" (completely processed) (the VBUK_WBSTK field is checked). In addition, you must be able to archive all shipments that are part of the same transportation chain as the current shipment.

Prerequisites for archiving

The V_TVARS table (see Figure 7.18) represents the Customizing table for the SD_VTTK archiving object.

Figure 7.18 Customizing of Residence Times for SD_VTTK

Residence times Different residence times can be defined according to the transportation planning point, shipment type, and the overall status of the shipment that is to be achieved. We can distinguish between two different residence times:

- ► **Creation**
  The period (in days) that must elapse after the shipment is created before the document can be archived. This period is calculated as the period between the date on which the shipment is created and the date on which the archiving session takes place.

- ► **Change**
  The period (in days) that must elapse after the last change is made to the shipment before the document can be archived. This period is calculated as the period between the date on which the last change is made and the date on which the archiving session takes place.

Deliveries (RV_LIKP)

Prerequisites for archiving
The RV_LIKP archiving object is used to archive deliveries. If a delivery is relevant for transportation planning, it must be part of a shipment and the shipment must be archived. The delivery must be posted if it is relevant for posting. If the delivery is relevant for billing, the billing documents must be generated first.

Residence times
The V_TVARL table (see Figure 7.19) represents the Customizing table for the RV_LIKP archiving object. It allows different residence times to be configured for each sales organization, delivery type, and form routine number (user exit).

The residence time is the period, in days, which must have elapsed since the delivery was created before it can be archived. The delivery creation date and the current date are used to calculate the residence time independently of the other characteristics of the delivery.

For more information about form routine numbers and the creation of *user exits* in the sales area, see the SAP Library.

Figure 7.19 Customizing of Residence Times for RV_LIKP

Billing Documents (SD_VBRK)

The SD_VBRK archiving object is used to archive billing documents. The billing document must have the status **complete** (posted in financial accounting).

Prerequisites for archiving

The V_TVARR table (see Figure 7.20) represents the Customizing table for the SD_VBRK archiving object. It allows you to configure different residence times based on the criteria sales organization, billing type, check accounting document and form routine number. The residence time is calculated in the same ways as for the RV_LIKP archiving object. The **Check accounting document** option ensures that the relevant accounting document is cleared and that the entire process is therefore completed.

Residence times

Figure 7.20 Customizing of Residence Times for SD_VBRK

Sales Documents (SD_VBAK)

The SD_VBAK archiving object is used to archive sales documents. The overall status of the sales document must be **complete** (meaning that the overall process status of the sales document is **complete** and the value of the field VBUK-GBSTK = C or blank).

Prerequisites for archiving

The V_TVARA table (see Figure 7.21) represents the Customizing table for the SD_VBAK archiving object. It allows you to configure different residence times based on sales organization, billing type,

Residence times

and form routine number. The settings correspond to those of the other archiving objects in the sales area. The **Check accounting document** option is missing in this case, but this check can be performed in the variant for the write program.

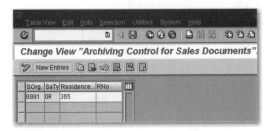

Figure 7.21 Customizing of Residence Times for SD_VBAK

Additional Requirements for Archiving Objects

Cross-application dependencies

In addition, you must check the cross-application business processes to determine whether information belonging to the sales document is still required in other applications. If this is the case, the documents from the sales application area cannot be archived until the other documents have been archived.

Documents may have different residence times

In a separate step, you must determine how long the various documents are to be stored in the system. From the perspective of the business department, it may, for example, be useful to remove deliveries from the system after a relatively short period of time, while it may be essential for accounting purposes that billing documents remain in the system as long as possible. Since the residence times of documents are customer-specific and depend on a variety of factors, you should compile an overview to indicate which types of business transactions are involved in sales and the average length of time it takes for a business process to be completed.

Access Requirements for Archived Data

Accessing archived data

In sales, special read programs are used to export the archive files and display them in list form. The standard programs are only provided as sample programs and may have to be enhanced in certain cases.

An additional option for evaluating and displaying archived sales data is provided in the form of the Archive Information System. Here the data can be displayed in a technical view or a business view. For more details, see Chapter 4.

Normally, no legal requirements apply directly to the documents in the sales area to be archived. However, certain requirements may apply indirectly to them (e.g., requirements from the financial accounting area) and these need to be identified.

Legal or business requirements

It is not possible to print archived sales-related documents. In any case, it does not make sense to do so, because the print program or relevant layout form may have changed since the document was first printed. It is therefore important to keep a copy of the document (either electronic or hard copy) the first time you print it. It is then irrelevant whether the data is archived at a later stage. If displaying the documents in the Archive Information System does not satisfy the requirements, you can enhance the evaluation program so that a list of archived documents can be generated.

Printing archived documents

You should also note that rebate settlement can no longer be executed in sales once the documents have been archived.

Defining the Archiving Sequence

After you have examined the individual sales objects in detail, you should work out a sequence concept for the sequence of the various archiving objects that are linked directly or indirectly to the sales archiving objects. In certain cases, there may be technical and business interdependencies between the various archiving objects, which make it necessary to adhere to a certain sequence.

Since these archiving and process chains are customer-specific, a sequence concept must be created in this phase to reflect customer-specific requirements. One example of a sequence concept is as follows:

Example of a sequence concept

SD_VTTK ⇨ RV_LIKP ⇨ SD_VBRK ⇨ SD_VBAK

7.5.4 Realization

In this phase, you implement and test data archiving in the development system. Since in sales this process is not application-specific, you can refer to the general process described in Section 7.5.7.

7.5.5 Final Preparation

In this phase, you make all required system settings and release them for transport into the production system. For more information, see Section 7.3.4.

7.5.6 Go-Live and Support

In this phase, the sales-related documents are archived in accordance with the solutions described above. This phase can be broken down as follows:

▶ **Initial data archiving**
In this step, all old documents up to a certain date are archived.

▶ **Periodic data archiving**
Data is then archived at regular intervals as defined in the detailed concept.

Preprocessing program   In the first phase of "initial" data archiving, you must determine whether the documents to be archived satisfy the requirements for archiving. To do this, start the preprocessing program with the **Detail Log** option selected and then analyze any problems that may appear in the log. SAP Notes often provide help with troubleshooting. To find SAP Notes, go to the SAP Support Portal on the SAP Service Marketplace.

Archiving   As soon as you have established that all documents to be archived can be archived, you can proceed with scheduling of the archiving programs. It is necessary to check when and how archiving of the sales-related documents is to be executed in the first phase.

Long-term concept   Once the initial data archiving has been successfully completed, you must develop a long-term archiving concept. This should allow you to maintain the data volume at a certain level through periodic archiving. This level must be acceptable to both the IT department and the business departments.

7.5.7 Example: Archiving a Sales Document

We will now illustrate how data archiving works in the sales area, using the example of a sales document (third-party order). We will also indicate any possible dependencies between the individual documents. We assume an appropriate level of expertise in using the

Archive Administration and therefore do not provide any detailed descriptions of archiving.

1. You start by using the preprocessing program (see Figure 7.22) to determine whether the document can in fact be archived.

Preprocessing

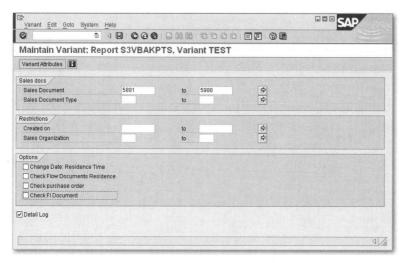

Figure 7.22 Selection Screen for Preprocessing

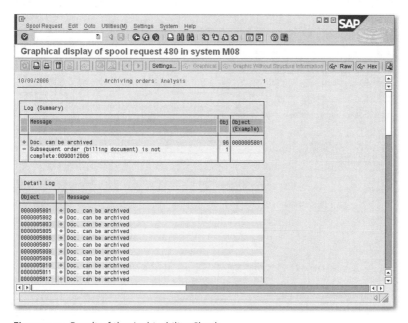

Figure 7.23 Result of the Archivability Check

Write program

2. If the archivability check returns a positive result (see Figure 7.23), you can archive the document by scheduling the write program in Archive Administration (transaction SARA) (see Figure 7.24).

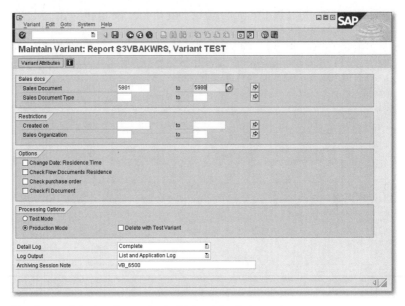

Figure 7.24 Selection Screen for Archiving Sales Documents

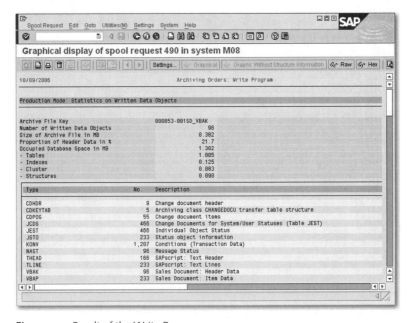

Figure 7.25 Result of the Write Program

The spool file of the write program provides an overview of all tables from which data was written into the archive during archiving.

3. Before you start the delete program, you can use the SD_VBAK archiving object to check that the archive file has been written correctly and can be analyzed. Figure 7.26 shows how the read program lists the archived documents.

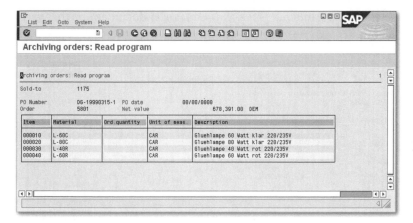

Figure 7.26 Result of the Read Program

4. Next, schedule the delete program for the relevant archiving sessions. Note that it may be advisable, depending on the configuration in Customizing, to create a backup copy of the archive file before deletion. Check the log of the delete job (see Figure 7.27). If the delete job has run without errors, no spool file is written.

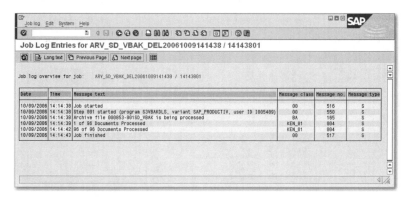

Figure 7.27 Log of the Delete Job

5. You must then verify that the document can be displayed with your chosen display and evaluation tools (reporting, Archive Information System, Document Relationship Browser). Figure 7.28 shows the display of the archived document in the original display transaction for sales documents (VA03), while Figure 7.29 shows the document in the relationship tree of the Document Relationship Browser. Here you can clearly see that the sales document has been read from the archive, while the other relevant documents (such as the material document or the warehouse transfer order) are still in the database.

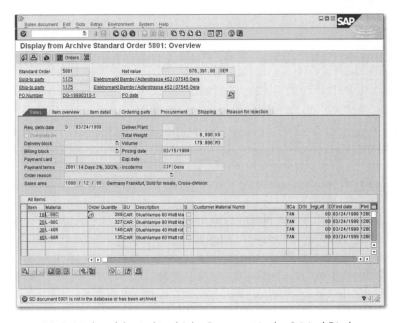

Figure 7.28 Display of the Archived Sales Document in the Original Display Transaction (VA03)

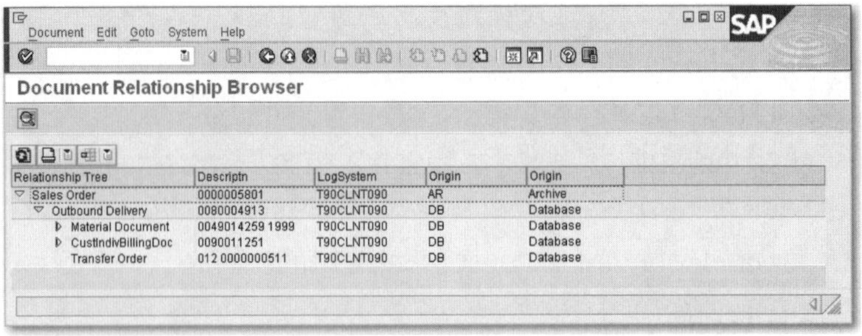

Figure 7.29 Document in the Document Relationship Browser (DRB)

7.6 Critical Success Factors for an Archiving Project

The following success factors and recommendations are based on our experience of countless successfully implemented archiving projects:

- ▶ Focus on a smaller number of key areas
- ▶ Direct involvement of those who will be affected by the project (include business departments and end users from the word go).
- ▶ Support from top management
- ▶ A skilled and experienced project team
- ▶ Project marketing and communication (to inform those involved in the project about the forthcoming archiving project and to promote it within the company)
- ▶ A competent and experienced project manager
- ▶ Appointment of a person with overall responsibility for archiving on the process/business side
- ▶ Do not underestimate project costs, in particular, in relation to data cleansing and coordination with the business department and auditing department.
- ▶ Regular review of project milestones
- ▶ Implementation of a quality assurance concept
- ▶ Competent and experienced consulting partners

7.7 Selecting the Right Residence Times

Since the data remains in the system for read access and does not simply "disappear" after archiving, you can select short residence times in many cases. Of course, this requires the approval of the business department, and this is often best achieved by clearly demonstrating the impressive access options that exist (see also the list of access options [DAACCESS] on the SAP Service Marketplace).

Some examples of applications in which short residence times are possible are provided below:

Examples of short residence times

▶ **Purchasing**
Short residence times can generally be selected in purchasing, because completed documents usually only need to be accessed in display mode.

▶ **Sales**
Short residence times can be configured here also. Orders and billing documents can be archived shortly after they have been completed. However, for rebate settlements, the documents must remain in the system and must not be archived. Archived billing documents cannot be printed.

▶ **Financial accounting**
Financial accounting documents can be archived after a short period, because only cleared documents can be archived, and the archived documents can be accessed from the original transaction. However, the corresponding secondary indexes may need to be retained for relatively long periods (for VAT audits).

▶ **Controlling**
For this application, we recommend that you check which data needs to be kept in the system for comparison with the previous year. Data from the previous year should remain in the system for these documents (for performance reasons).

> **Note**
>
> Due to the large data volume that is to be expected in an SAP production system, we recommend that you keep documents in the system for as short a period as possible. This concept is supported by the additional use of document storage in the form of print lists, outgoing documents, and so on.

Possible residence times for individual archiving projects or application areas:

Archiving Object/ Application Area	Residence Time
MM_MATBEL	current fiscal year
MM_EKKO	current fiscal year
RV_LIKP	current fiscal year

Table 7.2 Examples of Residence Times

Archiving Object/ Application Area	Residence Time
SD_VBAK	current fiscal year
SD_VBRK	current fiscal year
FI_DOCUMNT	current fiscal year plus previous year, secondary index for five years
CO	current fiscal year plus previous year (plus two years if required)
PCA	current fiscal year plus previous year (plus two years if required)
COPA	current fiscal year plus previous year (plus two years if required)

Table 7.2 Examples of Residence Times (cont.)

In these examples, archiving is executed on an annual basis after the year-end closing.

If the rate of database growth is very high, "aggressive" residence times may need to be employed:

Archiving Object/ Application Area	Residence Time
WM (RL_TA/_TB)	one month (RL_TA, RL_TB)
MM_MATBEL	three months
MM_EKKO	three months
RV_LIKP	three months
SD_VBAK	three months
SD_VBRK	three to six months (depending on when the invoices are settled)
FI_DOCUMNT	three months, secondary index for the current fiscal year (access via the Archive Information System for VAT audits)
CO	Line items three months, totals records for the current fiscal year plus the previous year

Table 7.3 Examples of "Aggressive" Residence Times

Archiving Object/ Application Area	Residence Time
PCA	Line items three months, totals records for the current fiscal year plus the previous year
COPA	Line items three months, totals records for the current fiscal year plus the previous year

Table 7.3 Examples of "Aggressive" Residence Times (cont.)

In this example, data archiving is executed on a periodic basis.

Note that these are all examples of residence times that can be implemented as part of a real-life archiving project without any additional effort. Residence times should normally be selected after all requirements have been defined for the project environment.

7.8   Selecting the Right Archiving Sequence

The sequence of archiving objects is defined in the analysis phase and set down in the detailed concept. The following steps will help you select the right sequence:

▸ Examine the relevant business processes.

▸ Check the network graphic (transaction SARA).

▸ Consult the documentation relating to the relevant archiving objects.

Example of an archiving sequence
An example of a sequence for the most important archiving objects is shown below:

1. RL_TA, RL_TB, RL_LUBU, RL_LINKP, RL_LINV

2. MM_MATBEL, MM_INVBEL, MM_REBEL

3. MM_EKKO ⇨ MM_EBAN ⇨ MM_EINA ⇨ MM_ASMD

4. SD_VFKK ⇨ SD_VTTK ⇨ RV_LIKP ⇨ SD_VBRK ⇨ SD_VBAK ⇨ SD_VBKA ⇨ SD_COND (*)

5. MM_ACCTIT

6. FI_DOCUMNT ⇨ FI_SL_DATA

7. CO_ORDER, PP_ORDER, PR_ORDER

8. CO_ITEM

9. COPA1_xxxx, COPA2_xxxx

10. AM_ASSET

11. IDOC

12. MC_Sxxx

13. MM_SPSTOCK ⇨ MM_MATNR

14. FI_ACCRECV, FI_ACCPAYB, FI_ACCOUNT

Note the following points:

- (*) SD_VBRK should be archived before SD_VBAK (see SAP Note 129310).
- A compulsory sequence within a line is indicated by an arrow (⇨).
- Example: MM_EKKO ⇨ MM_EBAN—MM_EKKO should be archived before MM_EBAN.
- The individual lines must be archived in the following sequence (or, alternativley, this sequence can be viewed as a suggestion only):
  - 2 ⇨ 3 (in accordance with the network graphic for MM_MATBEL)
  - 3 ⇨ 4
  - 4 ⇨ 14
  - 5 ⇨ 6, 5 ⇨ 13, 5 ⇨ 14
  - 6 ⇨ 7
  - 1 ⇨ 8
  - 7 ⇨ 8, 7 ⇨ 10

This archiving sequence is merely provided as an example and should not be simply adopted in its entirety in a real-life archiving project. The most important factors that will determine an archiving sequence are always the specific business processes used within a company and the specific requirements of the archiving project.

Appendix

A   Example of an Object Description for the Blueprint

Blueprint archiving objects are described in detail in the *Business Blueprint* phase (see Section 7.3.2). The following sections show a possible description using archiving object MM_MATBEL as an example.

1. **Description**

   Object MM_MATBEL is used to archive material documents for the MM (Materials Management) application in SAP ERP. A material document always consists of an MKPF record and at least one MSEG record.

2. **Relevant tables**

Table	Description
MKPF	Material document header
MSEG	Material document segment
NAST	Message status

3. **Available programs**

Program type	Program name
Write	RM07MARCS (transaction MBAR)
Delete	RM07MADES (transaction MBAD)
Administration	Transaction MBAV
Read	RM07MAAU (sequential access, transaction MBAL) RM07DOCS (direct access, transaction MB51)

4. Available display functions

▶ **Sequential reading**

Program RM07MAAU enables the sequential reading of material documents. For SAP R/3 version 4.0B and later, you can filter the output according to the material number.

▶ **Archive Information System**

The Archive Information System supports the display of material documents. Field catalogs SAP_MM_MATBEL01 and SAP_MM_MATBEL02 are available.

Field catalog ZSAP_MM_MATBEL is stored in the IR2 system. This field catalog is structured according to the requirements of the user department.

5. Reload functionality

None

6. Optional checks

None

7. Dependencies/sequence

None

8. Archiving-object-specific requirements

Accounting documents that are created when posting material documents are not archived using archiving object MM_MATBEL, but are archived in financial accounting instead.

9. Recommendations for the input parameters on the selection screen

You can use material documents to distinguish between goods receipt and goods issue documents (such as 4900000–4999999, 5000000–5099999).

Material documents (such as stock transfers) can exist in several plants.

You can start a test run by setting the **Test Mode** indicator in the processing options area.

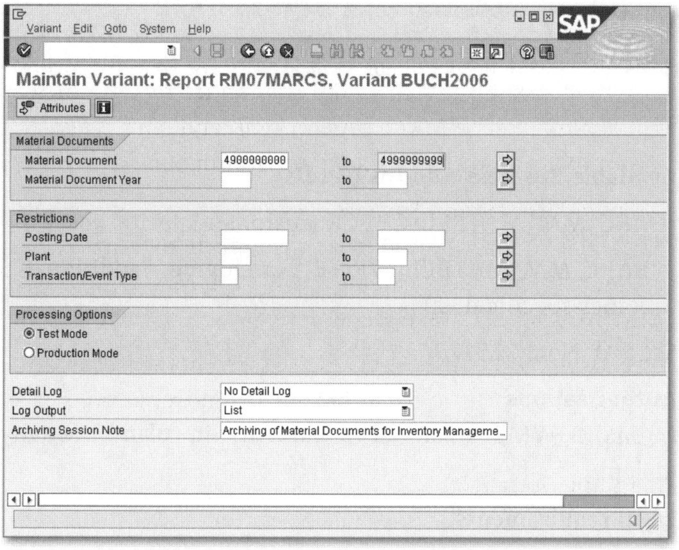

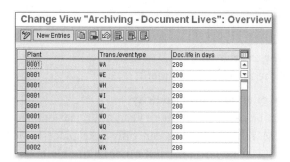

Figure A.1 Input Parameters for Archiving Material Documents

10. **Available Customizing settings**

    You can access Customizing either using transaction SARA or directly from transactions MBAR, MBAD, or MBAV.

    When setting document lives (see Figure A.2), the wildcard for the plant is "####," and for the transaction type, it is "##."

Change View "Archiving - Document Lives": Overview

Plant	Trans./event type	Doc.life in days
0001	WA	200
0001	WE	200
0001	WH	200
0001	WI	200
0001	WL	200
0001	WO	200
0001	WQ	200
0001	WZ	200
0002	WA	200

Figure A.2 Changing Document Lives for Material Documents

11. **Additional information or SAP Notes**

    Please read the documentation for the write and delete programs. There you will find notes on Customizing and on improving system performance during archiving.

SAP Note	Description	Release
518441	Performance during archiving MM_MATBEL: RM07MARC	from 4.0B

12. **Available Business Add-Ins (BAdIs)**

   ▸ ARC_MM_MATBEL_CHECK (customer-specific checks)

   ▸ EARC_MM_MATBEL_WRITE (archiving additional customer-specific data)

   See SAP Note 725173.

13. **Authorizations**
   M_MSEG_WMB (material documents in plant), activity 06 (delete)

14. **Legal requirements**
   None. However, various internal settlements are carried out based on the different material documents. These settlements are used to calculate VAT.

15. **Requirements for user departments concerning the storage period**
   The user department must be able to access the data up to three years after it was archived.

16. **Company requirements**
   The archive files must be retained in the archive or file system for 10 years.

17. **Print lists prior to archiving**
   To be defined by the user department.

18. **Date and time of archiving/periodicity**
   Archiving must be carried out once a year, after year-end closing (currently in March). Archiving can only take place in accordance with the user department and other components.

B   Checklist for Archiving Projects

The following checklist contains an overview of the activities that are generally important for planning and executing archiving projects. You can use this checklist to see what steps need to be carried out in the current phase of your project. The checklist is divided into the following project phases: *Project Preparation, Analysis, Preliminary Concept, Business Blueprint, Implementation, Final Preparation,* and *Go-Live & Support.*

Project Preparation	
▸ Project charter	☐
▸ Build project team	☐
▸ Project kickoff workshop	☐
▸ Project planning	☐
Analysis	
▸ Analyze inconsistencies between MM and FI (programs RM07MMFI and RM07MBST)	☐
▸ Analyze the database and tables (transactions TAANA, DB02)	☐
▸ Determine archiving objects (transaction DB15)	☐
▸ Determine dependencies	☐
▸ Determine archivable business objects	☐
▸ Project the anticipated data volume	☐
Preliminary Concept	
▸ Analyze additional archiving objects needed due to business requirements, such as legacy data	☐
▸ Determine the definitive archiving objects	☐
▸ Rough description of the archiving objects	☐
▸ Determine the archiving strategy (implementation phases, such as quick wins, transaction data, master data)	☐

Business Blueprint	
▶ Define the archiving sequence	☐
▶ Evaluate the storage media	☐
▶ Define the display functionality, including access times and requirements	☐
▶ Define the authorization concept	☐
▶ Define the residence times	☐
▶ For customer developments: program, perform tests	☐
▶ Create a concept for managing archive files	☐
Implementation	
▶ Customizing (in the test system)	☐
▶ Enter the logical file names and paths (transaction FILE)	☐
▶ ArchiveLink Customizing (if a storage system is used via the ArchiveLink interface)	☐
▶ Application-specific Customizing, such as setting the residence time (not necessary with all archiving objects)	☐
▶ Archiving-object-specific Customizing (transaction SARA)	☐
▶ When using a storage system: implement, configure, administrate	☐
▶ Test phase: Perform test runs in the test system; selective tests with small data volumes, full test with all documents (if available)	☐
Final Preparation	
▶ Transport the settings	☐
▶ Create a process description (company-internal documentation for users) for	☐
– Accessing archived business objects	☐
– Implementing analyses	☐
– Searching for and analyzing archived data	☐
▶ Pilot phase: Testing under real-life conditions (in the quality assurance system)	☐
▶ Report the test results to the user departments	☐
▶ User departments perform extensive tests (analysis/access to archived data)	☐
▶ Train end users	☐
▶ Release for live operation	☐

Go-Live & Support	
▶ Clean up data (if necessary from integration testing)	☐
▶ Create print lists that are needed before archiving	☐
▶ Execute archiving (job control)	☐
▶ Check whether new SAP Notes are available for the utilized archiving object	☐
▶ Check Customizing for the archiving object (both technically and in terms of residence times)	☐
▶ Start the preprocessing/write program in test mode	☐
▶ Analyze/check the logs	☐
▶ Clean up data (if necessary)	☐
▶ Start the write program in production mode	☐
▶ Analyze/check the logs	☐
▶ Save the archive files (if Customizing option **Delete Before Storing** was selected)	☐
▶ Maintain administrative data of the archiving run	☐
▶ Start the delete program (after performing a backup of the database, if possible)	☐
▶ Test access to archived data	☐
▶ Report to user departments	☐
▶ Postprocess after every archiving run	☐
▶ Update statistical data	☐
▶ Check if reorganization is necessary	☐
▶ Manually save and administrate archive files (if no storage system is used)	☐
▶ Implement a long-term archiving plan	☐
▶ Project-end workshop	☐

C   Additional Information and Services

C.1   Information

A wealth of additional information, documents, and presentations on SAP data archiving is available in SAP Service Marketplace, under the ILM *(Information Lifecycle Management)* quick link. The exact URL is as follows:

http://service.sap.com/ilm

Use the *ARCHIVELINK* quick link to access the SAP ArchiveLink area, where you will find the latest information on using ArchiveLink and the respective technology to store business documents.

SAP Data archiving in SAP Service Marketplace

C.2   Services

▶ **SAP Consulting**
When carrying out an archiving project, you may need the services of an external consulting partner. SAP Consulting has a number of competent consultants who have extensive experience in successfully completing archiving projects. You can also reach SAP Consulting via SAP Service Marketplace.

Consultancy with archiving know-how

▶ **SAP Data Volume Management**
SAP Data Volume Management (SAP DVM) provides a comprehensive portfolio of services for optimizing large data volumes in an SAP system with regard to a cost-efficient use of this data, i.e., total cost of ownership (TCO). One of those services is SAP Data Management that provides information regarding possible ways in which you can save storage space in your database. After analyzing your database in detail, the SAP service team will suggest how you can optimize the utilization of resources in your database.

Efficient management of large data volumes

The data management method suggested (see Section 1.5.2) may include preventing, aggregating, deleting, and archiving data in the sequence as specified here. This service is highly recommended for companies with large or fast-growing databases. You can reach the service from SAP Service Marketplace, using the DVM quick link.

▶ **SAP System Landscape Optimization**
SAP System Landscape Optimization (SLO) provides services for optimizing and harmonizing system landscapes. Those services facilitate and accelerate the implementation of business-relevant changes in customer systems, for example, caused by company mergers or internal reorganizations.

Archive migration

Sometimes this also includes the migration and implementation of archived data, which is also carried out by SLO. You can access the SAP SLO services in SAP Service Marketplace via the SLO quick link.

C.3 Training

Basic course

▶ **BIT660 — Data Archiving**
This three-day course gives you a thorough introduction to the technology and concept of SAP data archiving. You will learn about the most important SAP applications by studying practical, real-life examples. This course also provides you with detailed information about planning and carrying out archiving projects, customizing archiving objects, and storing and administrating archive files.

Course BIT660 is primarily intended for system administrators, consultants, and members of project teams who are involved in carrying out data archiving.

▶ **BIT670 — Data Archiving (Programming)**
This two-day course focuses on evaluating and reading archived data. You will learn how to write reporting programs (read programs) and how to adapt existing programs to reflect customer-specific requirements.

Course BIT670 is primarily intended for consultants and software developers who want to develop customer-specific read programs for archived data.

▶ **BIT614 Document Management with SAP: an Overview**
This two-day course provides an overview of the different document management options in an SAP system. You will learn about storing and managing documents using different SAP components, such as SAP Content Server, ArchiveLink, Records Management, Knowledge Warehouse, and so on.

Course participants are typically system administrators, consultants, and members of project teams, who will be asked to design and implement real-life scenarios for document management in their company.

▶ **BIT615 — Storing Documents Using ArchiveLink**
This four-day course provides an introduction to document storage using ArchiveLink, and is a good complement to the data archiving courses. It explains how original documents are stored in an external storage system, and how these documents are linked with business objects from SAP applications.

Course BIT615 is primarily intended for administrators, consultants, and members of archiving project teams.

▶ **BC680 — Data Retention Tool**
This two-day course introduces you to DART (Data Retention Tool), a tool that enables you to meet finance authority requirements regarding data access and auditability of digital documents. You will learn in detail how DART is closely connected with data archiving.

This course is intended for system analysts who are responsible for tax issues, and tax professionals. After attending the course, they will know how to configure DART, extract and retain data using DART, and use views for extracted data.

If you have any questions about course contents or dates, please contact the SAP International Training Center, or your SAP international subsidiary. For more information, please visit the education area in the SAP Service Marketplace.

D   Glossary

ADK   see *Archive Development Kit*

Administrative data   Additional information about → archive files and → archiving sessions, which is stored in the database. Examples: Number and size of the → data objects, archiving statuses, logical file paths, physical file names, all archive files that are included in a specific archiving session, and so on.

Archive   All data that is stored in → archive files.

Archive Administration   Central starting point for the majority of user activities in data archiving, such as scheduling → write and → delete jobs, building and removing the archive index, storing and retrieving → archive files, and so on. Can be called using transaction SARA.

Archive Development Kit (ADK)   Technical framework and basis of the SAP data archiving solution. The ADK is a software layer located between the SAP applications and the archive and it provides the runtime and management environment for all SAP data archiving functions. In addition, the ADK provides a programming interface (ADK API) for developing archiving programs at SAP or on the customers' side.

Archive file   Archive files are created by the write program in the file system of the SAP system and are used to store the archived data. The maximum size of an archive file can be defined by the user. An archive file can contain one or several → data objects and belongs to exactly one → archiving session.

Archive File Browser (AFB)   Data archiving tool for displaying the contents of archive files. The AFB provides a technical view of archived tables similar to that provided by the Data Browser (transaction SE16) for database data, and it supports administrators in finding solutions to problems with archive files.

Archive index   Application-specific database table that is needed for → direct access. The archive index provides the → read program with the exact position of a → data object in the → archive. A search can only be carried out by using the fields contained in the archive index. The archive index can be built up automatically in the → delete phase for → archiving objects that support the index function. The → archive information structure represents a special type of archive index that provides more comprehensive access options.

Archive information structure   Central element of the → Archive Information System (AS). It represents a kind of index that has been created on the basis of a → field catalog and that enables the search for archived data in the archive.

Archive Information System (AS)
Generic tool that is integrated in the data archiving environment and is used for indexing archive files, as well as for performing searches in archives. The search and display of data is based on → archive information structures that a user can define and fill with data from the archive.

ArchiveLink Service that is integrated in the Application Server ABAP technology. This service establishes a link between stored documents and the application documents that are linked to them in SAP NetWeaver AS ABAP (→ business objects).

Archive management Part of the → Archive Administration in which the → archiving sessions and archive files for a specific → archiving object can be displayed and managed. Can be accessed via the Archive Administration (transaction SARA).

Archive Routing Data archiving function that is used to define content repositories based on specific rules and conditions. The content repositories defined in this way are used to selectively store the archive files created during the archiving session. A content repository can be defined at the level of organizational units (e.g., company code) or according to time-based criteria, such as the fiscal year.

Archiving class An archiving class characterizes a specific type of data objects that have no business-relevant meaning, such as SAPscript texts, change documents, or classification data. The data that is identi-

fied via archiving classes is archived on the basis of an archiving object, along with the business objects that characterizes this data.

Archiving object Logical object of associated application data in the database. The data is written from the database into an *archive file* and deleted if the archiving process was successful. In addition, the archiving object contains the associated → archiving programs and Customizing.

Archiving program Generic term that is used for all programs used in the data archiving process, such as → write, → delete, → read, and → reload programs.

Archiving session Archiving unit that consists of a → write and a → delete phase. Optionally, it can also contain a → storage phase. In addition to the actual archiving process, the quantity of data that is written to the archive during the write phase is also referred to as an archiving session. This archiving session can be accessed in its entirety in → archive management based on a unique archiving session number.

Backup Creation of a copy of a database (or parts of a database) for the purpose of restoring the original database status in case of an error. See *Restore*.

BOR see *Business Object Repository*

Business Content Preconfigured role and task-based information models in SAP NetWeaver Business Intelligence (SAP NetWeaver BI) that can be customized according to the requirements of individual companies.

Business Content basically consists of roles, workbooks, queries, InfoCubes, InfoObjects, InfoSources, update rules, and extractors for SAP ERP and other selected applications.

Business object   Representation of a central real-world business object, such as a purchase order or an invoice. From a technical point of view, a business object is an instance of a business object type that contains actual values. Business objects are managed in the → Business Object Repository (BOR). See also *Data object*.

Business Object Repository (BOR) Service contained in SAP NetWeaver representing a directory of all object types (business object types, organizational object types, and technical object types) in hierarchical order. Each object type is assigned to a development package (hence indirectly to an application component).

Business view   View that is used in the → Archive Information System (AS) to display archived data. The display is similar to the display of data from the database. Not all → archiving objects contain a business view. See *Technical view*.

CCMS   see *Computing Center Management System*

Codepage   Vendor-specific and hardware-specific subset of a character set in which each character is assigned a hexadecimal value. ASCII, EBCDIC, or Shift-JIS are examples of codepages.

Computing Center Management System (CCMS)   Integrated tools for monitoring and managing SAP systems and independent SAP business components that can be used to automate the distribution of resources or the management of databases, for example.

Content   Documents of an application that are managed using SAP → Knowledge Provider.

Example: An HTML page contains a GIF. Thus, the managed document consists of two files—an HTML file and a GIF file. Both files together form the content of the HTML page that is managed as a physical document.

Content Management Service (CMS)   Component of → Knowledge Provider (KPro). The CMS enables the application-specific integration and administration of different types of content servers. As of SAP R/3 4.6C, the CMS is used by the data archiving system as an internal interface for the communication with → storage systems.

CRM Middleware   Software component in SAP CRM that is responsible for replicating, synchronizing, and distributing data between different systems. It connects the different producers of data with each other, such as mobile clients, SAP R/3 backend, SAP NetWeaver BI, APO, and CRM Server applications, and provides all systems involved with the required information.

CRM Server   Central software component in SAP CRM that provides all CRM online functions on the basis of SAP NetWeaver Application

Server, including the main components of → CRM Middleware. The CRM application data is validated and stored on the CRM Server.

Data object   Logical processing unit of data used in the ADK environment. The data object is stored by the → write program as a physical entity in the → archive file. From the point of view of the application, the data object basically corresponds to a → business object. The archiving object determines the database tables from which data records are to be transferred into a data object.

Delete job   Execution of the → delete program in the background. Depending on the Customizing settings, the delete job can be executed prior to or after the storage of the → archive file in the → storage system.

Delete phase   Part of the archiving session in which data is deleted from the database. The delete phase of an → archiving session begins with the launch of the → delete program for the → archive file that has been selected first. It ends when all files included in the archiving session have the status **Deletion completed**.

Delete program   Program that reads the data, which has previously been written to the archive by the → write program and then deletes the corresponding data in the database.

Direct access   Also referred to as *single-document access*. Read access to individual data objects in the archive. The pointer must be positioned at the beginning of the → data object in the → archive file. Only the data object that has been specified in the selection, such as a specific invoice, is read. This method is based on an index that can be generated using the Archive Information System (AS), for example.

Document storage   Electronic storage and management of documents such as original documents, outgoing documents, → print lists, etc., in an external → storage system. See *optical archiving*.

Field catalog   Collection of fields that can be used for the creation or maintenance of an → archive information structure.

HSM system   Hierarchical storage management system. Storage solution that automatically distributes data according to individually configurable rules (e.g., access frequency) within a hierarchy of different storage media (such as hard disks, MO disks, magnetic tapes). The accessing system perceives the HSM system as a file system that stores the files in a logically unchangeable file path.

ILM   see *Information Lifecycle Management*

Information Lifecycle Management (ILM)   Combination of processes and technologies that are intended to provide the right pieces of information at the right time and in the right place at the lowest possible costs across the entire data lifecycle.

Information structure see *archive information structure*

Jukebox Automated storage unit that contains different storage media, such as hard drives, storage partitions, and a robot mechanism to automatically change optical disks. A jukebox provides access to large data archives without the interference of an operator.

Knowledge Provider (KPro) Central service provided by *SAP NetWeaver Application Server* for storing and managing any document and document-like objects.

KPro see *Knowledge Provider*

Metadata Information that is stored in archive files and is needed to store and interpret data, irrespective of specific releases and platforms. Examples: schema of the database table, data type and length of a column, number format, → codepage.

Postprocessing program Program that can be executed once the → delete phase is finished in order to carry out an additional application-specific processing of the data in the database, such as the update of statistics, for example.

Preprocessing program Program that can be executed prior to the → write phase in order to check the data for archivability and to prepare it for archiving, for example, by setting a deletion indicator.

Print list Result of an application program, which is output as a list. The print list can either be printed

out on paper or stored in a → storage system via → Archive Link.

Offset Value in relative addressing that specifies how far a specific element or position is from the starting point. The starting point of a → data object in an → archive file is specified by an offset.

Optical archiving Commonly used, but incorrect, name for document storage. The → storage system used here is usually based on optical media (CDs, WORMs, etc.), hence the name optical archiving.

Read program Program that reads and evaluates or outputs archived data, for example, as a list.

Reload Activity in which archived data is read in the archive and then inserted into the current database. The concept of reloading data was designed for exceptional or emergency situations, such as an inadvertent archiving of data, and it should occur shortly after the → delete phase, if possible.

Reload program Program that reads archived data from the archive and reloads it back into the database.

Reorganization In the world of SAP R/2, this term was used to describe the physical deletion of application data during a reorganization of database tables. Today it generally describes the new arrangement of database tables with the purpose of a more efficient use of the storage space.

Residence time Period that must elapse before application data can be archived. Depending on the application, the basis for calculating the residence time can be the entry date, the posting period, the goods issue data, and so on. The residence time is usually specified in terms of days.

Restore The process of writing the backup copy back into the database in order to restore the original database status after an error. See *Backup*.

SAP NetWeaver Application Server (SAP NW AS) Technological advancement of the former SAP Basis system. SAP NW AS represents the underlying application platform for nearly all SAP Business Suite applications.

Sequential read Read access to archived data. The pointer is positioned directly at the beginning of the → archive file and moved on sequentially. The → Archive Development Kit transfers the → data objects read in this way to the → read program that compares the data with the selection specifications of the user and then analyzes or outputs the matching data. The read process ends when the end of the file has been reached. If several archive files or → archiving sessions are analyzed, the read process ends once the end of the last file has been reached.

Storage phase Optional part of the archiving process that consists of moving the archive files that were created in the write phase into a → storage system. Optionally, the

storage phase can also occur after the → delete phase.

Storage system External archiving system that is connected to the SAP system through a certified interface and stores the → archive files that were created in the → write phase. A storage system can contain different storage media, but it is usually based on optical storage media, such as CD-ROMs, WORMs, and so on.

Technical view View that is used in the Archive Information System (AS) to display archived data. The technical view is similar to the display via transaction SE16 and is available by default for every archiving object. See *business view*.

Tertiary storage All storage media such as CD-ROMs, magnetic tapes, optical disks, floppy disks, etc., which are located "below" magnetic disks (the secondary storage medium) in the storage hierarchy.

Write job Execution of the → write program in the background.

Write phase Part of the → archiving session in which data is written from the database into an → archive file. The write phase of an archiving session starts and ends with the execution of the → write program.

Write program Program that selects the data to be archived from the database and then writes this data into one or several → archive files.

E   List of Acronyms

ADK	Archive Development Kit
ALE	Application Link Enabling
AS	Archive Information System
ASAP	AcceleratedSAP
ASUG	Americas' SAP Users' Group
BAdI	Business Add-In
BAPI	Business Application Programming Interface
BOR	Business Object Repository
CBO	Cost Based Optimizer
CCMS	Computing Center Management System
CMS	Content Management Service
CRC	Cyclic Redundancy Check
DMS	Document Management System
DRB	Document Relationship Browser
DSAG	Deutschsprachige SAP-Anwendergruppe (German SAP user group)
HSM	Hierarchical Storage Management System
HTTP	HyperText Transfer Protocol
ICC	SAP Integration & Certification Centers
ILM	Information Lifecycle Management
IT	Information Technology
J2EE	Java 2 Enterprise Edition
KPro	Knowledge Provider
MDMP	Multi-Display/Multi-Processing
MO	Magneto-Optical
NAS	Network Attached Storage
OCR	Optical Character Recognition

OLE	Object Linking and Embedding
OLTP	Online Transaction Processing
OTF	Output Text Format
PDF	Portable Document Format
RAID	Redundant Array of Independent Disks
RFC	Remote Function Call
URI	Uniform Resource Identifier
WEBDAV	Web-based Distributed Authoring and Versioning

F   Bibliography

Acronym	Source
BE02	Buck-Emden, R.; Zencke, P.: *mySAP CRM 4.0. The Official Guidebook to SAP CRM 4.0.* SAP PRESS, Bonn 2004.
BRTOOLS	SAP Support Portal in SAP Service Marketplace, *SAP Note 12741*.
BÜR06	Bürckel, N.; Davidenkoff, A.; Werner, D.: *Unicode in SAP Systems*. SAP PRESS, Bonn 2007.
CCMS01	*CCMS Monitoring Architecture: Alert Monitor's Preset Monitors.* SAP White Paper, 2001.
DAACCESS	*Reports and Transactions for Accessing Archived Data.* SAP, 2006 *(http://service.sap.com/ILM, Data Archiving → Media Library → Literature & Brochures).*
DAPERF01	*Performance Aspects of Data Archiving—Factors for Optimal Results in Archiving Projects.* SAP White Paper, 2005 *(http://service.sap.com/ILM, Data Archiving → Media Library → Literature & Brochures).*
DAPERF02	Brinkmöller, B.; Fischer, G.: *Data Archiving Improves Performance — Myth or Reality?* SAP Insider, October 2005 *(http://www.sapinsideronline.com).*
DAPERF03	Brinkmöller, B.; Stefani, H.: *Data Archiving—The Fastest Access to Your Business Data?* SAP Insider, July 2005 *(http://www.sapinsideronline.com).*
DMG	*Data Management Guide.* SAP White Paper, 2006 *(http://service.sap.com/ILM, Data Archiving → Media Library → Literature & Brochures).*
GS01	Gersbacher, R.; Stefani, H.: *Data Archiving Essentials—What Every Administrator Needs to Know.* In: *SAP Professional Journal*, March/April 2001, pp. 3 – 28.
HEL06	Helfen, M.; Lauer, M.; Trauthwein, H.: *Testing SAP Solutions*. SAP PRESS, Bonn 2007.
RED02	Redford, M.: *Looking Forward to the Unicode Advantage: Internationalization and Integration.* In: *SAP Professional Journal*, January/February 2002, pp. 95 – 112.

Acronym	Source
SIMS2003	School of Information Management and Systems: *How much Information?* University of California, Berkeley, USA, 2003. (*http://www2.sims.berkeley.edu/research/projects/how-much-info-2003/*).
WEBDAV	*http://www.webdav.org: HTTP Extensions for Distributed Authoring —WEBDAV RFC2518*, February, 1999.

G   The Authors

Dr. Veit Bolik holds a doctorate in technical and inorganic chemistry from the University of Kaiserslauten, Germany. After graduating, he worked as a software developer in a company that specialized in media asset management. He joined SAP in 2004, where he has worked as a software developer for data archiving solutions with a focus on CRM and data archiving technology.

Dr. Bernhard Brinkmöller studied physics at the University of Münster, Germany, and went on to graduate from the University of Bonn, Germany. He then worked for the University of Minnesota and the University of Karlsruhe (Germany), with research placements at the Los Alamos National Lab and the Paul Scherrer Institute (Switzerland). He joined SAP in 1994, where he worked as a performance specialist until he assumed the position of Data Archiving Development Manager in 2000.

After studying communications engineering in Karlsruhe, Germany, Gerd Buchmüller worked for three years as a hardware developer in the telecommunications industry. He joined SAP in 1996. During his first two years, he worked as an information developer in the business process modeling field and then in the area of database administration. Since then, Gerd has worked as a software developer in the data archiving technology area.

Georg Fischer has been responsible for Data Archiving Product Management at SAP since 1998. In 2003, he also assumed responsibility for the areas of performance, data management, and scalability. After studying information technology at the Darmstadt University of Technology, Germany, he worked at Digital Equipment Corporation (DEC) in document management, optical archiving, and data archiving. Before he switched to product management, Georg worked for companies in Europe and the US as a project manager responsible for implementing archiving in an SAP environment.

Dr. Martin Fischer studied at Ruprecht Karls University in Heidelberg, Germany, graduating with a degree in Digital Image Processing in Physics. He joined SAP in 1997 as a developer in the financial accounting area, where he was primarily responsible for data archiving and the Archive Information System. Currently, he works as a developer in the Performance, Data Management, and Scalability department.

Reto Gentinetta is head of the SAP Customer Competence Center at Schweizerische Post (Swiss Postal Services) in Switzerland. Before assuming this position, he worked as a Consulting Manager and Senior Consultant for SAP NetWeaver Technology Consulting at SAP (Switzerland) AG. Reto has many years of experience in managing international archiving projects. Since 1996, his work has focused on technology consulting and data archiving in the SAP ERP environment. He is a highly sought-after expert in the field of data archiving, and has contributed to advances in the field through numerous consulting projects and lectures.

Dr. Axel Herbst has been a data archiving technology developer, a project manager, and a Development Architect at SAP since 1997. After studying information technology, he worked at IBM on data integration projects. He graduated from the University of Kaiserslautern (database group) in 1996, and then became a product data management consultant. Today he works at SAP where he develops concepts for service-oriented archiving as part of SAP's Information Lifecycle Management (ILM), focusing on XML, JEE, and the usage of innovative storage architectures.

Dr. Gernot Kuhr studied physics and business administration at the universities of Münster, Heidelberg, and Mannheim, Germany, and graduated from the University of Heidelberg in medicinal physics. Then, he worked in the medicinal physics department at the German Center for Cancer Research in Heidelberg. Since 2001, he has worked as a software developer in the area of FI data archiving at SAP. He has also moved to the Performance, Data Management, and Scalability department where he is responsible for ADK archiving, among other things.

Iwona Luther studied computer science at the University of Applied Sciences in Cologne, Germany. Since 1997, she has worked as a software developer at SAP—at first in the area of data archiving in financial accounting, and since 2004, she has worked in the central area of data archiving technology. Today she is responsible for the table analysis tool, TAANA, quality management within archiving development, and for archiving solutions for multiple applications.

Dr. Jan Nolte-Bömelburg studied chemistry at the Technical University of Berlin, and graduated in the field of physical chemistry. He joined SAP AG as a Support Consultant in 1997, where he worked in technical support mainly for database systems and data archiving technology. Since 2001, he has worked as a data archiving technology developer.

Thorsten Pferdekämper studied information systems at the University of Mannheim, Germany. Since 1995, he has worked as a software developer at SAP. Initially, he was responsible for data archiving in financial accounting, the Archive Information System, and the Document Relationship Browser. In 2005, he moved to SAP Custom Development.

Gerhard Scherer was the SAP Development Manager responsible for ArchiveLink, which he has been involved in developing and designing since its inception. In addition to his development responsibilities, he also focused on consulting and product management. Having worked for SAP for 10 years, he left the company in 2002 to establish xft GmbH together with three partners. This company specializes in add-on products and consulting for SAP NetWeaver, with a particular focus on the document processes and SAP Records Management areas.

Helmut Stefani studied applied linguistics at the Johannes Gutenberg University in Mainz/Germersheim, Germany, where he graduated as a technical translator for English and Spanish. After working in England he returned to Germany to work for an American company as a CAD software localization specialist. He has worked at SAP as an information developer and product management specialist in data archiving since 1997, and has jointly authored several publications on this subject.

Rainer Uhle studied mathematics and geography at RWTH in Aachen, Germany, where he graduated with a degree in education. He joined SAP in 1987, where he first worked as a trainer in the areas of customer education and internal training. In 1996, he became a Curriculum Development Manager for the Logistics Information Systems (LIS) and SAP Business Information Warehouse (SAP BW) fields. In 2001, he moved into SAP NetWeaver product management, where he is now responsible for the Enterprise Data Warehousing (EDW) area.

Dr. Michael Wulf studied physics at the University of Hamburg, Germany. After graduating with a degree in physics, he joined SAP in 1995 in the area of Human Capital Management (HCM) development (i.e., for the basic principles of payroll accounting). During that time, he was a member of the team that was responsible for developing archiving solutions in HCM. Since 2003, he has worked as a Product Manager in HCM, and since 2005, he has been responsible for the basic functionality area (master data, time management, and payroll).

Dr. Peter Zimmerer studied physics and mathematics at Justus Liebig University in Giessen, Germany. After graduating with a degree in physics, he joined SAP in 1992, where he was involved in developing Report Writer. At the end of 1999, he joined the SAP NetWeaver BI department. As a Development Architect, he oversees data archiving and nearline storage in the data staging area.

Index

Detailed methodology for developing and implementing functional and load tests

Functionality and implementation of eCATT, SAP Solution Manager, SAP Test Data Migration Server, and more

367 pp., 2007, 69,95 Euro / US$ 69,95
ISBN 978-1-59229-127-4

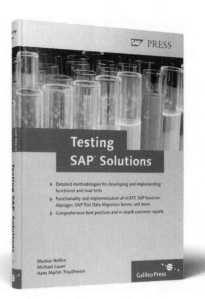

Testing SAP Solutions

www.sap-press.com

Markus Helfen, Michael Lauer,
Hans Martin Trauthwein

Testing SAP Solutions

This book provides you with comprehensive coverage of all testing requirements and techniques necessary for implementing, upgrading or operating SAP solutions. Readers get an overview of all existing tools, their functionalities, and best practices for utilization. The authors focus mainly on SAP Solution Manager, Test Workbench and eCATT, and their use in functional and load tests is highlighted in detail.

>> www.sap-press.de/1408

Complete technical details for upgrading to SAP NetWeaver AS 7.00

In-depth coverage of all upgrade tools and upgrade phases

Includes the brand-new upgrade procedure for double-stack installations

approx. 350 pp., 2. edition, 79,95 Euro / US$ 89,95
ISBN 978-1-59229-144-1, Aug 2007

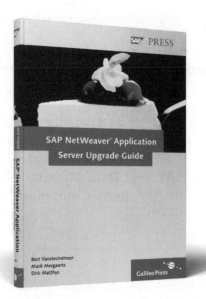

SAP NetWeaver Application Server Upgrade Guide

www.sap-press.com

Bert Vanstechelman, Mark Mergaerts, Dirk Matthys

SAP NetWeaver Application Server Upgrade Guide

With release 7.00 (the basis of SAP ERP 2005), SAP undertook a complete revision of the upgrade procedure of NetWeaver AS. Now, it is also possible to upgrade so-called „double-stack" installations with an ABAP and a Java stack under the hood. This book is your comprehensive guide to all kinds of SAP upgrades. It describes a complete project, explains project management questions, provides technical background information (also on the upgrade of other systems like CRM, Portal, XI, and BW), and then goes through a project from A to Z.